BEHAVIORAL FORMATION

Volatile Design Processes & the Emergence of a Strange Specificity

ROLAND SNOOKS

TABLE OF CONTENTS

ESSAYS	STRATEGIES	PROJECTS

ACKNOWLEDGMENTS

Behavioral Formation has evolved from the design work of my practice, which spans Kokkugia, Studio Roland Snooks, and the research I lead at RMIT University. Jonathan Podborsek, Robert Stuart-Smith, and I established Kokkugia as an experimental design research practice in 2004, with an ambition to explore the architectural implications of complex systems through algorithmic design. The body of formally complex architecture that emerged from this collaboration became the catalyst in 2012 to launch Studio Roland Snooks and a research agenda at RMIT University. These more recent modes of practice were established to expand this algorithmic design agenda into experimental tectonics and built architectural form.

Many of the design concepts, experiments, and projects from the early period of my work are entwined with those of Robert Stuart-Smith through our years of collaboration. Rob, thank you for your unwavering friendship, intellectual curiosity, and tireless ambition to rethink all aspects of architecture. Thank you to Jono, whose insight, wit and irreverence were crucial to the formation of Kokkugia and establishing this trajectory of work.

RMIT Architecture has provided a vitally supportive structure to expand my design research into digital fabrication and robotic construction. This research agenda has evolved into the RMIT Architecture | Tectonic Formation Lab, to explore a synthesis of generative design and additive manufacturing. I am grateful to Vivian Mitsogianni, Martyn Hook, and Richard Blythe who have believed in this work and created an environment for it to develop over the past eight years. I also acknowledge, and appreciate, the RMIT School of Architecture and Urban Design for their support in the production of this book.

Architecture is dependent on the collaboration and commitment of the design team, and I am grateful to all the talented people who have brought these projects into being. The project teams and collaborators are listed in the Catalogue of Projects. In particular, I would like to thank Marc Gibson, Cam Newnham, Charlie Boman, Fleet Hower, and Casey Rehm whose years of dedication and skill were crucial in the development of this work.

I am grateful to everyone who contributed to the production of this book and persisted throughout the lengthy process of editing and design. Thank you to Ricardo Devesa, Ramon Prat, and Marga Gibert at Actar for your guidance and patience.

This book has grown out of the PhD that I completed at RMIT in 2014, Behavioral Formation: Multi-Agent Design Strategies, and has since evolved and incorporated work from the subsequent five years. Thank you to my PhD supervisors, Paul Minifie and Pia Ednie-Brown – who are also partially responsible for catalyzing this line of research in 2002 – for your advice, criticism, and intellectual generosity in challenging my conceptualization of this body of work.

During the 18-year evolution of this design research, I have been influenced by many colleagues and mentors. In particular, ongoing conversations with Cecil Balmond, Karl Chu, Marc Fornes, Ed Keller, François Roche, and Tom Wiscombe have informed and shaped this work over the years. Crucial to the development of my work has been the curation, exhibition, and commissioning of these projects notably by Ewan McEoin, Frédéric Migayrou, Marie-Ange Brayer, and Fleur Watson.

Finally, to Laura Harper, who has revealed many new insights, become an increasingly frequent collaborator, and fundamentally impacted the development of my work: your advice, which I have come to rely upon, is truly invaluable; thank you.

Dedicated to Graeme and Loma

PREFACE

The body of work presented here defines a behavioral approach to architectural design—one in which architecture emerges from the behavior of complex systems and their interaction with design intention. This is an approach I have developed over the past eighteen years of architectural practice.

At the core of this practice is a series of algorithmic design processes developed through architectural projects, before being extracted as more generalizable strategies. These strategies are not posited as ideological imperatives in themselves. Rather, they are evaluated through the characteristics of the architecture they create: an architecture defined by emergent qualities, strange characteristics, and affects that exceed the projects' concepts and processes.

This book lies somewhere between a monograph, a methodological treatise, and a manifesto on the architecture of swarm intelligence. It presents an assemblage of interleaved essays that position the work, design strategies that posit their methodological underpinnings, and key projects that exceed their theoretical or methodological origins. The intention of this structure is to reinforce the interrelationship of ideas, processes, and forms that define my practice.

This practice developed as part of an emerging generation of designers for whom the interaction of complex systems and algorithmic processes catalyzed a new direction in experimental architecture: focused on the design of intricate geometries, tectonics, and expressive form. Within this generation, the original contribution of my body of work is the development of a design methodology based on the logic of swarm intelligence that operates by encoding design intention within multi-agent algorithms—referred to here as Behavioral Formation. This methodological development, which I began in 2002, has played the pioneering role in establishing a multi-agent algorithmic approach to architectural design. More importantly, Behavioral Formation enables a departure from the contemporary adoption of indexical algorithms: defining, instead, an approach that embeds and intertwines the architect's design intention within emergent processes.

Over the past decade, the multi-agent design strategies of Behavioral Formation have been disseminated and adopted more broadly within algorithmic architecture. The work outlined in this book documents the sustained development of this approach into the authoritative position on behavioral design methodologies within architecture. In developing this work through architectural design projects, my practice has shifted from the original concern for methodology to focus instead on drawing out the strange specificity of the projects themselves.

INTRODUCTION

BETWEEN EMERGENCE AND INTENTION

Emergent processes of formation create intensive, heterogeneous, intricate, complex phenomena. These processes have come to define our contemporary understanding of the nature of becoming, which stands in contrast to established notions of design and intention. The experimental design research posited here speculates on this relationship between emergent processes of formation and architectural design intention, and explores the strange and specific qualities of the architecture that is drawn out of this interaction.

This design research operates within a larger architectural and cultural concern for complex systems and their role in algorithmic design processes. The original contribution of this work to the larger milieu is the articulation of a design process in which architectural intention is embedded within emergent processes. This is a reconceptualization of design intention as behaviors that interact in a self-organizing process of formation – ***Behavioral Formation.*** Intention, in this process, is recast as discrete, micro-scale architectural decisions, relationships, or procedures that are encoded as behaviors within multi-agent algorithms. The local interaction of these agents self-organizes architectural design intention at the macro-level.

Behavioral Formation develops, and exploits, an intricate intertwining of intention and emergence. The design intention of the architect is both encoded within algorithmic systems of emergence and operates externally to the algorithm in a feedback loop conditioned by explicit decisions and the evaluation of emergent outcomes. This approach is an important shift from the dominant contemporary architectural use of algorithms where design intention is limited solely to iterative evaluation. The implications of working through these highly iterative, non-linear, computational design processes are manifest as a compression of hierarchies, a blurring of geometric types, and the uncoupling of geometric elements from architectural roles.

This body of work aims to establish both a behavioral approach to architectural design and to tease out the *strange specificity*[1] of its architecture through the interaction of self-organization and subjective intention. Ultimately, the ambition of this architectural design work is not processual; instead, it is concerned with the specific qualities, characteristics,

RMIT Mace, 2015–2016.
Detail of the titanium printed
fibrous mass.

and affects of the architecture created through this approach that exceed—but are integrally dependent upon—their generative processes.

EMERGENCE

Complex systems are created through the interaction of elements that gives rise to behavior greater than the sum of its parts. The self-organizing behavior of these systems generate complex order and emergent phenomena. As Manuel DeLanda has pointed out, these have been playing an increasingly important role in our conception of formation for several decades: 'We are beginning to understand that any complex system, whether composed of interacting molecules, organic creations or economic agents is capable of spontaneously generating order and of actively organizing itself into new structures and forms'.[2]

As a discipline engaged in designing complex organization, structures and form, emergent processes of formation are increasingly being explored as potent techniques within architectural design.[3] Instrumentalizing these processes within architecture is an intellectual engagement with complexity and with the processes of formation that operate within the world. The compelling aspect of complex systems for architects, however, is not the theoretical explanation of becoming, but the phenomena of emergence and its intensive, intricate, and affective capacities.[4] Examples of these emergent characteristics include the turbulent nature of tornadoes, the intricate networks of slime mold, and the complex order of cellular automata rule 110.[5] The application of emergent processes to architectural design has the capacity to create spaces that are experienced in a fundamentally different way to the spaces of Classicism or Modernism—affects defined by an emergent rather than reductive order.

Complex systems have permeated the contemporary psyche, being understood through the cities we live in, the social media through which we communicate, and the algorithms that suggest what we buy, listen to, or read. This milieu has given rise to a popular understanding of authorship that has shifted significantly over the past fifteen years. Open source, crowd sourcing, and notions of collective intelligence have undermined the individual author and formed a new understanding of distributed authorship.[6] While working through similar underlying complex systems, the approach described here is not about distributed authorship, but rather about the distribution of the author's design intent and its reconceptualization as behaviors that interact in a non-linear system of self-organization.

INTENTION

The volatile nature of self-organizing processes represents an apparent conflict with the established notions of architectural intention. In establishing the modern concept of architectural design, Leon Battista Alberti separated design from craft through notation, establishing the authority of the master architect that is still a dominant understanding within the discipline.[7] While the certainty of authorship has come under various attacks, the relationship of authorship to digital generative processes are most relevant here. Greg Lynn's seminal animate form projects of the mid-1990s reconceptualized design processes through animation. This approach drew criticism for the perceived loss of authorship, or intention, in working with dynamic processes, including issues such as the 'stopping problem'.[8] The problem, however, was not insufficient logic for stopping the process; on the contrary, it was the difficulty of encoding subjective design intention—the architect's will—within the systemic animate processes.[9] In Lynn's animate form projects, design intention operates through, or is translated into, a series of simulated natural forces external to the pliant surfaces that they inflect. This is a morphodynamic process in which the surfaces are receptors of formal influence, and the degree of design intention is limited by the capacity to translate this intention into physical forces, such as winds, gravities and vortices. A similar limitation is evident within another important influence on this work—the form-finding 'material computation' of Antoni Gaudi and Frei Otto[10]—where generative authorship is limited to physical laws and material properties. The inability to embed architectural decisions within a generative model remains a primary limitation of contemporary algorithmic processes, and substantially defers architectural intention to the evaluation of these generative models.

At this point it is worth defining 'intention' in further detail. Intention is used here to describe an architect's imperatives, desires, sensibilities, or design criteria. Intention can be propositional, as a desire is, or a constraint, such as a criterion. The sensibility of an architect is an accumulation of their tropes, biases, and tendencies—their intuition. Intention as discussed here relates to aesthetics, form, program, structure, ornament, affects, or any other aspect of architecture.[11]

In much of contemporary algorithmic design, processes are adopted, and occasionally adapted, from biology or computer science and applied to architecture, where the dominant interface with architectural intention is the evaluation of the iterative outcomes of the algorithm. These adopted algorithms do not operate on any architectural logic. Instead, it is the architect's role to adjust their parameters iteratively in an attempt to navigate their outcomes to a successful architectural result. A further retreat from intention within computational design is in the prevalent ambition to remove the designer from this feedback loop, automating evaluation[12] based on quantitative criteria, such as structure, in an attempt to optimize the engineering performance of buildings.

Behavioral Formation instead posits a primarily morphogenetic[13] design methodology in which distributed architectural intention self-organizes in a generative algorithmic process. The self-organized intention that emerges from this process is cast into a feedback loop with more direct intention through qualitative evaluation and interaction with explicit design decisions. Consequently, the primary form of intention operates at the micro-scale of algorithmic behavior and is conditioned by macro-scale decisions. This process is a balance between volatile, self-organizing, intention that is encoded within the algorithm, intuitive evaluations, and more stable, explicit decisions. All of these forms of intention are subjective and qualitative; however, the intention encoded within the behavior of the algorithm operates systemically, while the evaluation of its outcomes operates intuitively.

Babiy Yar Memorial, 2010.
Bronze memorial space.

This algorithmic approach draws on a subset of complexity theory known as 'swarm intelligence', which can be defined as the local interaction of autonomous agents from which collective behavior emerges.[14] The translation of this logic into architectural design involves encoding the architect's design intent as numerous discrete behaviors distributed within a population of agents; it is the local interaction of these agents that leads to the self-organization of a meta-level design intention. The design intention embedded within these behaviors can range from specific tectonic decisions to more abstract behaviors designed to produce emergent behavior at a larger scale.

This behavioral approach to architectural design enables an integration of intention with the volatility of emergence. This is not a process of creating emergent form that can later be applied to, or crafted into, architecture. It is a methodology of creating a specific and intentional architecture that is designed through, not after, emergence. The implications of this behavioral approach have been explored over the past eighteen years through the architectural projects described here.

COMPLEXITY

Behavioral Formation draws on the volatility of complex systems that operate at the 'edge of chaos'[15]. These far-from-equilibrium[16] states have the greatest potential for emergence and the generation of new forms and organizations, generating behavior that is not given within their starting conditions or parameters. Working with volatile systems is inherently experimental. These processes are never pure or essentialist; they create chaotic conditions and catastrophic shifts. The intensive processes at work in Behavioral Formation inextricably tie the process and object, imbuing the emergent forms with intricate, complex, and affectual qualities. This intensity is evident in the fibrous mass of the RMIT Mace or the bronze memorial space of the Babiy Yar project,[17] where the intricate organization of the bodies melts into a continuous, highly differentiated surface.

There is no single scientific definition of complexity, while emergence is even harder to define. As John Holland points out: 'It is unlikely that a topic as complicated as emergence will submit weakly to a concise definition, and I have no such definition to offer'.[18] Despite James Crutchfield's claim that 'Defining structure and detecting the emergence of complexity in nature are inherently subjective', the argument posited here is that emergence is a real phenomenon independent of the observer—although not quantifiable.[19] Stephen Wolfram demonstrates that the edge-of-chaos conditions in cellular automata cannot be quantitatively evaluated or recognized: they are qualitative.[20] This is crucial for design, as it foregrounds the importance of the architect's interaction in teasing out emergent qualities from complex systems, given that the complexity of a system is not a determinant of its qualitative emergent characteristics.

SPECIFICITY

While the design processes posited here are algorithmic and consequently systemic, the architectural intent and underlying behaviors are highly subjective. These architectural decisions relate to such concerns as the topology of space, intricacy of structure, and the expressive characteristics of form. These qualitative concerns exceed the pragmatic issues of building science—and, in this regard, Behavioral Formation departs significantly from many computational design approaches that relinquish design intent to the pragmatics of optimizing building performance. The performance of architecture, relative to environmental, structural, or fabrication imperatives, is necessary, but it is argued here that these should not be elevated to the position of the driver of architectural design. The projects contributing to this body of work negotiate pragmatic concerns; however, their subjective, intuitive architectural intention is never abandoned to a set of pseudo-objective performance criteria.

An argument for generative design is often made by using the somewhat dubious claim that the process overcomes preconceived architectural forms, organizations, or tectonics. The work here does not claim to be beyond preconception. However, the generative processes do produce a specific characteristic of form and articulation that resists being explicitly drawn

Composite Wing, 2014.

or modeled. These characteristics, and their negotiation with more explicit intention, lead to the strange specificity of the projects.

Designing through volatile algorithmic processes shifts the nature, but not the degree, of authorship. Design intention within behavioral processes of formation does not relate to the exact dimension or topology of architecture, but instead to the characteristics of architecture: those that emerge from the behavioral process. Form remains within flux for long periods through these processes, while emergent formal characteristics are more resilient and reoccur across iterations.[21] This is a shift in focus from designing the form of the object to designing the nature of the object, where the form is teased out as an emergent property of the process.

It is the emergent properties of self-organizing systems and their affectual capacities that make them compelling. However, the ability of these systems to negotiate complex problems, such as the self-organization of programmatic or structural systems, is a significant contributor to their robustness as architectural design tools.[22] The capacity to negotiate pragmatic concerns within a highly volatile process enables an integration of both the wild and the practical.

The design strategies posited here are not intended to create indexical[23] forms or purist outcomes from complex systems.[24] Instead, these projects are the outcome of subjective decisions applied in a process of negotiating between emergent behavior of complex systems, pragmatic concerns, and direct formal and aesthetic intentions. Subjective intention engages directly in this design process through a strategy of *strange feedback*, in which the outcome of direct modeling processes becomes the input to algorithmic processes, and vice versa. It is a process of constant feedback between bottom-up algorithmic processes and top-down modeling. This recurring operation iteratively creates a synthesis or correlation of direct and generative operations.

Subjective formal and aesthetic intention operates both external to, and integrated within, the algorithmic behavioral process of formation. One reoccurring trait, which is external to the process, is the mute, faceted, geological forms that are employed in several projects[25] as an attempt to resist the discrete reading of separate architectural elements, and to destabilize

RMIT Meeting Pavilion, 2015.

the building's relationship to the ground.[26] Although the geological example is a formal language appropriated from outside architecture, other tendencies emerge from the processes themselves. These emergent tendencies, or characteristics, are coaxed out and refined to become a set of procedural operations, which are redeployed across multiple projects. The *agentBodies*[27] research began as an experiment in blurring the relationship between line, component, and surface. The capacity of this process to generate intricate and ornamentally expressive woven tectonics has since become the focus of the strategy, which has been redeployed in projects including Flinders Street Station and the NGV Pavilion.[28]

The tendencies and limitations of the agent-based algorithms developed within this research have been exploited, exaggerated, and developed into a highly personal formal language. This language of hairy, fibrous, blurred, and geological articulations is not an indexical outcome of agent-based processes, but the interaction of individual subjectivity and the generative capacity of these algorithms.[29] As this research has evolved, the concern has shifted from the development of a broadly applicable behavioral design process to the specificity of the projects and their strange qualities. These qualities are teased out of the interaction of behavioral processes and somewhat idiosyncratic intention.

The design strategies and projects posited here have a complex relationship to biology. The algorithms that underlie this work are not dissimilar to those that underlie many natural phenomena, such as the flocking of birds, the behavior of social insects, or slime mold. Although, it is the logic of collective behavior emerging from local interactions that has been appropriated from swarm intelligence rather than any specific biological behavior. Similarly, the geometry that is created by the accumulation of many small strands though the *fibrous assemblages* strategy has been informed by an understanding of the fibrous character of biological material from electron microscope imaging. However, there is no direct imitation of specific biological conditions or processes. Instead, these images become another way of conceptualizing and describing geometry: a shift from the mathematical description of surface to the computational accumulation of vectors.

NGV Pavilion, 2015–2016.

Behavioral processes of formation work by accumulating architectural geometry or matter, such as the assemblage of strands or agentBodies. This description of architectural matter is characterized by its small scale relative to the whole: a network of interconnected parts that weave together to form irreducible assemblages. These interconnected parts have specific, designed, geometry, distinct from simple computational geometry such as voxels or particles. However, these tectonic assemblages are not compatible with the way in which we currently construct buildings, as they do not privilege surface or the standardized building components used in construction.

The feasibility of behavioral processes of formation is dependent on the development of procedural approaches to construction that mirror this logic of design. A key aspect of this is the appropriation of an emerging set of direct-deposition and robotic fabrication techniques. Reprogrammable robotic construction enables intricate, non-standard assembly of parts, while direct-deposition techniques open up a new space of formal possibility. These techniques allow the accretion of material to be thought of in a similar manner to the digital process—as behavioral.[30] The logical extension of this behavioral conception of the robot is explored in the *stigmergic robotics* strategy. This approach operates by programming behaviors directly to a robot that senses and responds to the accretion of material in real-time, creating a feedback between computational and material behavior.[31]

IMPLICATIONS

Complex systems are inherently processes of negotiation. The non-linear interactions within behavioral processes of formation simultaneously embed multiple criteria or intention within a single form. This negotiated whole departs from the discrete articulation of architectural elements and roles that has dominated architecture from antiquity to Modernism. The mutual interconnectedness of architectural roles blurs the distinction between parts and creates irreducible assemblages.

This interconnectedness extends to drawing conventions. Modernism rejected the privileged perspective of the Renaissance in favor of the objectivity of the axonometric, and in particular the exploded axonometric (the notational device of discrete articulation). The architecture of Behavioral Formation is interconnected and irreducible; it cannot be drawn with exploded axonometrics. Instead, it is described through its behavioral logic, tectonic prototypes, and saturated images intended to convey emergent affects.

Behavioral Formation resists known architectural expressions by undermining the hierarchies and recognition of architectural signifiers. The geometry of Behavioral Formation does not relate to a given architecture role: it is not a beam, column, or façade, but potentially a negotiation of all these. These roles do not have a linear relationship to geometry within the design process; instead, geometry negotiates between these roles, recast as behaviors, creating hybrid geometries embedded with multiple intents. The concrete shell of the Fibrous Tower[32] is simultaneously structural, ornamental, sun shading, and inhabitable. This separation of architectural role from geometry is amplified through the repetition of the same process of formation at multiple scales—a *polyscalar tectonic* strategy. Within this process the role of geometry changes from one scale to another (for example, from spatial to ornamental), while the geometric expression is consistent.

This blurring of roles extends to the blurring of geometric descriptions. The generation of geometry from the bottom up—from fibrous assemblages—blurs the distinction between line, component, and surface. These conditions are no longer conceptually different; rather, they are different instances of the accumulation of the same geometry. A line is the linear accumulation of points rather than a mathematical description of connectivity between two points. Likewise, a surface is the matting together of lines or fibers in a manifold topology, rather than the description of u and v isoparameters.[33] This enables architectural geometry to subtly shift or blur between surface, line, and component.

Redundancy is a characteristic of complex systems, such as the routing networks of the internet, or the minimal path networks of slime mold. The role of redundancy in Behavioral Formation is in opposition to contemporary concepts of optimization that isolate and

Fibrous Tower 2, 2009. Shell detail.

quantitatively evaluate specific minima or maxima conditions,[34] such as structural efficiency or solar gain. Discretely articulating and designing a series of systems[35] is contrary to strategies such as fibrous assemblages that negotiate between different architectural roles such as enclosure, structure, and ornament within the one body of geometry—strands. The structural excess of a fibrous assemblage operates ornamentally, while the ornamental excess may operate structurally. This redundancy is also inherently robust, as it can deal with change that the optimization of specific conditions cannot. The integration of multiple roles into a single malleable geometry creates efficiencies, such as the integration of skin and structure in a semi-monocoque. This is not, however, an argument for the efficiency or optimal capacity of Behavioral Formation;[36] instead, it is the qualitative characteristics of these redundant conditions that are of interest. There is an ambiguity in the geometry of the Fibrous Tower 2 and the Fibrous House:[37] the redundancy of the fibers blurs the distinction of structure, skin, and ornament, in favor of a reading of intricate mass.

Through the development of this body of work, new problems are constantly created. The most significant of these is *global ignorance*, which arises from privileging the local interactions of agents to the exclusion of global conditions—a necessary protocol for creating complex systems. This local interaction of agents is problematic in the design of architectural concerns that rely on a global-scale comprehension of the architectural project, such as enclosure or structure. This limitation has become the catalyst to develop strategies to deal with these fundamental architectural concerns and open up new experimental potential. For example, the strategy of *manifold swarms* was developed to deal with the inability of agents to know their topological relationships, while *the agency of structure* is a response to the need for global structural analysis within emergent design processes. Through the development of these new strategies, specific architectural characteristics emerge.

Behavioral Formation is not an attempt to represent the complex nature of formation in the world. Rather, it is an attempt to instrumentalize this understanding as a generative process. This is a concern for an emerging generation of architects. A trait common among others of this generation is the use of complexity as a generative tool, which is applied directly to the reductive body of modernity. Instead, the ambition of this work is to explore the architectural possibilities that emerge from this behavioral approach, and their wider architectural implications. These implications for architectural form, tectonics, spatial conditions, characteristics, and affects should be evident within, and best understood through, the projects themselves. The interaction of non-linear computational processes and subjective design decisions creates an architecture that is rich with intricate order and the strange characteristics that emerge from these processes.

1 This is discussed at greater length in the section Strange Specificity.

2 DeLanda 1995.

3 A short history outlining the relationship of complex systems and architecture is described in my PhD dissertation 'Behavioral Formation: Multi-Agent Algorithmic Design Strategies' (Snooks 2014, pp. 19-28).

4 'Affect', 'affectual' and 'affective' are used to refer to the emotional effect of architectural space on the subject; see Glossary of Terms.

5 See Glossary of Terms.

6 Distributed authorship in architecture, and its analogy to Web 2.0 concepts, is discussed by Mario Carpo in the essay 'Digital Indeterminism: The New Digital Commons and the Dissolution of Architectural Authorship' (Lorenzo-Eiroa 2013, pp. 47–51).

7 Mario Carpo posits that Renaissance humanists, and in particular Alberti, 'invented architecture as an art of drawing, and the notion of the modern architect as a new kind of humanist author—a thinker and maker of drawings' (Lorenzo-Eiroa 2013, p. 48).

8 The stopping problem was a critique of animate processes, which questioned the logic for stopping the process at any given frame or point in time.

9 Lynn's work has been hugely influential within generative architectural design and is an important precursor to this research. This is discussed further in the Multi-Agent Algorithms section.

10 In particular, this is a reference to Gaudi's catenary models and Otto's soap-film models, which are discussed in greater detail in the Volatility section.

11 The nature of the design intention within this body of work is most clearly described through the individual projects and their descriptions.

12 With the growing adoption of machine learning, and the pattern recognition capacity of neural networks, the automation of pseudo-qualitative evaluation is increasingly feasible. However, this typically presupposes an a priori body of training data, which inherently limits the speculative capacity of the design search.

13 See Glossary of Terms.

14 Swarm intelligence is discussed in greater detail in the Behavioral Methodologies section.

15 'Edge of chaos' refers to the state of a system that is between order and chaos. This is a state of maximum complexity.

16 Far-from-equilibrium systems are those in a state of dynamic equilibrium. The term was coined by Ilya Prigogine in relation to thermodynamics.

17 See RMIT Mace and Babiy Yar Project sections.

18 Holland 1999, p. 3.

19 Crutchfield 1994.

20 The qualitative nature of Wolfram's classifications is discussed in greater depth in the Volatility section.

21 These formal characteristics include properties such as the curvature or local organization of parts, and their behavior can be illustrated through the example of liquid foam. In generating foam, the topology or size of the bubbles is unpredictable, but their foaminess is a stable emergent characteristic. This concept is described in greater detail in the article 'Observations on the Algorithmic Emergence of Character' (Snooks, in Abruzzo 2007, pp. 92–101).

22 The Composite Wing is an example that integrates structural heuristics within a generative algorithmic process. See Composite Wing Project section.

23 'Indexical' is used to describe an object that indexes, or refers to, its process of formation in which there is a causal relationship between formation and the characteristics of the object.

24 A critique of the purist application on indexical algorithms is outlined in the Volatility section.

25 These projects include the RMIT Meeting Pavilion, Babiy Yar, and Malibu House. See the corresponding project sections and the Catalog of Projects.

26 This use of geological forms is discussed in greater detail in the Strange Specificity section.

27 See the AgentBodies Strategy section.

28 See Catalog of Projects and NGV Pavilion Project section respectively.

29 The messy, hairy characteristics developed in this work have been influenced by the work of Jason Payne and Francois Roche.

30 An argument for procedural fabrication is expanded on in the Behavioral Composites Strategy and AgentBody Prototypes Project sections.

31 See Stigmergic Robotics Strategy section.

32 See Fibrous Tower Project section.

33 This is the logic of describing a spline surface.

34 Contemporary multi-objective optimization algorithms enable the negotiation of a series of different criteria; however, these algorithms are limited to dealing with quantitative rather than qualitative concerns.

35 This discrete articulation of systems is a typical characteristic of Modern architecture, which reached its apex in British high-tech, with architects such as Norman Foster, Richard Rogers, and Nicholas Grimshaw.

36 Although it is worth noting that structures in nature that evolve through self-organizing processes, such as the formation of bone, are highly optimal.

37 See Catalog of Projects.

ESSAY

BEHAVIORAL METHODOLOGIES

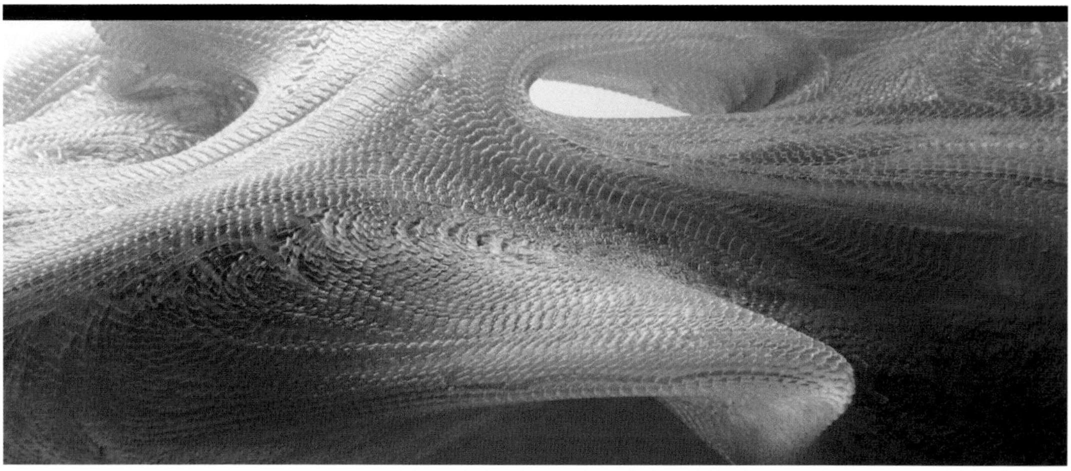

Behavioral Formation intertwines emergence and intention in the design of an architecture characterized by its strange specificity. Central to this specific approach is a more generalizable, generative design methodology that draws from the logic of swarm intelligence and operates through a multi-agent algorithmic process. This strategy functions by encoding simple architectural intents, or decisions, within a distributed system of autonomous computational agents. The interaction of these local decisions generates a complex, self-organized, design intention, giving rise to a form of collective intelligence and emergent behavior at a global scale. The development of this behavioral methodology represents a reconceptualization of design agency and posits an approach that integrally ties intention, self-organization, behavior, geometry, and material.

Developed within a broader milieu of generative design, this approach is a rejection of computational architecture's propensity for interdisciplinary appropriation of algorithms complete with their indexical relationship to known and inherently selected forms. This is not a concern for the appropriation of emergent pattern or form; instead, this methodology is fundamentally a speculative approach. It is premised on the importance of the architectural logic of algorithms and the relationship of the generative process and object, where an object's qualities and tectonic characteristics are understood to be integrally tied to its process of formation. This behavioral methodology has been distilled into a series of strategies that instrumentalize a self-organizational approach to architectural design.

Swarm intelligence describes the decentralized, local interaction of autonomous agents that self-organize in generating emergent collective behavior. The term 'swarm intelligence' was originally used to describe cellular robotics, but is now more broadly associated with the collective behavior that emerges from biological, social, and computational processes. The complex order that is created by the logic of swarm intelligence is vividly expressed in natural systems such as the schooling of fish, flocking of birds, behavior of social insects, and the self-organization of slime mold.

The appropriation of swarm algorithms to architecture is not an attempt to introduce biology as a metaphor, or to make architecture swarm-like.[1] It is not the particular biological

National Art Museum of China, 2010.

rules or behaviors underlying these algorithms that are appropriated; instead, it is their algorithmic structure and the logic of spatial interaction, negotiation, and self-organization. Behavioral Formation is premised on the design of architectural, rather than biological, behaviors as the basis for a generative process. The architect's design intention is recast as a set of procedures, or behaviors, that interact in generating a self-organization of design intent. Importantly, encoding architectural intent within an algorithm is fundamentally different to the contemporary appropriation of known, indexical algorithms that create abstract templates for architecture. The purist appropriation of the form or pattern of these templates is devoid of architectural logic or intention, and necessitates a subsequent interpretation into architecture, rather than producing an architecture that emerges from an algorithmic process driven by architectural decisions.[2]

The architectural nature of these behaviors can vary significantly: from pragmatic rules regarding issues of structure or programmatic adjacencies, to more abstract behaviors that create macro-scale effects such as architectural form. For instance, structural intention can be encoded as behaviors designed to locally bundle a network of strands. In this example, intention might reside solely at the micro-level as bundling behaviors designed to create specific, local, tectonic conditions. Alternatively, turbulent flows emerging from the interaction of agents in the generation of form represent a more abstract level of intention. This intention may have less to do with the specific micro-level conditions than with the emergence of complex order at the macro-scale.

Intention operates through both the design of the underlying rules or behaviors and the evaluation of the emergent outcomes of their interaction. The non-linear, or complex, operation of these systems opens a volatile space of possibility between the parameters of the system and its outcome, which resists causal relationships and predictable results—instead provoking a speculative approach. Ultimately, it is the iterative feedback between these two modes of intention that guides the design process. The local behaviors are evaluated through their capacity to generate successful architectural forms and organizations, with this evaluation then being fed back to alter and fine-tune these underlying behaviors. Behavioral processes are at their most volatile during their initial iterations. While there are no causal

Malibu House, 2011–2013. The behavior of the strand-based, multi-agent model deployed in the generation of this ceiling is designed to create a specific, localized character of pattern and tectonics.

links between parameters and their effects, an intuitive understanding of a behavioral algorithm develops over the course of the design project, and across projects.

It is the multitude of agents and their interactions that lead to emergent behavior. If emergence is dependent on the creation of discernible macro-level behavior[3]—if it is a qualitative phenomena—then, for an emergent architecture to have an affective capacity, it must emerge at a scale at which the architecture is experienced. Consequently, the agents need to operate at a scale at which the perception of the individual agents recedes, allowing the dominant reading to be of the emergent organization generated by the agents. This suggests that the agent needs to operate at a scale significantly smaller than that of an architectonic element (wall, column or fenestration) and foregrounds the importance of high-population models. While the 'three body problem'[4] might demonstrate a minimal definition of a multi-agent system capable of complex order, it is in the extreme population models, such as weather systems, that volatility and chaotic behavior are most evident. This has been a catalyst for increasing the population of the multi-agent algorithms developed over the course of this research, leading to highly intricate emergent forms.

The translation of an algorithm into geometry establishes the project's indexicality, or registration of the process, in form. Cellular automata, for example, mapped in its typical state (a grid of black and white squares), always index their generative process regardless of the emergent capacity of its rules. The generation of formal characteristics that are neither indexical to the algorithm, nor geometric substrate, requires an enmeshed relationship of the two. This necessitates a process in which form emerges from the interaction of the algorithm and geometric substrate, rather than geometry simply being applied to the outcome of an algorithm. While multi-agent algorithms usually consider the point or vector to be the substrate of the agent, this is a significant constraint for architectural design that is typically constructed from higher-level geometry such as line, plane, and volume. The spatial nature of architectural intention, and its instantiation as behaviors within behavioral design processes, necessitate defining the computational agent through geometry and its connectivity: topology. Consequently, this research explores how agency can be encoded within the malleable substrates of lines (strands and splines), networks (meshes, graphs, and surfaces),

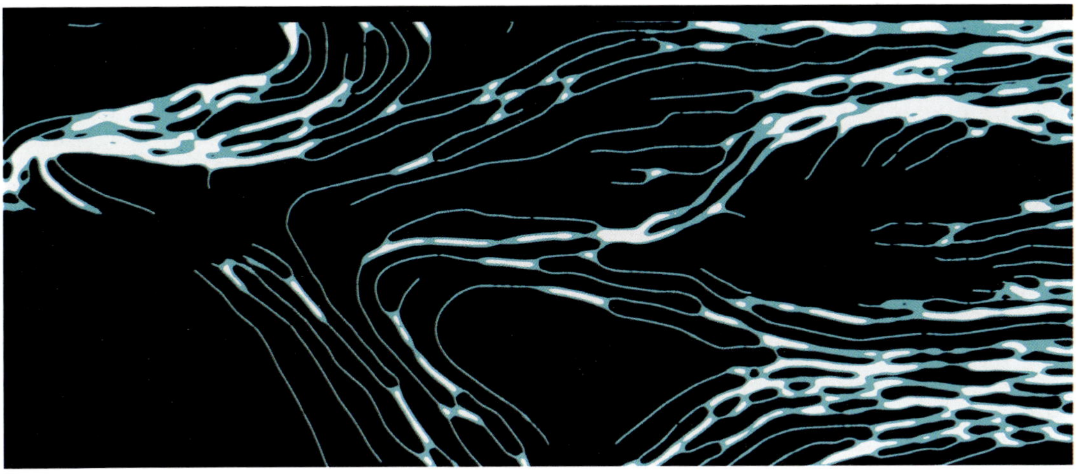

and bodies (components), in the generation of form that exceeds its process and creates specific, non-indexical, formal characteristics.[5]

POSITING A BEHAVIORAL PARADIGM

The behavioral design processes posited here fundamentally differ from the broader lineage of generative design methodologies, through their capacity to integrate architectural intention within the core of the generative process. This reconceptualizes generative design, and its relationship to architectural intention, through the self-organizational capacity of algorithmic behaviors. It is a process that neither appropriates external behavior, nor seeks known conditions or optima—it is experimental and volatile. The capacity to encode behavior within geometry avoids the appropriation of known mappings and applied geometry; instead, it enables behaviors to negotiate through the substrate of geometry. This methodology establishes the basis for a behavioral paradigm of architectural design.

While the bulk of this research involves the design and interrelation of form, structure, and ornament, the original impetus for this work came from a concern for programmatic self-organization. This research into behavioral design strategies began in early 2002 with experiments and research for the Emergent Field project.[6] The project was premised on an understanding of Melbourne's laneway urbanism. The center of Melbourne has an active street life that is prevalent in the laneways rather than in the planned streets of the Hoddle Grid. These laneways were originally intended as service alleys, which have more recently been re-appropriated by bars, cafes and shops. Understanding this as an emergent condition, the ambition of the project was to develop a strategy of emergent urbanism to redesign a desolate Modernist plaza in the Melbourne CBD. A multi-agent algorithmic process was developed to self-organize the distribution of program at a fine grain. Each small volume of program was encoded with behaviors that related to its relative cohesion, attraction, and repulsion from each programmatic type. The interaction of these agents generated a self-organized distribution of program.[7] While the project's initial premise was programmatic, many aspects of this current design research—such as embedding agency within lines and

Emergent Field, 2002–2003.
Composite views.

surfaces, and the generation of emergent form, structure, and ornament from multi-agent algorithms—have their origin in this project.

As both program and form can be encoded as behaviors within a single generative process, these concerns—which are often cast in binary opposition—are able to simultaneously interact. This mutual interaction creates non-linear rather than binary or sequential relationships. The inherently inclusive nature of this approach is flexible enough to absorb a multitude of influences or design intentions, and need not privilege a single generator. This approach enables all aspects of architecture to be thought of as having their own independent, but mutually negotiating, agency.[8] This mutual negotiation resists individual dogmas regarding the source of formation, and is contrary to any form of purity or essentialism[9]—whether this be the purity of the Modernist mantra of 'form follows function'; the physical form-finding of Gaudi, Otto and their computational acolytes; or the indexical templates of the algorithmic expressionists[10]. Behavioral Formation is a highly iterative process of negotiation that creates a coherent assemblage—maintaining difference within a continuous whole.

The non-linear operation of behavioral methodologies is capable of, and indeed characterized by, chaotic shifts within a continuous system, as opposed to parametric strategies that create gradient differentiation within a known range. The *woven composites* research, developed for the Aalto University project[11], demonstrates this non-linear capacity. The agentBodies[12] change their behavior in kind, rather than simply degree, causing a shift from a knitted to a woven expression. These expressions are not collaged or composed, but instead are expressions of a single system. The mutual interaction and negotiation of the bodies maintain a coherent and continuous order despite changes in expression.

Through behavioral design processes, intentions, or parameters, that do not explicitly relate to form, become intrinsic to the generation of form and its affectual capacities. The local behavior of agents are responses to decisions regarding program, form, structure, materiality, tectonics, ornament, and fabrication techniques; the interaction of these concerns gives rise to form and its affects. Consequently, the affects of an architectural space are

Aalto University, 2012.
Woven composites studies.

an emergent outcome of a series of formal and non-formal behaviors in the process of formation: a condition akin to Sanford Kwinter's description of 'true formalism'[13]. Behavioral methodologies liberate matter from the imposition of form, enabling digital matter to be encoded with architectural intent, and thus to be thought of as an active agent in the process of formation.

The non-linear nature of Behavioral Formation differentiates it from the linear causal relationships established between parameters and geometric change in parametric design or associative modeling. Within linear parametric design, all possibility is already given in the starting condition. This is a paradigm of development, rather than inception, as it offers no active process for something new to emerge. Parametric design is currently the dominant mode of digital design, reducing computation simply to a flexible tool of manipulation, and neglecting the ability of computation to deal with complexity and processes of formation. Parametric design becomes an act of selection, rather than emergent formation.

Appropriating and developing behavioral systems for architectural design should not be misunderstood as the use of multi-agent algorithms to simulate human occupation or action. Any simulation of human occupation is simply a tool of analysis rather than generative design.[14] Behavioral methodologies do not attempt to predict the behavior of people, but instead to re-conceptualize design intention through algorithmic behaviors. Similarly, these methodologies are not an attempt to assign literal behavior or action to kinetic form; rather, it is an abstract approach to the generation of form from behavior.

BEHAVIORAL TECTONICS

The non-linearity of Behavioral Formation is at odds with the sequential or hierarchical nature of many processes and relationships within architecture. A non-linear process that is in a constant state of mutual negotiation resists establishing subservient or hierarchical relationships. A single behavior within this process may carry greater significance or relative importance, although it is always operating in a mutually effecting feedback. As such, a

Fibrous Tower, 2008. The concrete shell negotiates between form, structure, and ornament, to decouple the relationship of architectural role and geometry.

single behavior does not dictate or structure the others. This non-linear, or non-hierarchical, nature of Behavioral Formation resists tectonic hierarchies and refocuses tectonic concerns on the assemblage at the micro-scale—from which tectonics emerges. Through this behavioral approach to tectonics, a synthetic relationship is established between scales, and a blurring between diverse tectonic elements. The motivation for this is to resist the normative frame through which we read architecture, and to develop a formal and aesthetic vocabulary for an architecture that emerges from complex systems.

The negotiation between many behaviors resists a linear relationship between architectural elements and a singular architectural role. For example, columns and beams have a specific architectural role that they typically signify or index. However, a topologically complex surface could be generated by behaviors that include the resistance of vertical load (as a column does) and enabling horizontal span (as a beam does). Consequently, these behaviors are not indexical to a specific architectural or geometric element. Instead, these design intentions are influences that negotiate in the process of forming the topology.

This uncoupling of the individual identity of an architectural element, and its relationship to an architectural role, can operate at two scales: that of a single architectural concern (such as structure), or across concerns (such as program, structure, and ornament). At a single scale, rather than articulating primary, secondary, and tertiary structure, a single body of geometry negotiates structure at various scales within a continuous whole. This is not to suggest that Behavioral Formation involves a complete flattening of hierarchy. Instead, hierarchy is an emergent property of a decentralized system, rather than being predetermined and based on sequential scales.

This compression of tectonic hierarchies in itself is not novel. Examples of this can be seen in Felix Candela's dissolution of the individual articulation of shell, beam, and column, and in the erosion of the hierarchy of form and structure within the form-finding experiments of Frei Otto.[15] Otto's work with membrane structures created a negotiation between form and structure through the minimization of surface tension within the material computation of soap-film models. However, a fundamental difference between the agency of Behavioral

Nine Elms: Retroactive Form Study, 2017–2018. Detail.

Formation and material computation is the ability to encode behavior that is not limited to the physical laws within which material computation operates. This shift from physics to behavior opens new possibilities in form generation, and resists reductive notions of optimization.[16]

BEHAVIORAL STRATEGIES

The behavioral processes of design posited here were developed over the past seventeen years through design projects, and refined into a series of re-deployable strategies. These strategies relate to the interaction of behavior and geometry, processes of feedback, material behavior, and procedural fabrication. The *fibrous assemblages* and *agentBodies* strategies describe the capacity to encode behavior within specific geometric substrates—strands and bodies respectively—with their tectonic implications explored through projects such as the Fibrous Tower projects[17] and RMIT Mace[18]. The *manifold swarms* and *polyscalar tectonics* strategies operate through the interaction of agents to create emergent spatial and tectonic conditions. A series of strategies—*strange feedback*, *agency of structure*, *painterly formation*, and *stigmergic robotics*—have been developed primarily in response to the global ignorance of multi-agent algorithms.[19] These strategies disrupt the purity of the algorithmic process by establishing a feedback with other forms of intention or agency.

Within the design process, the various strategies are frequently combined or operate in parallel. In particular, the compression of surface topology, structure, and tectonics has been explored through an integration of the manifold swarms and agentBodies strategies. This has been exploited in projects such as the NGV Pavilion[20], and Nine Elms (Retroactive Form Study)[21] to create an irreducible relationship between form, structure, and articulation.

While the specificity of the projects are created through the interaction of these strategies and project-specific design intention, the strategies themselves are more generalizable approaches independent of any given project. This is not to suggest that the strategies are generic or without design bias, behavior, or intention. Quite the contrary, in fact: they have been developed through specific architectural concerns.

Behavioral processes of formation reconceptualize the relationship between architectural design intention and generative algorithms—recasting intention as behaviors embedded within self-organizing, multi-agent systems. A primary concern of this research is to develop design methodologies that engage with emergent phenomena and explore the architectural processes implicit within swarm intelligence. Ultimately, however, it is the emergence of architecture from these systems—with complex order, and rich with intricate detail—that is of greater interest than its process of becoming.

Nine Elms: Retroactive Form Study, 2017–2018.
The manifold swarms and agentBodies strategies are integrated in the design process to create a turbulent, thick, fibrous mass. This retroactive form study was designed for the Coder Le Monde exhibition at the Centre Pompidou. It was developed as an intensification of the process used in the Nine Elms Bridge project.

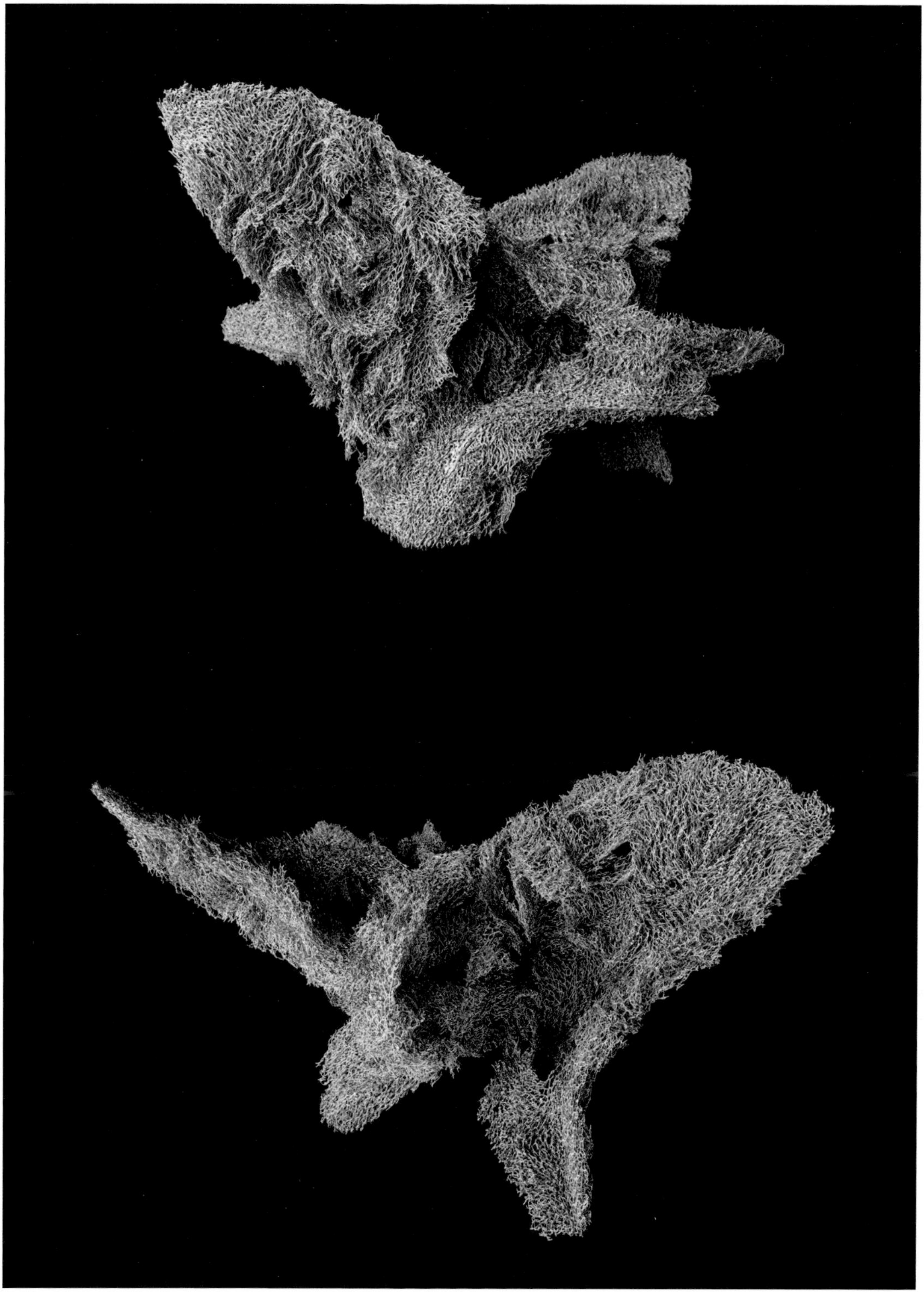

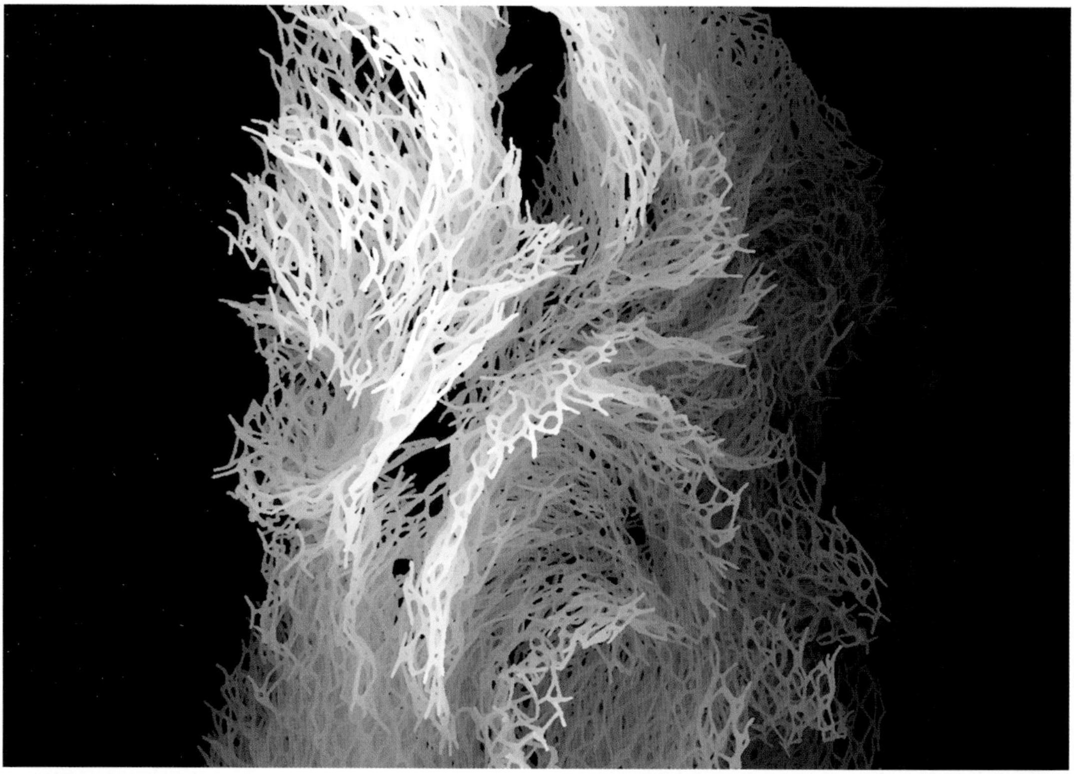

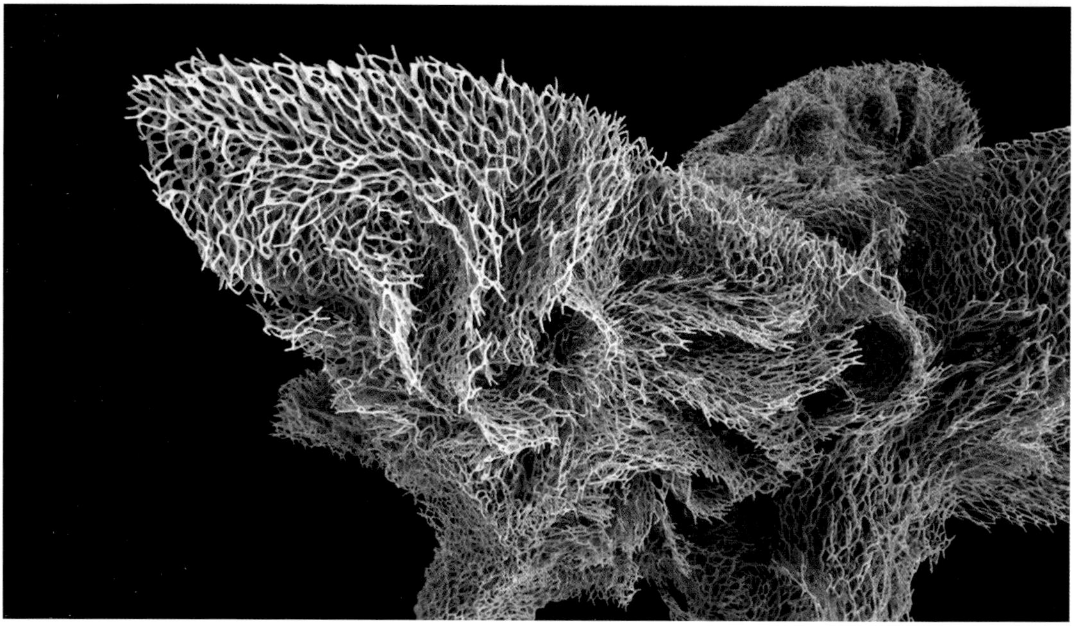

Nine Elms: Retroactive Form Study, 2017–2018.
Agents are distributed through a manifold swarm strategy.

The interconnection of agentBodies creates a complex structure and intricate ornamental characteristics.

1 The relationship of this work to biology is discussed in greater detail in the Introduction: Between Emergence and Intention, and the Strange Specificity section.

2 This distinction is discussed further in the Volatility section.

3 As argued by Steven Johnson (Johnson 2002, p. 19).

4 The 'three body problem' describes the mutual interaction of three bodies with mass. Poincaré's work on the three body problem in 1887 demonstrated indeterminate behavior arising from the non-linear interaction of three bodies. The non-linearity of the three body problem and the non-periodic orbits that it creates led Poincaré to posit the concept of sensitivity to initial conditions—the basis of chaos theory. See Mitchell 2009, pp. 21–22.

5 The nature of encoding behavior within a geometric substrate is discussed further in the Multi-Agent Algorithms section.

6 Emergent Field was submitted as Roland Snooks's Major Project (undergraduate thesis) at RMIT University in June 2003 (supervised by Paul Minifie).

7 These programmatic agents also negotiated with the existing urban fabric.

8 Within this body of work there are two approaches to encoding independent agency within a population of agents: as an 'ecology of swarms' or as a 'contextually differentiating swarm'. With the ecologies approach, each aspect of architecture (e.g., tectonic, structural, or programmatic) is treated as a separate population of agents—conceptualized as separate species of agents that interact in a mutual feedback loop. The contextually differentiating approach involves a homogenous population of agents that locally differentiate based on their context. For example, in the Nine Elms Bridge project (See Catalog of Projects), the agents shift between tensile and compressive behaviors based on their specific structural condition.

9 These traits are increasingly evident in computational architecture, as witnessed through the array of pure compression or tension structures designed with the aspiration of a faithful reification of engineering constraints. This is discussed in further detail in the Volatility section.

10 'Algorithmic expressionists' are defined here as those who deploy the algorithm to create expressive templates, which remain in their indexical, pure, or typical instantiation or mapping. A critique of this is further developed in the Volatility section.

11 See Catalogue of Projects.

12 AgentBodies is a generative tectonic strategy discussed at greater length in the AgentBodies Strategy section.

13 Kwinter 2008, p. 146.

14 What is being argued for here is in contrast to Patrik Schumacher's recent adoption and promotion of crowd modeling as a method of evaluating the use of space (Lorenzo-Eiroa, Sprecher 2013, pp. 53–60). Schumacher's logic has evolved from crowd simulations that have been used in character animation and egress engineering for more than a decade. This logic is that of evaluation of design rather than as a design generator.

15 Examples of this dissolution in Candela's work include La Iglesia de la Milagrosa (Mexico City, 1955) and Caseta de Ventas (Valle Verde, Guadalajara, Mexico, 1960), while Otto's work includes the Munich Olympic Stadium (1972) and Stuttgart Railway Station (2021).

16 A critique of form-finding and optimization is elaborated on in the Volatility section.

17 See Fibrous Tower Project section and Fibrous Tower 2 in Catalog of Projects.

18 See RMIT Mace Project section.

19 'Global ignorance' in this context refers to the privileging of local interactions over a global, or macro, understanding of the population of agents within multi-agent models. This is discussed at greater length in the Volatility section.

20 See NGV Pavilion Project section.

21 The Nine Elms: Retroactive Form Study was exhibited as part of the Coder Le Monde exhibition at the Centre Pompidou in 2018. It has since been acquired for the permanent collection of the Centre Pompidou. See Catalog of Projects.

STRATEGY

FIBROUS ASSEMBLAGES

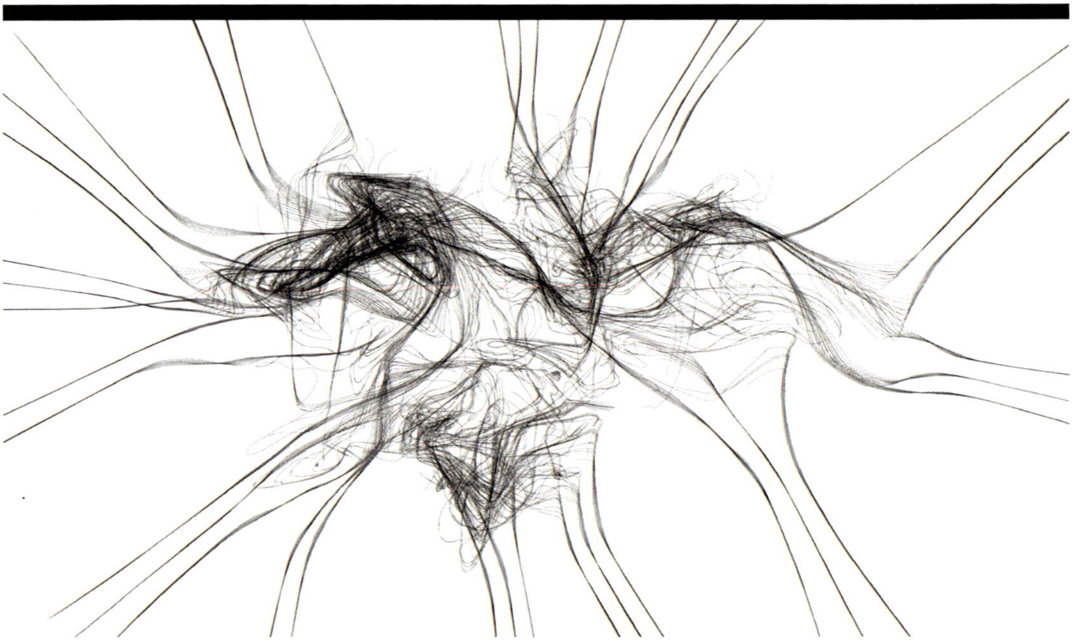

Fibrous House, 2012.
Strand geometry plan.

Materials are not homogenous bodies of matter, but instead are assembled from complex micro-scale elements, forming intricate structures which imbue materials with their bias and specific capacities. This understanding of material, or matter, has been vividly rendered with the advent of the electron microscope; such imagery has been a useful conceptual and aesthetic reference in this work. Conceptualizing matter as the assemblage of micro-scale elements was the catalyst for developing *fibrous assemblages*: a multi-agent design strategy that encodes agent behavior within the geometry of strands.[1] This strategy draws upon Frei Otto's self-organizing woolen strand experiments, but extends the agency from localized bundling based on surface energy minimization (of water) to a complex set of architectural design decisions or behaviors.[2]

Within behavioral design processes, fibrous assemblages are created through the local interaction of strands in the generation of architectural form, surface, structure and ornament. Fibrous assemblages can either be deployed at the scale of a single architectural concern, such as structure or ornament, or they can operate across these scales, exhibiting structural or ornamental behavior according to the specific local conditions. Taken to its logical extreme, this design strategy offers a conceptual approach to creating all facets of architecture from a single geometric type – the strand.

Fibrous assemblages are structurally non-linear, and are not defined by prescribed hierarchies of primary, secondary, and tertiary elements. Instead, hierarchies emerge from the non-linear

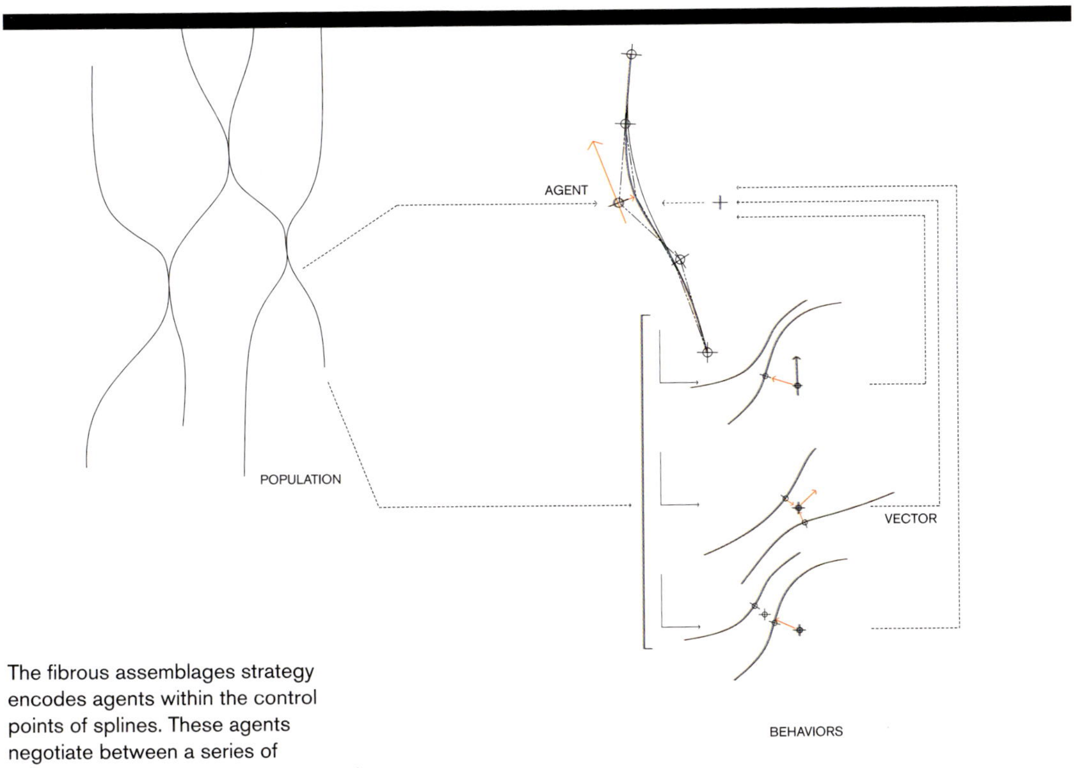

The fibrous assemblages strategy encodes agents within the control points of splines. These agents negotiate between a series of behaviors, both spatial and topological.

interaction of strands as variations in intensity, intricacy, and density. Within the assemblage of strands comprising the Fibrous Tower 2,[3] features such as thick surfaces, dominant bundles, and weaker horizontal links emerged from a less articulated field.

Strands within fibrous assemblages weave to form surfaces, while surfaces delaminate into strands. This relationship between surface and strand contributes to a related blurring of the distinction between architectural roles such as skin and structure. The excess and redundancy of fibrous assemblages enable the strands to operate in multiple roles simultaneously. The strands negotiate between structural, topological and ornamental behaviors encoded within each strand. Each of these architectural imperatives become embedded within the final form. For example, within the Fibrous House,[4] the highly networked nature of the thin strand geometry creates strength through its structural depth and connectivity. While this is not in itself structurally optimal, the geometry concurrently embeds other architectural imperatives such as ornament and surface. This creates a condition in which every strand operates structurally within a redundant, highly ornamental assemblage.[5]

A volatile approach to fibrous assemblages was developed through the Fibrous House project as a speculation on the tectonics and aesthetics of designing exclusively through strands. The project's form is intentionally chaotic, a wild and intricate assemblage that is a vivid expression of the intensive algorithmic process of its formation. The fibrous tentacles of the house extend from the landscape, converging in a turbulent flow that wraps to enclose the program of the

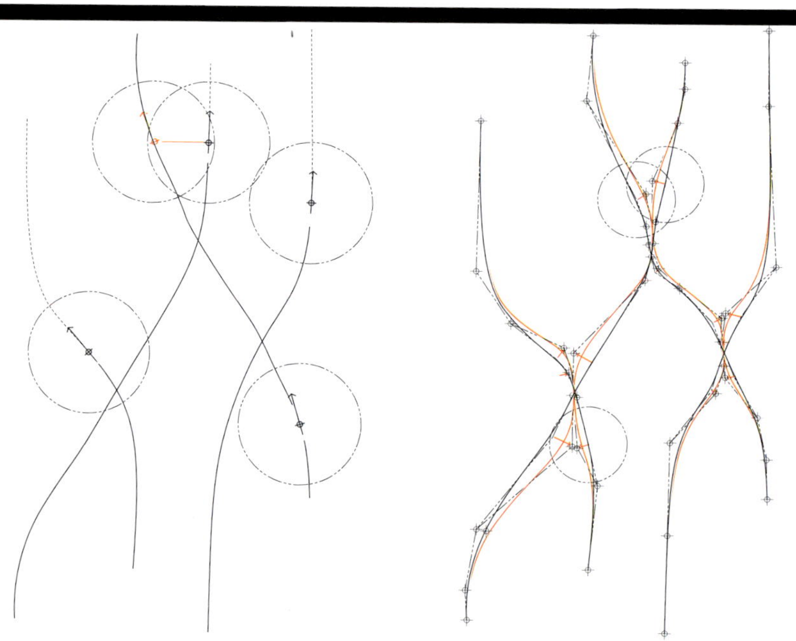

Agents operate at two scales within fibrous assemblages: the generation of strands, and the self-organization of strands.

house. While the project is not deliberately referential or metaphorical, characteristics generated through the process lie somewhere between the reading of the natural fibers of plants and the tissue of flesh – disquieting qualities that were teased out of the process.

At its extreme, as in the Fibrous House, fibrous assemblages lead to a singular architectural expression. However, this is not a homogenous expression; it is a field capable of supporting emergent internal differentiation. This differentiation emerges as sub-expressions, where the assemblage expresses locally differentiated characteristics, such as the coexistence of the cellular and striated conditions in the fibrous towers. The non-linear feedback within the design process of fibrous assemblages enables them to absorb competing imperatives – imperatives that generate locally differentiated characteristics within a continuous whole.

Fibrous assemblages have a complicated relationship to surface. While strands can matt together to generate surface, it is very difficult to create a coherent surface topology without relying on a surface as an a priori input, or attractor in the system. However, this is precisely the appeal of these geometries: they resist the simple geometric expression of a surface. Fibrous assemblages maintain a fuzziness; they blur the boundaries between surface and line, resist enclosure as a definitive edge, are topologically vague, and weave and unravel in complex and subtle ways.

Fibrous assemblages rely on a sufficient population of elements to enable an emergent expression: that of the assemblage rather than the expression of the individual line. While fibrous

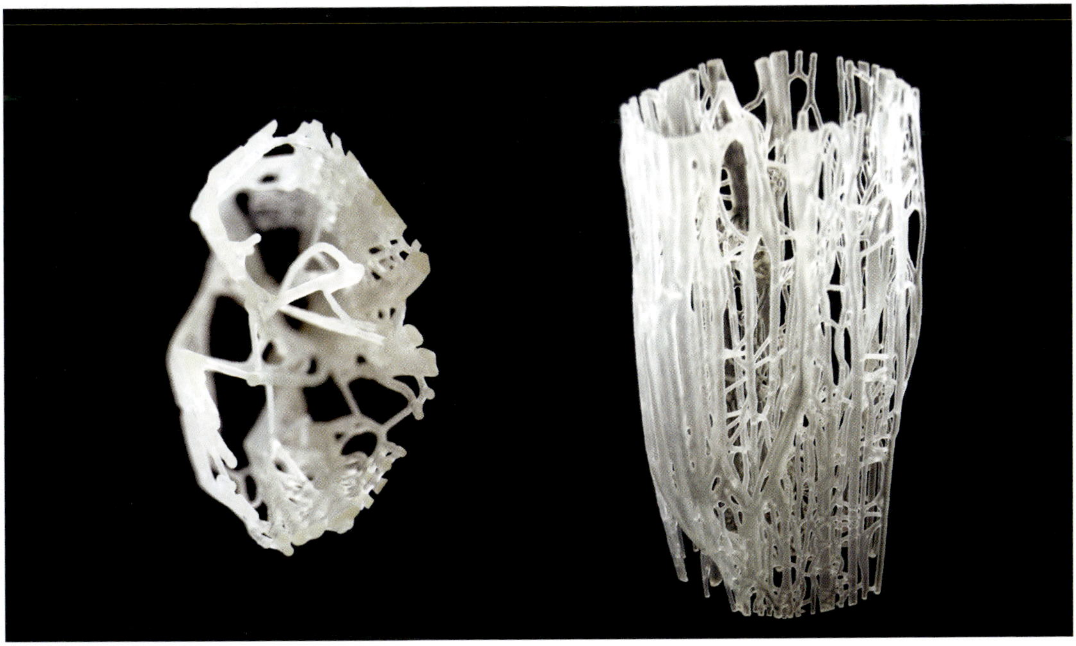

Fibrous Tower 2, 2009.
Shell study model.

assemblages often exhibit interesting local characteristics through the bundling and weaving of strands, it is the expression of the system's self-organization that is most compelling: the emergence of complex order that is readable at the building scale.

The volatility and intricacy of this fibrous assemblages strategy has been increasing as this lineage of research projects progress. At the scale used in the Fibrous Tower,[6] the strands are subservient to the surface geometry of the tower. The strands in Fibrous Tower 2 are less constrained and exhibit a less applied characteristic. However, it is not until the high population assemblage of the Fibrous House that the emergent order of the strands becomes the dominant expression: a condition where surface and form are inseparable from strand.

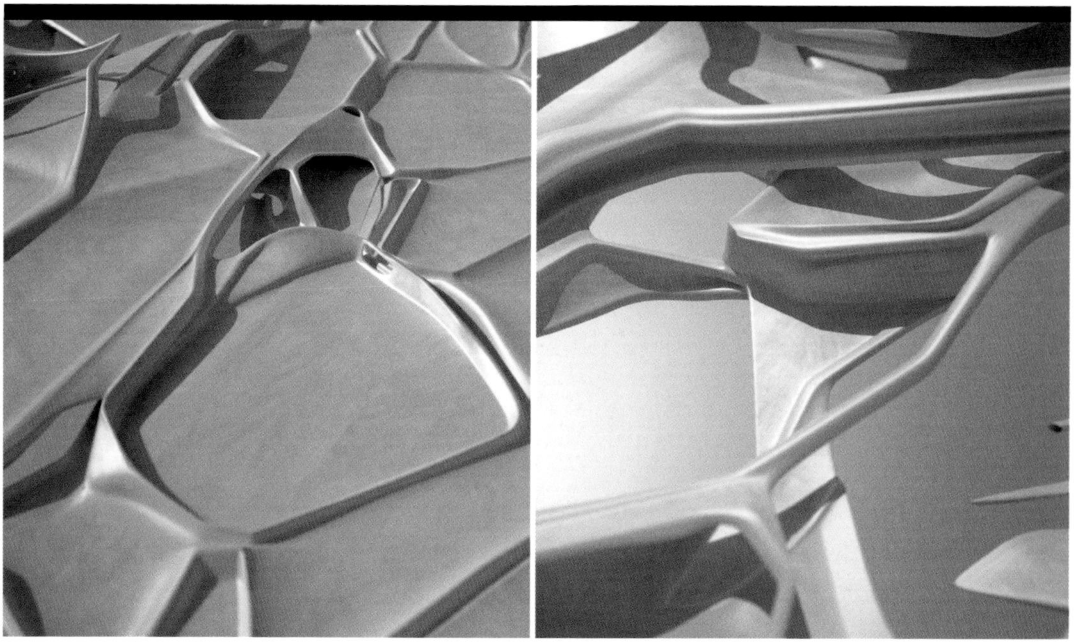

New Taipei Museum, 2011. Façade studies exploring the relationship of strand and surface.

1 For a technical description of the strand-based multi-agent algorithm, see Multi-Agent Algorithms section.

2 Frei Otto's wet grid experiments (Otto 1996) explored self-organization by coating an arbitrary distribution of woolen strands in water so that the surface tension of the water would locally bundle the strands and self-organize their position relative to their neighbors.

3 See Catalog of Projects.

4 See Catalog of Projects.

5 The role of redundancy is discussed at greater length in the Introduction: Between Emergence and Intention.

6 See Fibrous Tower Project.

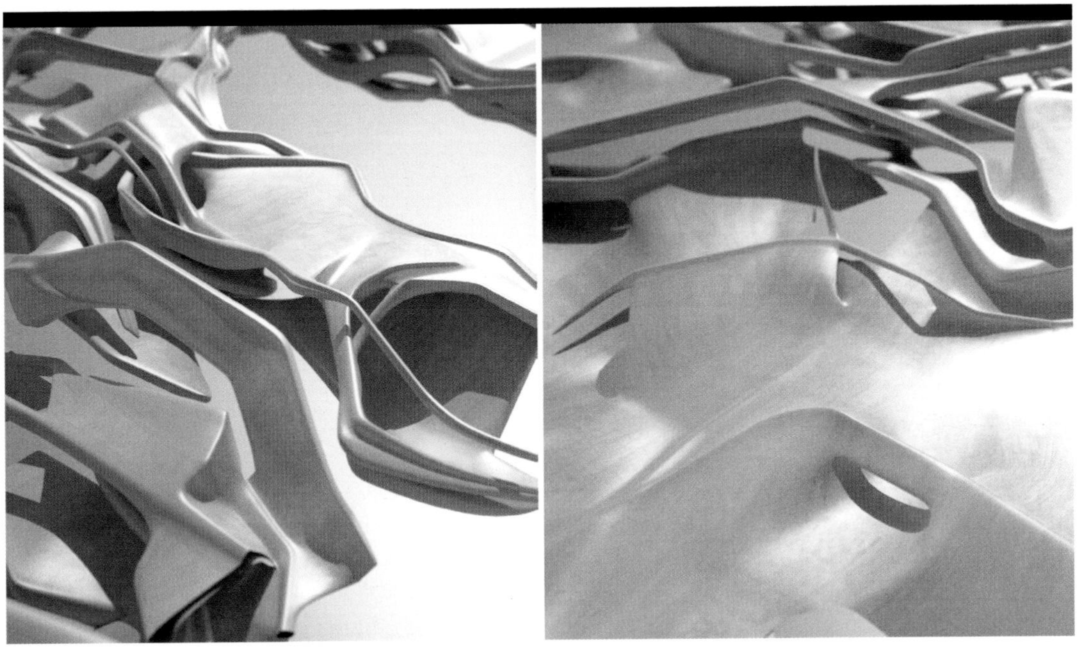

Fibrous Tower 2, 2009. The project is part of a series of studies into fibrous tower skeletons, which explores the generation of ornamental, structural, and spatial order through the fibrous assemblages strategy. This iteration is concerned with the spatial possibilities of woven interior structure and atriums, which delaminate from an exterior shell.

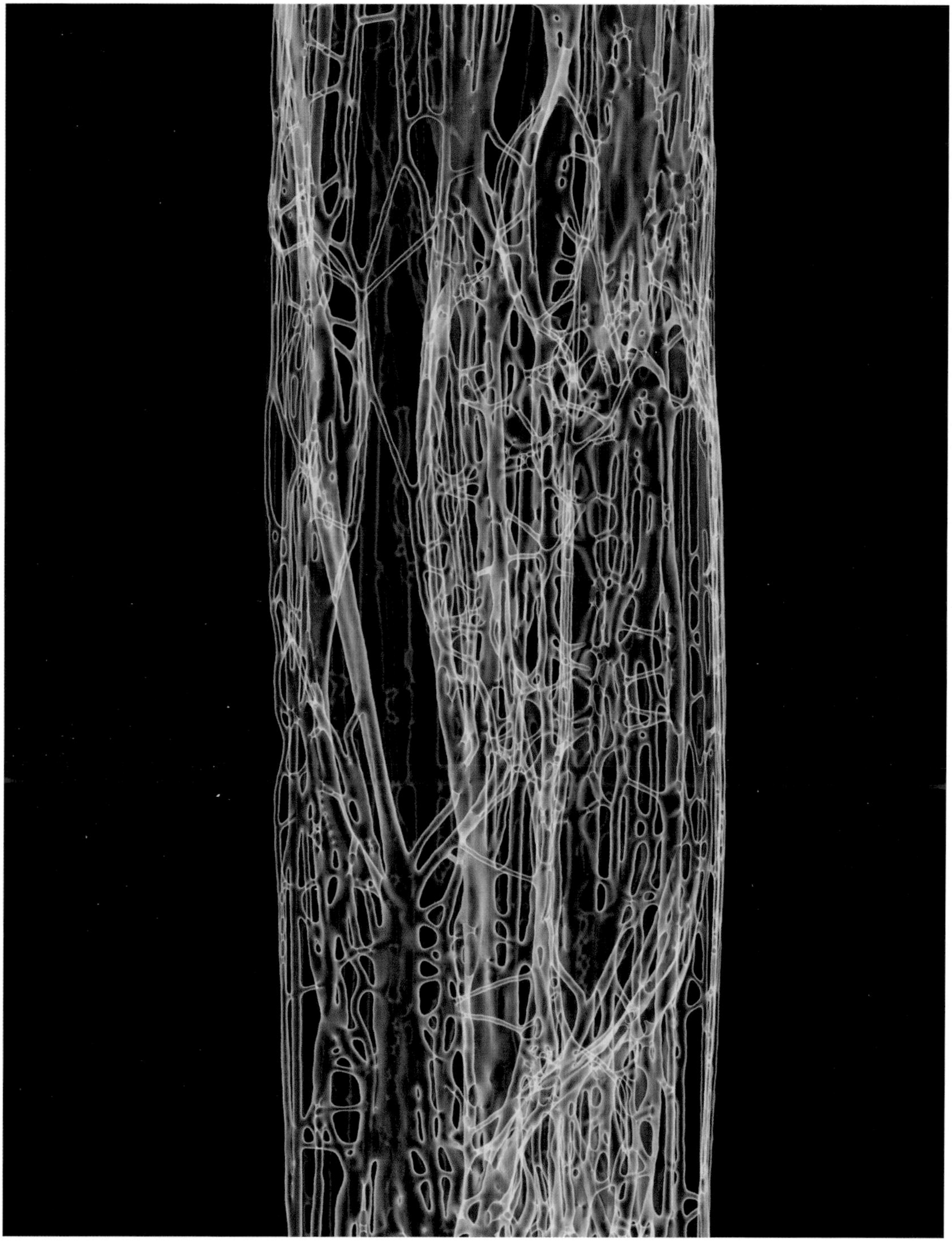

Fibrous Tower 2, 2009.
Shell study drawing.

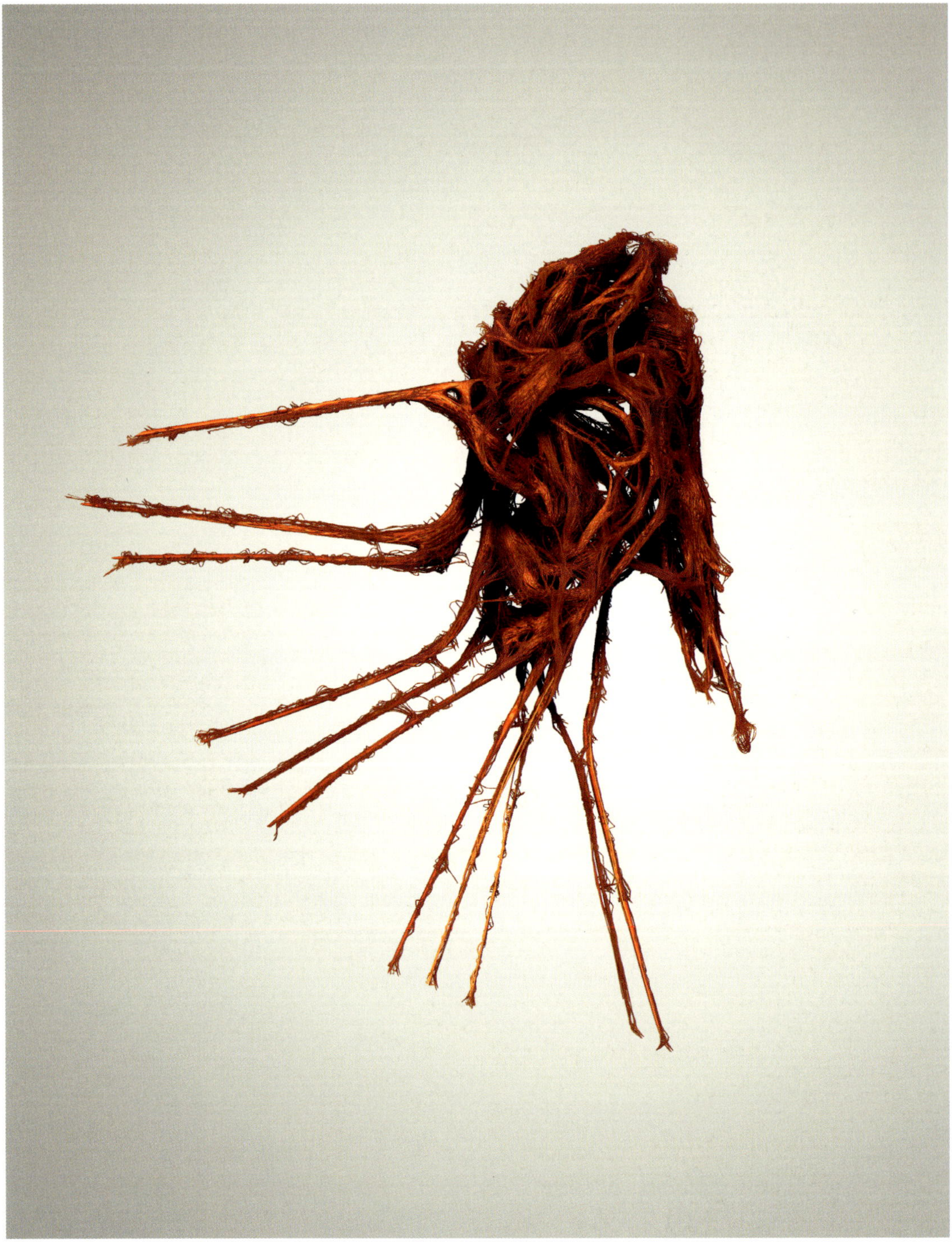

Fibrous House, 2012. The project is an experiment in the generation of volatile fibrous assemblages. It is a speculation on the tectonics and affects of designing an entire project from a single geometric type, the strand. The form is intentionally chaotic, a wild assemblage that expresses its intricate internal order without smoothing over or taming its process of formation. The project indulges in excess, and opportunistically takes advantage of the redundant nature of the geometry that is produced.

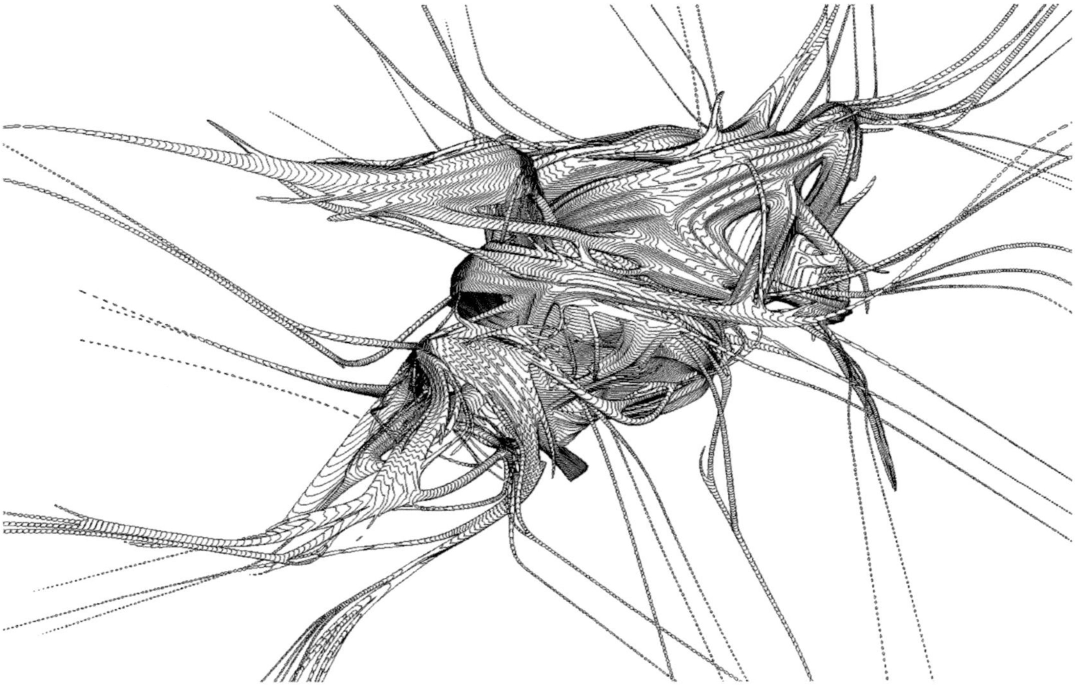

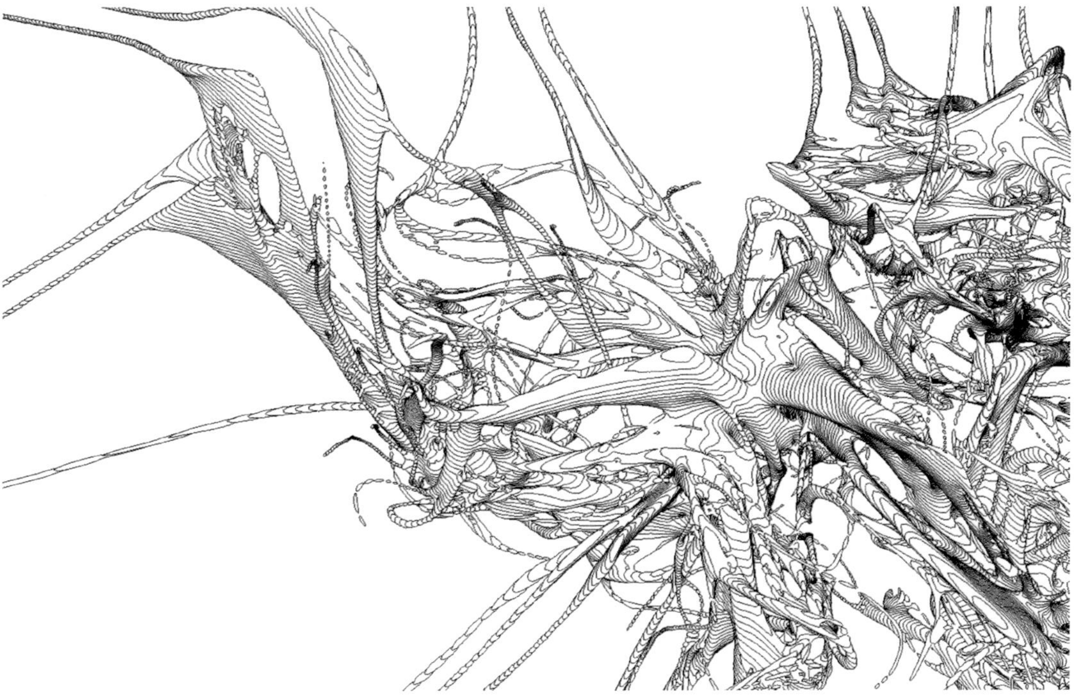

Fibrous House, 2012.
Chunk studies.

PROJECT

FIBROUS TOWER

Aerial perspective.

Tectonic hierarchies of structure, skin, and articulation are compressed within the intricate concrete shell of the Fibrous Tower. The formal characteristics of the shell evolved in response to both the emergent behavior of its algorithmic design process, and the capacities of concrete casting techniques. This speculative proposal for a commercial office tower was a deliberate attempt to engage highly expressive approaches to articulation within a rational system of construction.

The concrete shell negotiates between structural, environmental, ornamental, and spatial imperatives; these are conceptualized as behaviors that interact to influence a single body of geometry. This concept of negotiating architectural concerns or behaviors within geometry was developed through the design of the Fibrous Tower, and now underscores many of our projects. This concept has since expanded into a broader conceptualization of the uncoupling of geometry from architectural roles or purposes.[1]

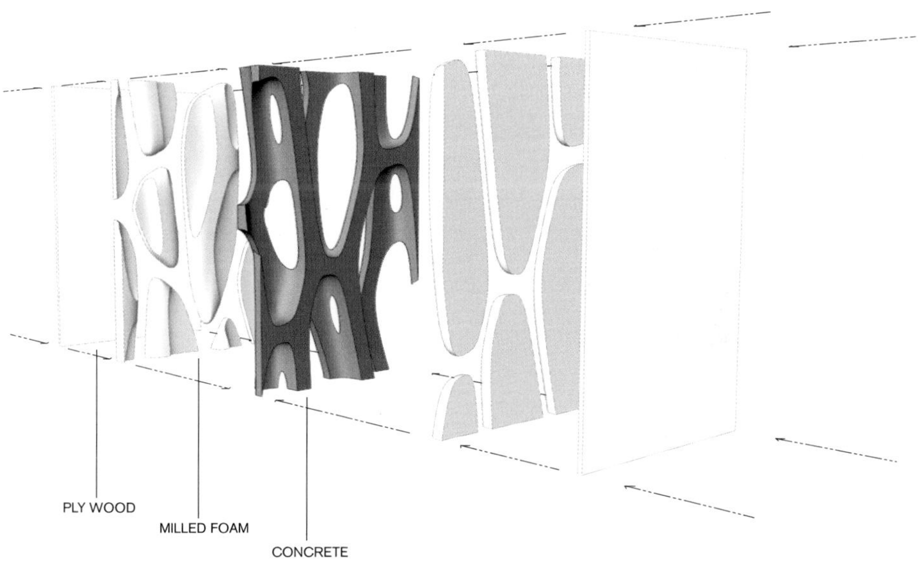

Concrete formwork diagram

The Fibrous Tower was the first of our *fibrous assemblages* projects. The development of this strand logic was an attempt to create an ordering system and give directionality to a pattern of perforations in the concrete shell. The continuation of the parapet and the narrow moat around the base of the shell were intended to create a reading of a continuous, unbounded field of strands. Hierarchies emerged through the strands' self-organization, rather than being prescribed as an a priori condition. We orchestrated this bundling to create shifting scales of visual and structural order. Different geometric types were generated across the shell, with zones of cellular and laminar characteristics integrated into a continuous pattern. Structurally, the shell transfers the static load from the floor plates, freeing the interior from columns.

The shell operates as the structure and façade of the Fibrous Tower, with the glazing inset one meter. Detaching the glazing from the shell maintained the purity of its geometry,

Aerial perspective.

enabling the use of standardized glazing systems, and avoiding the need to incorporate window framing and lining into its complex form. The floor slabs, which are connected to the shell through a series of tabs, are cut away in several locations to provide communication across floors, breaking up the monotony of the tower's floor plates, and creating a more immersive internal experience of the shell.

A cast, in-situ, concrete construction process was proposed, using plywood formwork for the face of the shell, and insertion of foam molds to form the intricate pattern of openings. Despite the complicated geometry of the shell perforations, the generative design logic enables the foam molds to be fabricated on a three-axis CNC mill without undercuts. The specific character of the perforated geometry is generated through the intersection of these molds, thus creating creased edges that define the complex interior of the perforations.

1 This is discussed in greater detail in the Behavioral Methodologies section.

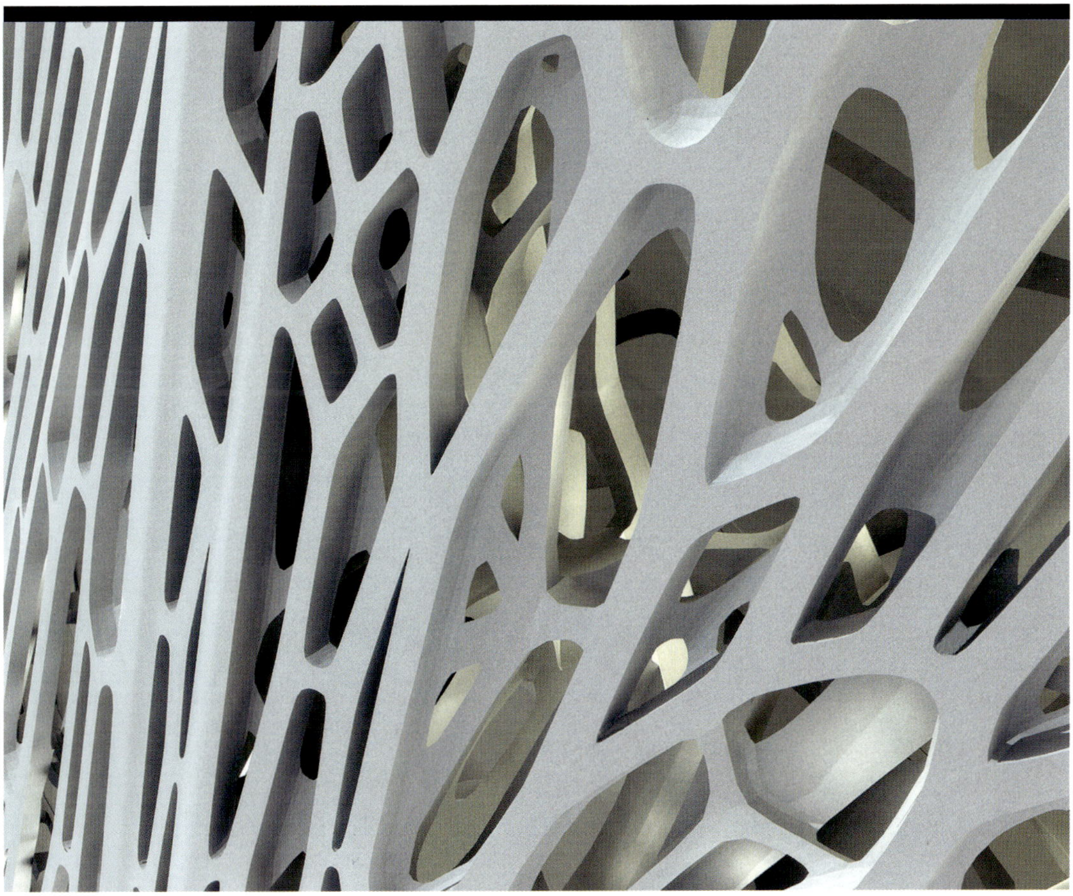

Concrete shell detail.

STRATEGY

POLYSCALAR TECTONICS

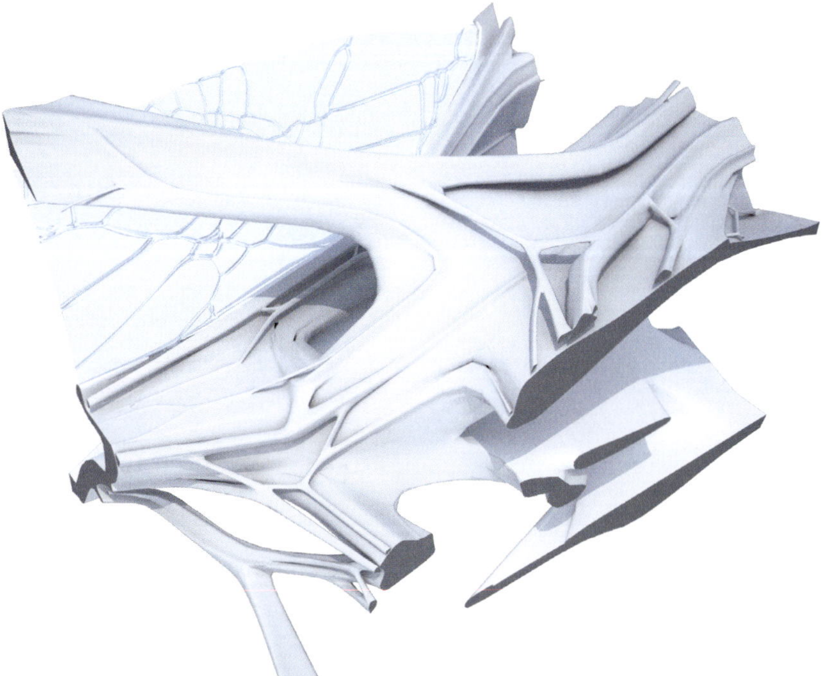

Polyscalar tectonics is a design strategy that maintains a consistent process of formation or expression across scales. The strategy is part of a larger agenda in this research to separate architectural purpose from discrete geometric elements.[1] Polyscalar tectonics repeats the same operation at multiple scales, which necessarily separates geometry from an indexical relationship to any specific purpose. This strategy creates an ambiguity or blurring between the formal, structural and ornamental roles of geometry.

This approach is typified in the Yeosu Pavilion,[2] where the same formal language of surface and strand is deployed across scales, creating a singular expression. In this blurred condition, the geometry operates as a redundant hybrid, where any pleat or strand is always partly structural and partly ornamental, never purely one or the other. This strategy compresses tectonic hierarchies and resists the application, or the subservient nature, of ornament to structure. This is not a disguise for the various tectonic systems, but a strategy for blurriness in operation, as much as for legibility.

Polyscalar tectonics are not unique to Behavioral Formation. The gothic can be considered to contain a polyscalar approach, where the constant subdivision of structure becomes ornamental and creates a continuous reading or operation across scale. It is perhaps not unusual, then, that many of the polyscalar tectonic projects can be thought of as having gothic tendencies: the sectional poché of the Yeosu Pavilion's bundling strands has a distinct gothic figure.

Yeosu Pavilion, 2009. A near-gothic poché, evident in this chunk study, is created through the polyscalar bundling of fibers.

Polyscalar tectonics operates either in a self-organizing or a fractal manner. Fractal operations repeat the same procedure recursively at decreasing scales. The agent-branching logic of Yeosu Pavilion exhibits this approach, where each bifurcation locally decreases the scale of behavior and geometry. The fibrous assemblages projects operate through a self-organizing logic. Unlike the operation of the fractal approach, there is mutual feedback between strands regardless of scale, where small and large-scale strands interact and bundle.

A polyscalar approach is important in this design research, both conceptually and aesthetically. The blur between architectural elements is a clear expression of a non-linear process of negotiation. This process produces an aesthetic that is representative of formation more than form, a characteristic evident in the negotiated strands of Fibrous Tower 2.[3] The expression of this singular strategy is continuous but not homogeneous, with local differences emerging from within the continuous whole. This lack of reference renders the work strange and often alien, as there is no recognition of a specific or singular purpose assigned to geometry.

Within high-resolution behavioral models, polyscalar tectonics generates an architectural language, where something novel emerges from the excess of something known. The sheer mass of strands that bundle to form the Fibrous House[4] changes the definition, or the way the project is perceived, from discrete strands to the emergent assemblage of those strands. The house is perceived as a turbulent flow rather than an accumulation of parts, blurring the relationship between form and articulation. This emergent macro-level reading takes on a

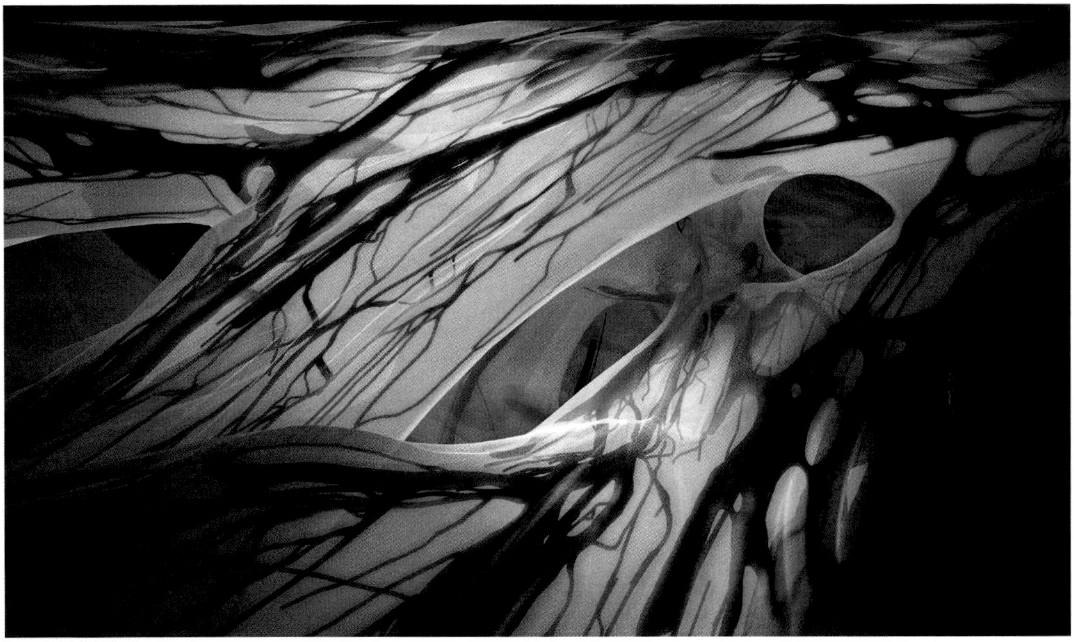

Cliff House, 2012.
The polyscalar strands are silhouetted within the back-lit translucent skin.

new and strange set of qualities and characteristics that are closer to that of flesh or fibrous material than to the composition of architectural elements. The Cliff House, which was developed in parallel to the Fibrous House, employs the same polyscalar tectonic and fibrous assemblage strategies to create significantly different characteristics. The strands of the Cliff House are constrained to a surface, with the two elements unified through a process of *strange feedback*.[5] This shifts the reading from fibrous mass to surface and creates a network of polyscalar pleats through the negotiation of surface and strands.

The operation of polyscalar tectonics is not necessarily legible within the characteristics it creates. The memorial space of the Babiy Yar project[6] is generated through a polyscalar agentBody approach,[7] where bodies are nested at fractal scales. Unlike the fibrous assemblage projects, the various scales are not individually expressed in the Babiy Yar Memorial. The finer scale of agentBodies is not legible as a separate system; instead, they create a highly intricate articulation of the whole.

1 The separation of architectural purpose from geometry is discussed in more depth in the Introduction: Between Emergence and Intention, and in the Behavioral Methodologies section.

2 The Yeosu Pavilion project is a competition entry for the thematic pavilion for the 2012 Yeosu Expo. The project was designed in collaboration with Tom Wiscombe.

3 See Catalog of Projects.

4 See Catalog of Projects.

5 See Strange Feedback Strategy section.

6 See Babiy Yar Project section.

7 See AgentBodies Strategy section.

Cliff House, 2012.
The surface of the pleated skin reveals an imprint of the fibrous strand geometry below.

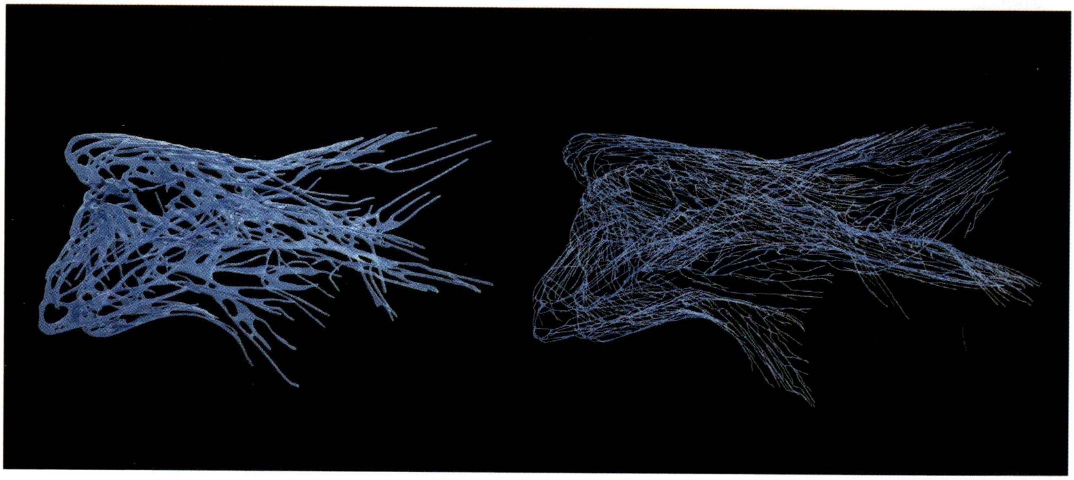

Above: Cliff House, 2012. A tectonic chunk illustrating the polyscalar strand and pleat geometry.

Below: Cliff House, 2012. The two primary scales of strand geometry have a mutual interaction in the process of formation.

Cliff House, 2012.
Perspectives.

ESSAY

MULTI-AGENT ALGORITHMS

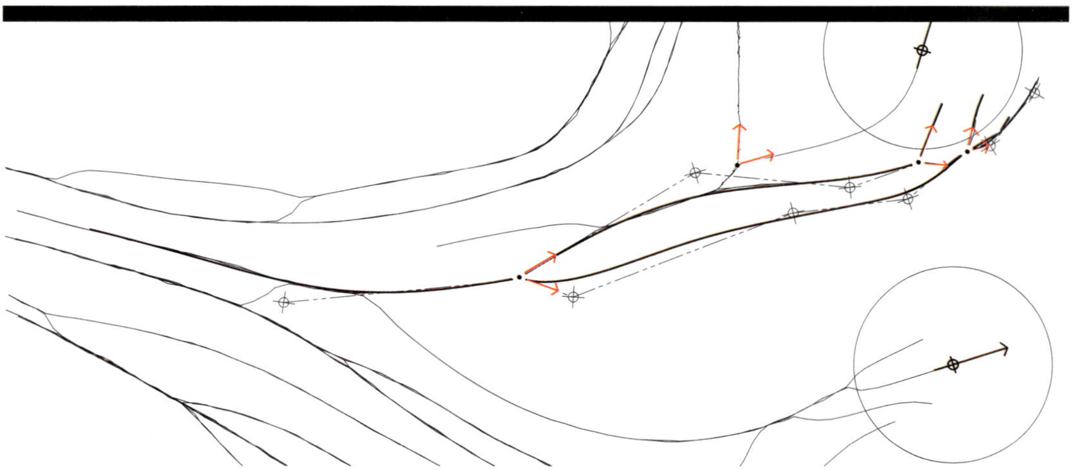

Multi-agent algorithms form the procedural underpinning of Behavioral Formation, which constitutes a pioneering adaption of these algorithms to architectural design. Our sustained development of multi-agent design processes began in 2002 with my thesis design research at RMIT University, and was subsequently expanded through the work of Kokkugia,[1] Studio Roland Snooks, and my PhD dissertation (2014). Multi-agent algorithms operate through the local interaction of autonomous computational agents, which self-organize and generate emergent behavior at the global scale. These algorithms establish a non-linear relationship where each agent is responding to the neighboring agents without hierarchical, or top-down, control. Conceptualizing and encoding architectural intention as behaviors within these algorithms demonstrates a significant departure from the algorithmic design processes employed within architecture over the past three decades.

Computational multi-agent systems were first developed by John von Neumann in the form of cellular automata in the 1940s,[2] and further developed in John Conway's *Game of Life* in the 1970s.[3] However, it is the work of Craig Reynolds that holds most significance for Behavioral Formation. Reynolds made an important contribution to the computational understanding of swarm systems through the development of behavioral models of simulation in the mid-1980s.[4] Reynolds's *boids* algorithm simulates the flocking or schooling behavior of birds and fish. The agents, or 'boids', respond to their neighboring agents with three basic behaviors: alignment (to match the speed and direction of the neighbors); cohesion (to steer toward the centroid of the neighbors); and separation (to avoid collision with the neighbors). This algorithm creates a vivid demonstration of the bottom-up nature of swarms and the lack of any centralized, or global, control. In discussing Reynolds's work, Philip Ball states that within flocks and swarms, 'the coherent group behavior emerges from simple, purely local interactions between individuals, who have no sense of what the whole group is doing.'[5]

Multi-agent algorithmic branching logic.

AGENT BEHAVIOR

Multi-agent algorithms operate through the interaction of individual agents that respond to the state or actions of their neighboring agents by changing their own state or actions. These algorithms are premised on the mutual interaction of agents to create the feedback necessary for self-organization and the generation of emergent behavior.

The agent models developed through this Behavioral Formation research operate in Cartesian space, and navigate through vector calculations. The simplest version of the agent is defined by a point in space that has a series of parameters, including its velocity and range of vision. This basic agent is then extended in various ways to embed it within high-level structures such as a strand, network or body. However, it is the individual point within these structures that is the primary location of active agency. The agent's motion is controlled by the negotiation of numerous behaviors. Most behaviors calculate a vector to undertake a given intention, which is then assigned a priority, and used by the agent to influence its change in state, such as velocity and position. This operation is undertaken iteratively, where each agent updates its state at every time-step; typically, these simulations will run for thousands of steps.

A simple behavior is described in the alignment behavior diagram (see below): through a spatial diagram, a vector diagram, the pseudo code (plain English description of the code), and the code written in the Java programming language. This alignment behavior is attempting to match the speed and direction of an agent to the agents within its range of vision (which is described by the circle around the agent). The multi-agent diagram (see opposite) indicates how each behavior responds to a population of agents, with the vectors calculated by those behaviors used to determine the future velocity and position of the agent through the negotiation of their forces.

The multi-agent algorithms developed through this research were primarily written in Java and have been released publicly as the *Kokkugia Agent* library in various versions from 2007 onwards.[6] This open source access has enabled the dissemination of the technical aspects

Alignment behavior diagram. Behaviors are developed through diagramming, programming, and writing of pseudocode.

DIAGRAM

VECTORS

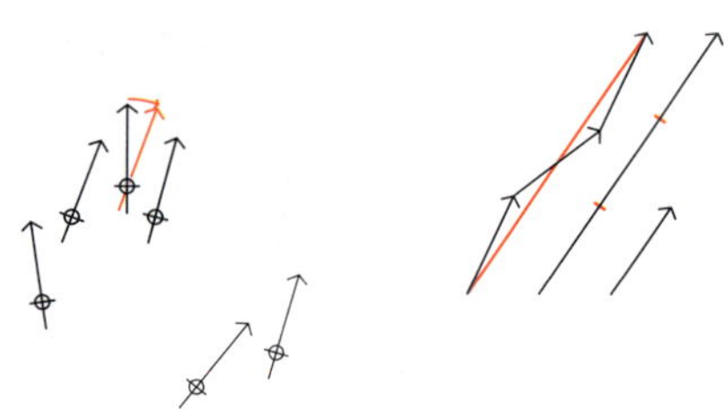

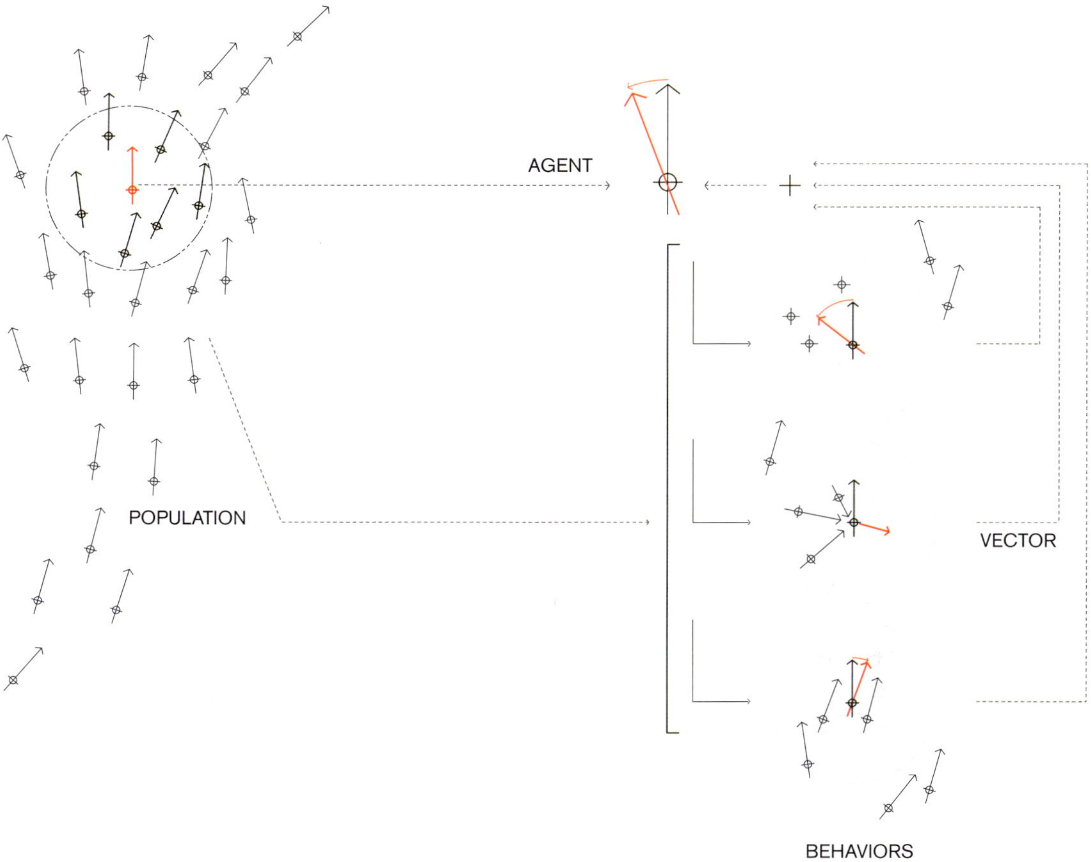

The actions of an agent emerge from the interaction and negotiation of numerous behaviors.

PSEUDOCODE

loop through a population of agents

calculate the distance to the agent

if the agent is within a range of visionget the agent's velocity

sum the agent's velocity with the other in range agents

divide the sum of the agents velocity by the number of agents within range

get the average velocity of the agents

return the average velocity

CODE

```
public Vec3D alignment(ArrayList<kNode> neighbours, Float range,
        Vec3D sum = new Vec3D();
        float count = 0;
        for (kNode n: neighbours) {
            if(pos.distanceTo(n.pos) <= rangeOfVis*range){
                sum.addSelf(n.vel);
                count++;
            }
        }
        if (count > 0) {
                sum.scaleSelf(1/count);
                sum.limit(maxForce);
                sum.scaleSelf(scale);
                acceleration.addSelf(sum);
                return sum;
            } else {
                return new Vec3D(0,0,0);
            }
        }
```

of this research and its proliferation into a wider community of architects working on algorithmic design processes.

THE SUBSTRATE OF AGENCY

Embedding design intention within geometry requires computational agency to be encoded within sufficiently complex and hierarchical substrates. Strands, networks and bodies define specific topological relationships between agents, and embed the agent as the active component within a specific structure.

Strands are a collection of point-based agents in a specific linear order. Within this structure, it is the agents that are active rather than the strand. The agents move in response to their local conditions, and inherit attributes, additional behaviors, and constraints from the strand. The strands are encoded with internal behaviors (typically related to factors such as elasticity, bending, or material capacities) that control how agents on the same strand interact.

Networks are a collection of point-based agents that are associated through a specific network topology, which defines the neighborhood of interaction. A spring network is a typical example of this, where an agent responds to those agents connected to it rather than responding to agents within a spatial proximity. A mesh can be thought of as a subset of a network, where the springs form connected polygon faces.

AgentBodies are a collection of strands, while the strands are a collection of point-based agents (strand agents). These bodies are structured hierarchically, with a host agent dictating the position and orientation of the body. It is this host agent and the strand agents that are active, while the strands and the body are hierarchical control structures. This structure allows the agent to operate at two scales of agency; in the Composite Swarm project,[7] for example, the distinction is between topology and tectonics. These strand-based agentBodies enable an expressive body design, capable of readable topological change at the scale of the body.[8]

Within Behavioral Formation, agency is encoded through a series of substrates.

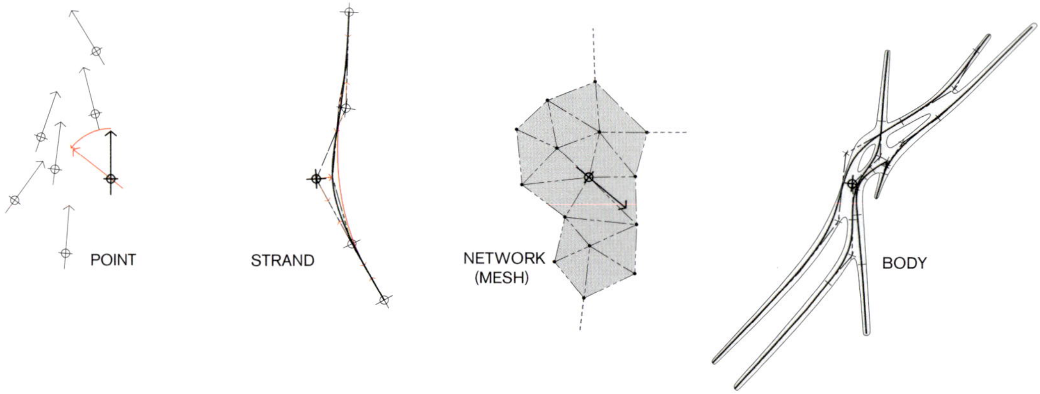

STIGMERGIC AGENTS

Stigmergy describes the self-organization of a system through the indirect interaction of agents. Pierre-Paul Grasse introduced the term 'stigmergy' in 1959 to describe the indirect coordination of social insects, such as the construction of mounds by termites, or the self-organization of ant's pheromone trails.[9] The stigmergic formation of ant trails, for example, operates through the ants' deposition of a chemical pheromone trail, which other ants then respond to and follow. As successive ants reinforce this pheromone trail through positive feedback (trail attracts ant, ant increases attraction of trail), a self-organized order emerges. Stigmergic systems also generally include negative feedback, such as the evaporation of pheromone, so when trails fail to be reinforced regularly, they evaporate and create less attraction. It is the balance between positive and negative feedback that keeps a system in a dynamic equilibrium, from which complex order emerges.

During the construction of termite mounds, the termites interact indirectly through the matter of the mound. Termites move particles of dirt and secrete pheromone where they deposit that dirt; this in turn stimulates other termites to deposit more dirt in that location, generating a positive feedback loop. The termite mound has some obvious parallels to the possible construction of architecture. However, the interest here in stigmergy is not metaphorical or literal: it is an interest in the self-organizing capacity of stigmergic systems.

The use of algorithmic techniques in architecture often creates a discontinuity between the logic of the algorithm and the development of architectural geometry. For example, a flock of birds is self-organized at any given instance. The interesting emergent behavior of a flock, however, lies in its macro-scale behavior over time (the motion of the flock). But herein lies the problem for the designer using swarm algorithms. To extract the positions of a swarm at any given moment in time ignores this emergent behavior. An alternative to this is to extract the history of the flock, for instance by drawing a line that traces the path of the agent. While this technique captures a trace of the emergent behavior and motion, the lines have no ordered relationship to each other, as this spatial description ignores the agents' relationship in time. The agent has no recognition of its own path or the paths of others; in

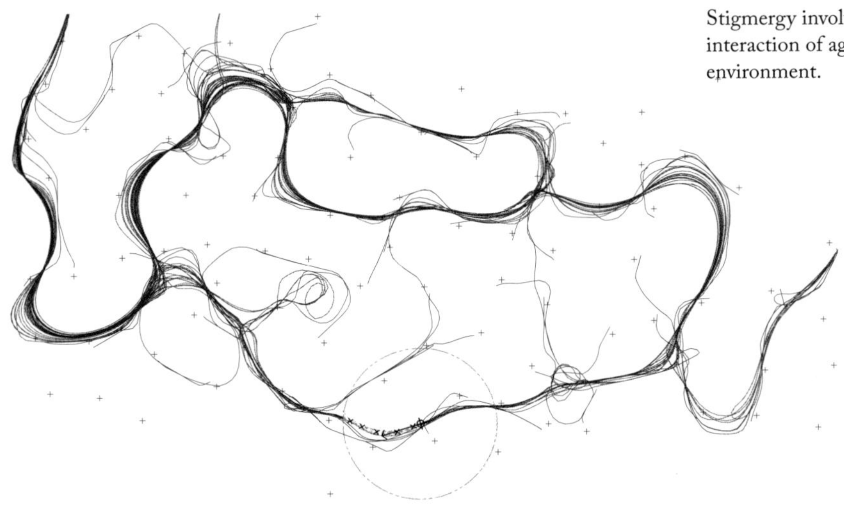

Stigmergy involves the indirect interaction of agents through their environment.

drawing a new path, it does not respect the existing lines. Consequently, the self-organizing flocking or swarm algorithm does not lead to self-organized geometry (paths or lines); in fact it is often quite the opposite, as the lines intersect each other arbitrarily. This is not dissimilar to drawing with one's eyes closed, and being unable to respond to the lines already drawn.

Stigmergy is an important technique in Behavioral Formation, as it provides a method of incorporating architectural geometry in the generative process. The bird-flocking example above can be reconstructed as a stigmergic system by establishing feedback between the agents and motion paths. In this case, the agent is affecting its environment by drawing a path, and the environment is influencing the agent as it responds to the existing paths. The paths that emerge from this process create a self-organized, complex order.

The design projects developed through this Behavioral Formation agenda use either stigmergy or self-organization of architectural geometry as the primary mode of feedback that leads to the generation of complex order. The *fluid turbulence*[10] and *strand* projects[11] operate through a stigmergic process of feedback between agents and strands. Likewise, the generative algorithm developed for the Babiy Yar Memorial[12] landscape operates in a similar manner to ant trail systems.

The non-stigmergic algorithms, such as those used in the agentBodies or the *manifold swarms* projects, use self-organization of geometry to generate emergent order. These projects do not trace geometry from the behavior of a system; the geometry itself interacts to achieve a higher degree of emergent order. For example, in the RMIT Mace project,[13] the agentBodies move in response to the neighboring bodies. Over time, this feedback results in the generation of a self-organized manifold and tectonic network, with geometry being intrinsic (rather than applied) to the behavioral process of formation.

In addition to its role in digital design, stigmergy provides a powerful concept for self-organized fabrication, where the generative algorithm or decision-making is encoded directly as robotic operations, triggered by the local conditions of the material it is

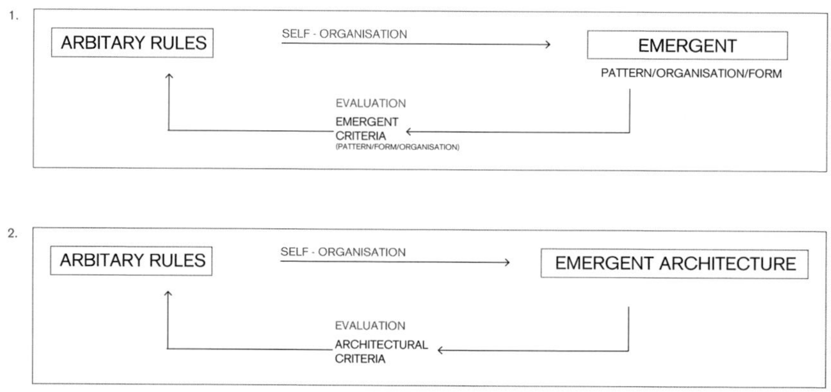

Approaches to encoding architectural intent.

fabricating. This logic is the basis for the *stigmergic robotics* strategy,[14] which operates through the interaction of volatile material behavior and algorithmic processes.

APPROACHES TO ENCODING ARCHITECTURAL INTENT

The arguments posited here are contingent on the ability to encode architectural design intent within an algorithmic process.[15] With the dissemination of multi-agent algorithms in architecture over the last few years, the ways in which they are being applied can be observed and categorized based on the role of architectural decisions or intent within the process.

Four categories of application are described in the encoding intention diagram (see below), all of which assume that there is a feedback loop of evaluation that influences the parameters of the behaviors.[16] The first category involves the use of arbitrary behaviors that self-organize to create emergent patterns, organizations or forms. These behaviors are arbitrary with respect to architecture; they are not specific to either local or global[17] architectural design intention. Often this technique involves appropriating algorithms from biology, such as flocks or ant-trails. The evaluation of the emergent output is based on the emergent qualities of the pattern or formation. This approach, while useful in generating pattern, is most often naïve in an architectural context, as the generated pattern must be applied to, or manipulated into, architecture, rather than architecture being intrinsic to its formation.

The second category is similar to the first in its operation and selection of the behaviors, but the evaluation is determined by architectural criteria. The various iterations of the algorithm are assessed against the architectural objectives of the project, and the behavioral parameters are adjusted accordingly. While architectural design intention is at play in this approach, it remains at the level of the emergent whole – not an emergent architecture, but an emergent formation that is fit for architecture. With this approach, there is no architectural intention encoded within the system itself, and consequently, it has little capacity for architectural sophistication. Nevertheless, it can be a powerful generator of abstract form.

3.

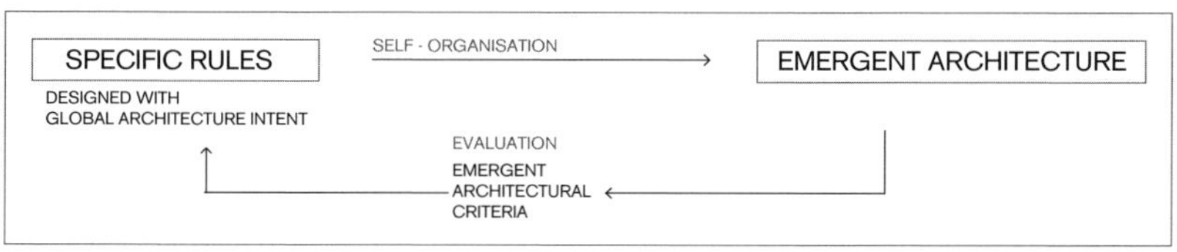

4.

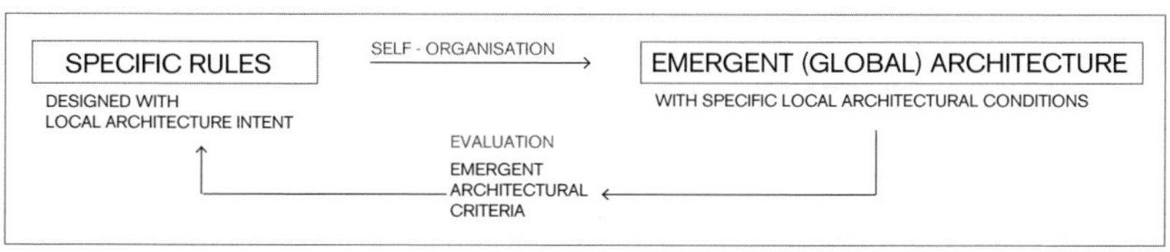

The third category involves designing specific behaviors with the intention of creating a particular global architectural outcome. The design iterations are evaluated against those architectural outcomes, and the behaviors are iteratively redesigned in response. An example of this approach is the manifold swarm strategy, where behaviors are designed so that the agents self-organize into coherent manifold surfaces. While the outcome is highly volatile and emergent in this case, the particular intention of creating manifold surfaces is achieved.

The final category is the design of behaviors that encode specific local architectural relationships. The architecture that is designed through this approach exhibits emergent characteristics at the global scale, while maintaining specific local architectural conditions. These local behaviors and conditions can relate to issues such as form, program, structure, tectonics, and ornament. The iterative outcomes are evaluated based on the architectural capacities and qualities of both the global formations and the local conditions. This approach is evident in the agentBodies of the RMIT Mace project, which interact with the adjacent bodies to create an intricate structural network.

The algorithmic design strategies in this research fit into the third and fourth categories. Encoding architectural design decisions within multi-agent algorithms establishes a conceptual relationship between emergence and intention that is fundamental to this research. This is an important point of difference to other algorithmic approaches to architecture, including the increasingly popular, simplistic use of multi-agent systems to generate abstract pattern and form.

THE ARCHITECTURAL CONTEXT OF MULTI-AGENT ALGORITHMS

The multi-agent algorithmic design processes described here, and which underlie Behavioral Formation, were developed out of the broader context of architecture's digital turn,[18] the discourse of complex systems, and processual ontology. This work evolved in response to the generative digital design experimentation that emanated from Columbia University in the 1990s, and in particular, the Animate Form project of Greg Lynn.[19] Behavioral

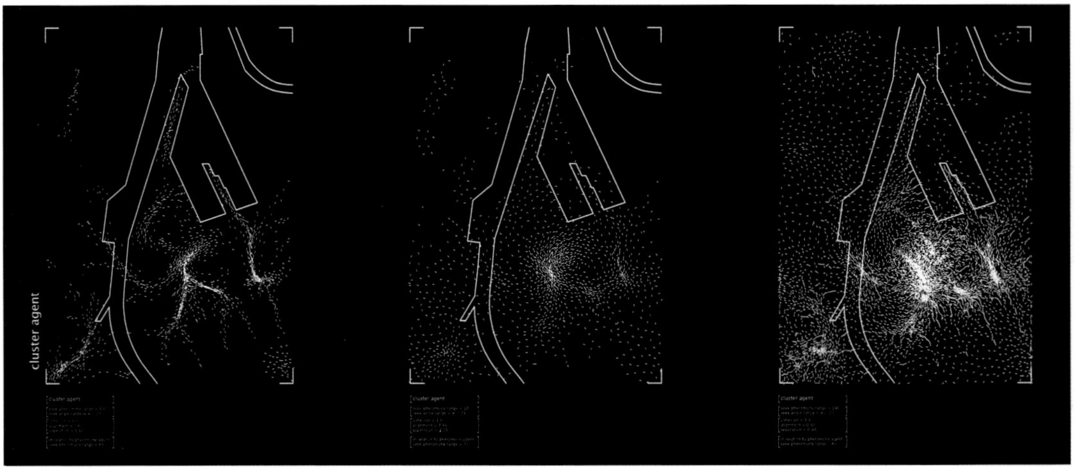

Swarm Urbanism, Melbourne Docklands, 2008. This conceptual proposal posits an urban design methodology based on the emergent capacities of Swarm Intelligence.

Formation is part of a second wave of generative digital design that is concerned with algorithmic approaches, scripted techniques, and emergent order. This shift from dynamic systems to self-organization is important both for the characteristics of what is designed and for the method of extracting form from a dynamic process. Self-organizational models lead to emergent phenomena, and tend toward more organized states. In these processes, form is not frozen or mapped from a dynamic process; instead, it emerges from the system. Rather than the ambition of animate form to register "motion and force at the moment of formal conception,"[20] self-organizing processes lead to emergent characteristics, or an aesthetic of emergence. Complex order and intricate assemblages of micro-scale parts define these characteristics; aesthetically, these are closer to fur or the bundling of fibers than the smooth and pliant surfaces of architecture's first digital turn. The self-organizing capacity of behavioral processes of formation is inherently morphogenetic. This involves the negotiation of internal behaviors – the interaction of design intentions encoded within the agents[21] – as opposed to the negotiation of external forces in the morphodynamic operation of animate processes.[22] Within these self-organizational processes, architectural geometry is active, rather than either a passive receptor of form or an index of force.

Algorithmic design approaches in architecture can be traced through the earlier pioneering work of protagonists such as John Fraser and Karl Chu in the latter decades of the twentieth century.[23] However, in the first few years of the new millennium, algorithmic design processes shifted from a predominantly conceptual and technical concern to an engagement with design practice and the formalism of architecture's digital turn.

Within this algorithmic context, the original contribution of the Behavioral Formation project I have developed has been the adoption and development of multi-agent algorithms into a design methodology that reconceptualizes intention through behavior.[24] The catalyst for the development of this multi-agent design approach was a reference Stan Allen made to Reynolds's work in his seminal essay, 'From Object to Field.' Allen cites the discussion of Reynolds's boids algorithm[25] in Mitchell Waldrop's 1993 book, *Complexity: The Emerging Science at the Edge of Order and Chaos.*[26] Stan Allen posited 'field conditions' as bottom-up

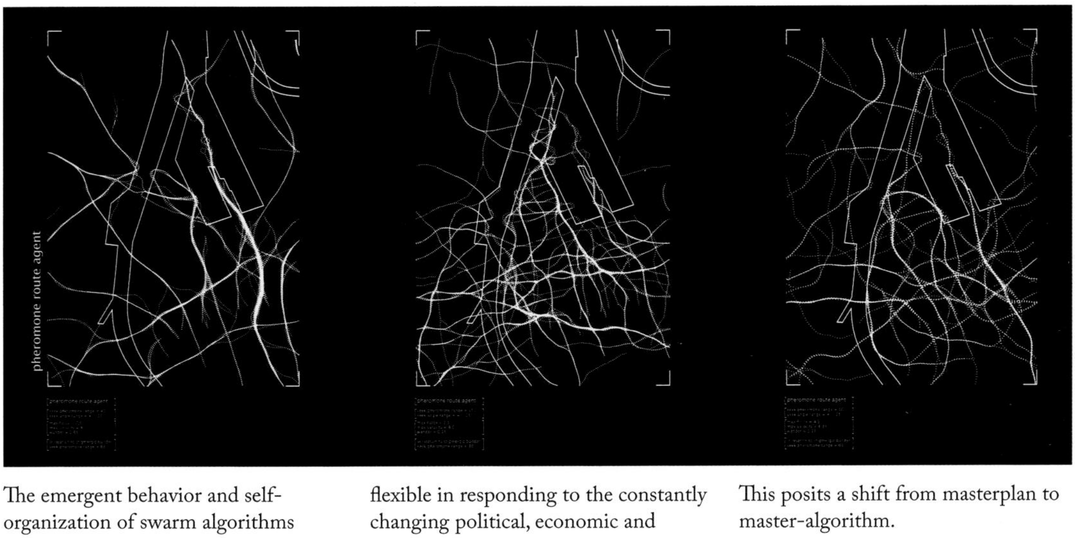

The emergent behavior and self-organization of swarm algorithms can generate urban systems that are flexible in responding to the constantly changing political, economic and social pressures of urban development. This posits a shift from masterplan to master-algorithm.

phenomena that are relational rather than figural. Allen postulates that field conditions refer 'to mathematical field theory, to non-linear dynamics and computer simulations of evolutionary change. It parallels a shift in recent technologies from analogue object to digital field.'[27]

Multi-agent algorithms are the procedural embodiment of a general model of self-organization through mutual interaction. This generalizable nature of multi-agent algorithms, and the capacity to encode specific architectural intentions, importantly differentiates behavioral processes of formation from the larger body of algorithmic experimentation within architecture. These traits are essential to creating a coherent algorithmic design methodology. One that is capable of negotiating the often-conflicting intentions and requirements of architectural projects, and fully engaging with the fundamental concerns of architecture.

1 The experimental work of Kokkugia was undertaken in collaboration with Robert Stuart-Smith.

2 Waldrop 1993, pp. 217-220.

3 Waldrop 1993, pp. 219-220.

4 Reynolds 1987.

5 Ball 2009, p. 126.

6 The publicly released Kokkugia Agent library has been developed to work with Processing (www.processing.org). Aspects of this code have also been developed in a number of programming languages operating on various platforms including Rhino3D, Maya, and 3DS Max.

7 See Composite Swarm project.

8 An alternative structure for defining bodies, based on small networks without host agents (described as bodyTopologic), has been developed by Robert Stuart-Smith, and applied to projects for the Busan Opera and Helsinki Library (www.robertstuart-smith.com).

9 Camazine et al. 2003, p. 56.

10 Fluid turbulence projects include National Art Museum of China, and Kazakhstan Symbol – see Catalog of Projects.

11 Strand projects include Fibrous Tower 2, and Fibrous House – see Catalog of Projects.

12 See Babiy Yar Memorial project.

13 See RMIT Mace project.

14 See Stigmergic Robotics Strategy section.

15 This does not imply that Behavioral Formation is exclusively digital. Algorithms are simply instructions; the medium in which they operate is conceptually irrelevant. Practically, however, the level of iteration and the population size experimented within this research would be far beyond the capacity of manual calculation.

16 An iterative evaluation and feedback loop forms the simplest interaction between the algorithm and design intent.

17 Global is often used in this research to describe the macro-scale of a system.

18 This digital paradigm shift is articulated by Mario Carpo in *The Digital Turn in Architecture 1992-2012 (Carpo 2015).*

19 Greg Lynn's pioneering application of dynamic systems to generative design is outlined in his seminal publication *Animate Form* (Lynn 1999).

20 Lynn 1999, p. 11.

21 Although multi-agent algorithms generate complex order without external influence, many of the multi-agent algorithms developed in this research also respond to input from outside of these systems.

22 Karl Chu articulates this difference between morphogenetic and morphodynamic design strategies in (Chu 2006). This distinction is discussed at greater length in the Introduction: Between Emergence and Intention.

23 John Frazer outlined an evolutionary approach to architectural design (Frazer 1995). Karl Chu established the Institute of Genetic Architecture at Columbia University (GSAPP), and posited the conceptual basis for a genetic approach to architecture (Chu 2006).

24 Since this pioneering adaptation of multi-agent algorithms to architectural design, several architects have made crucial contributions to the development and expansion of this area of research; most notably Alisa Andrasek, Robert Stuart-Smith, and Francois Roche. Andrasek's work has focused on high-resolution models and the purity of the complex order that emerges from these systems. In addition to Stuart-Smith's work with Kokkugia, he has advanced behavioral approaches through research and teaching, primarily at the Architecture Association Design Research Lab (AA.DRL), and more recently through his work with swarm robotics. Roche, while less concerned with technique or tooling, has developed a conceptually sophisticated body of work that explores the implications of swarm systems through crypto-fictional scenarios. This work with multi-agent algorithms has been disseminated largely through the academic engagement of this group of protagonists within architecture schools, including the University of Pennsylvania, Columbia University, Architectural Association, RMIT University, and the Bartlett, resulting in their adoption by a younger generation of architects. This dissemination of multi-agent algorithms is demonstrated through the publication *Swarm Intelligence: Architectures of Multi-Agent Systems* edited in collaboration with Neil Leach (Leach and Snooks 2017). A prior application of multi-agent algorithms to design processes, that I am now aware of, was undertaken by Paul Coates and Pablo Carranza published in 2000 (Carranza 2000). This focused on the technical development of generative processes rather than a behavioral conception of architectural design and encoded intention.

25 To my knowledge, this is the first reference to Reynolds's work within architectural discourse, cited in Stan Allen's essay, 'From Object to Field', published in *Architecture After Geometry* (Bates 1997, pp. 24–31).

26 Waldrop 1993.

27 Bates 1997, p. 24.

STRATEGY

AGENTBODIES

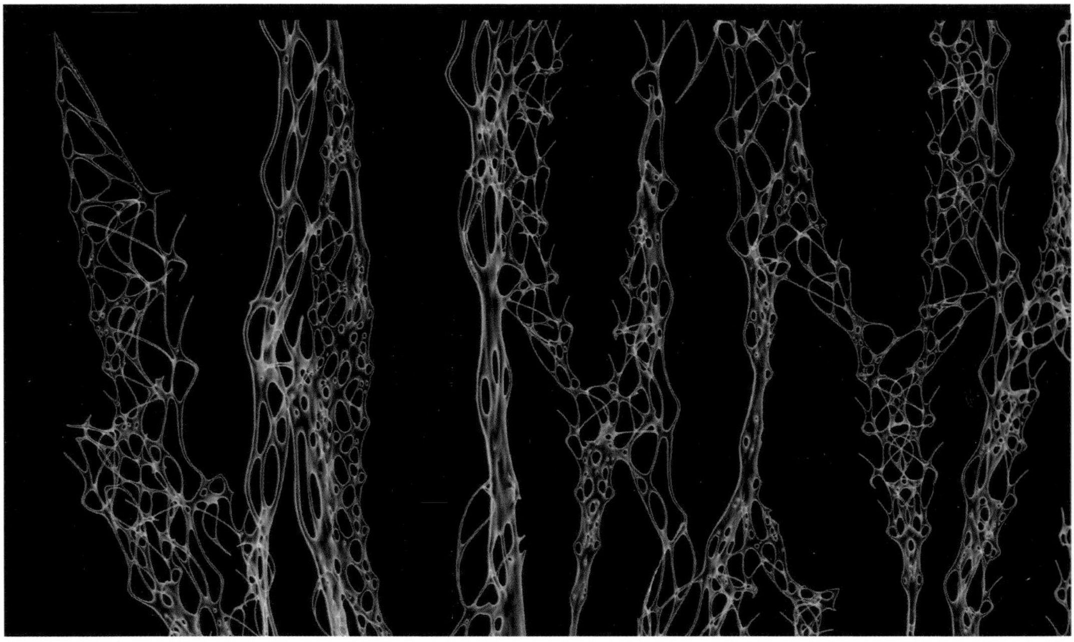

Swarm Matter, 2009.

AgentBody algorithms embed tectonic geometry within algorithmic processes and algorithmic agency within geometry. We developed this reciprocal strategy through the design of intricate tectonics and complex formal articulation. The enmeshed relationship of geometry and agency establishes a self-organizing methodology in which structural, material and fabrication logic can be encoded within the geometry of the agent.

This conceptualization of the agent draws on the logic of ant bridges, where it is the interconnected geometry of the ants' bodies that creates architectural or structural matter. AgentBody algorithms developed out of our earlier Behavioral Formation strategies that encode agency within simple geometry, such as points or strands. The strand is a hierarchical structure, where the agent is embedded as a vertex or control point within the strand. AgentBodies have an additional level of hierarchy: they are composed of several small interwoven strands that form a skeleton, which is assigned to a host agent. Embedding the geometry of the bodies within the volatile generative process provides an additional site of direct design intention, and enables a tight integration of geometry and behavior.

This strategy distributes agency throughout the strands of the skeleton. Consequently, each control point in the skeleton operates with a degree of autonomy, rather than being hierarchically linked or guided by the tip of the strand (as is the case with inverse kinematics). This distributed agency creates considerable organizational and geometric differentiation at both the level of the body and the interaction between bodies. The interaction of self-organizing bodies

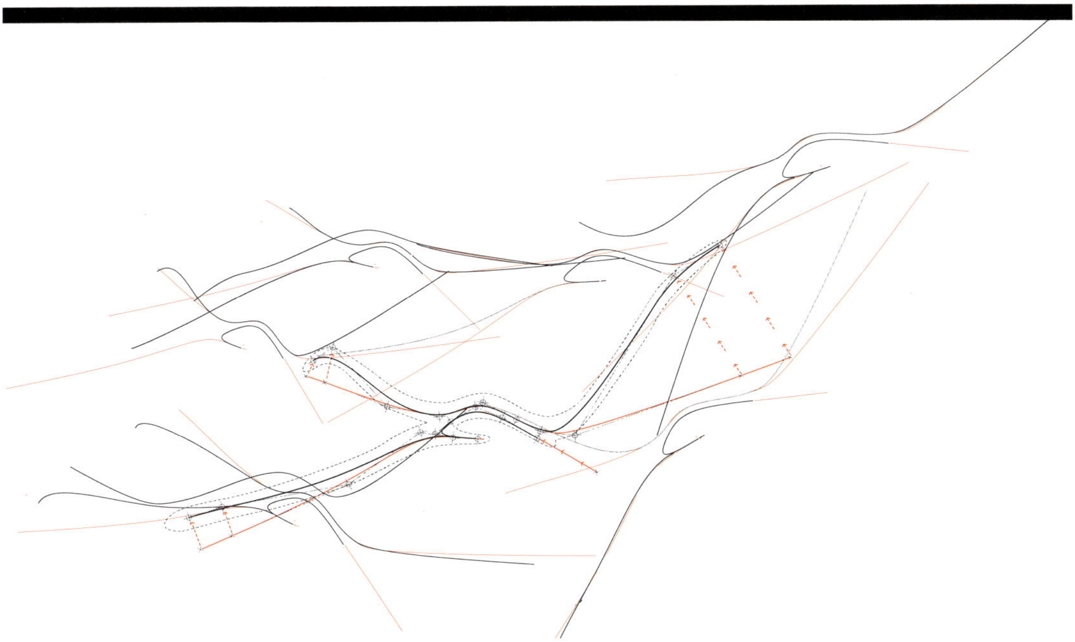

AgentBodies operate through a hierarchically embedded agency, where each limb interacts with its environment and adjacent bodies.

within the self-organizing swarm of host agents creates constantly varying geometries at the local scale: strange families of forms mutate and shift in and out of recognizable repetition.

The skeleton creates an internal organizational and behavioral logic for the body, enabling its skin to have a fluid surface topology.[1] The interaction of adjacent bodies generates emergent surface topologies, regardless of whether the body is designed with a topologically fixed or free skeleton. AgentBodies are inherently architectonic. Their logic of connection leads to highly intricate assemblages that we have leveraged for their ornamental and structural potential. The relatively constant underlying morphology of the skeletons provides sufficient repetition within a field of bodies to create recognizable patterns and ornamental effects.

AgentBody algorithms were first developed through the Swarm Matter research project as an ornamental strategy. Swarm Matter exhibits emergent order at several scales. At the macro-scale, a figure emerges from a field of bodies; at the micro-scale, strange and unique characteristics arise from the local interaction of bodies. The emergent macro-figure is largely the result of the interaction of the host agents (to which the bodies are assigned), while the local conditions are created by the interaction of the bodies' skeletons. The underlying structure of the body enables the entire topology of the skinned body to radically re-form. This dissolves the recognition of the individual body in favor of the emergent order of the field. The local conditions that emerge in the Swarm Matter project are characterized by periodic repetition, emergent symmetries, or unique expressions. Bodies that are arrayed in a linear arrangement

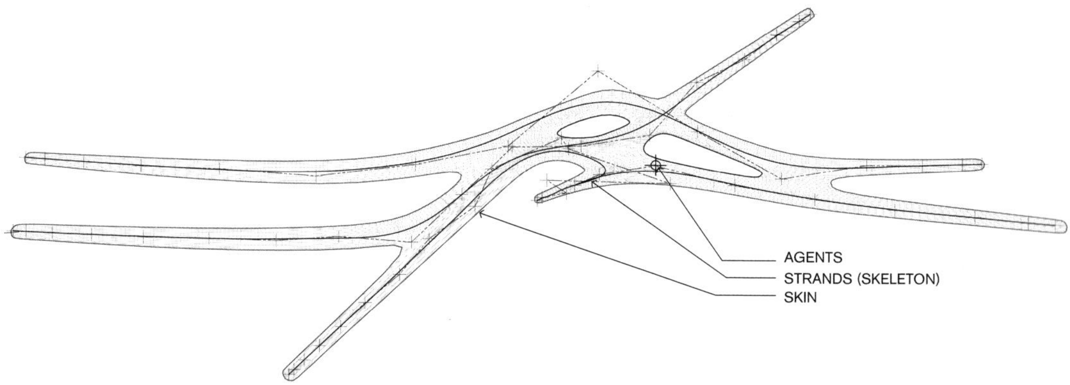

AgentBodies consist of networks of splines, with agency encoded within their control points.

and are subject to a similar set of local conditions create periodic order. Symmetries are not encoded into the logic or geometry of the bodies; instead, the emergence of symmetry is dependent on highly specific interaction of two or more bodies. While these symmetries are uncommon, their immediate recognition renders them an important property of the system. Unique expressions, such as the wing-like formations, are conditions that emerge from the interaction of agents, but have a specificity that renders them with a degree of autonomy from the continuity of the field.

The interconnection of agentBodies generates complex structural networks that operate through redundancy and create non-linear load paths. These networks exhibit, and shift between, the structural behavior of spaceframes, shells, and membranes. The design of the Composite Swarm and Composite Wing projects exploit this structural capacity through surface.[2] A network of foam agentBodies creates a continuous interconnected network of ridges and structural depth that generates the necessary stiffness within a fiber composite skin. These projects create structural strength through a composite of geometries rather than simply through a composite of materials.

Geometry is integral to the behavior of agentBody algorithms; they do not defer geometric character or tectonic logic to secondary meshing algorithms or applied components. This integrated nature of geometry and algorithm enables material, structural, and fabrication constraints to be encoded within the agentBody. Material properties, such as flexibility and elastic deformation, are encoded within the digital bodies of the Composite Swarm algorithm

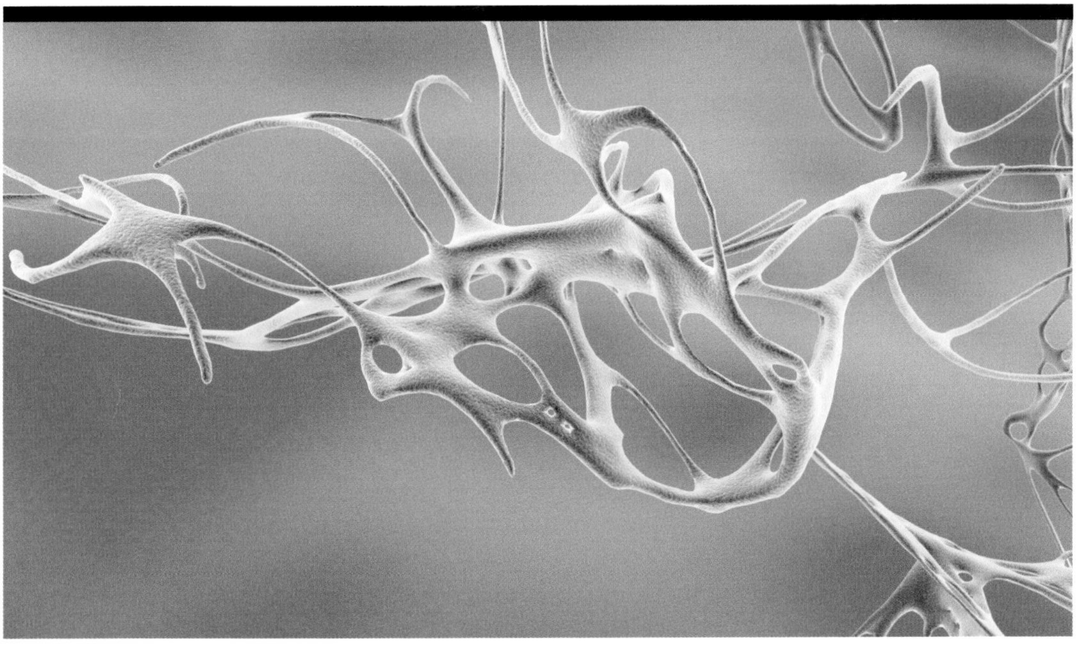

Swarm Matter, 2009. Detail.

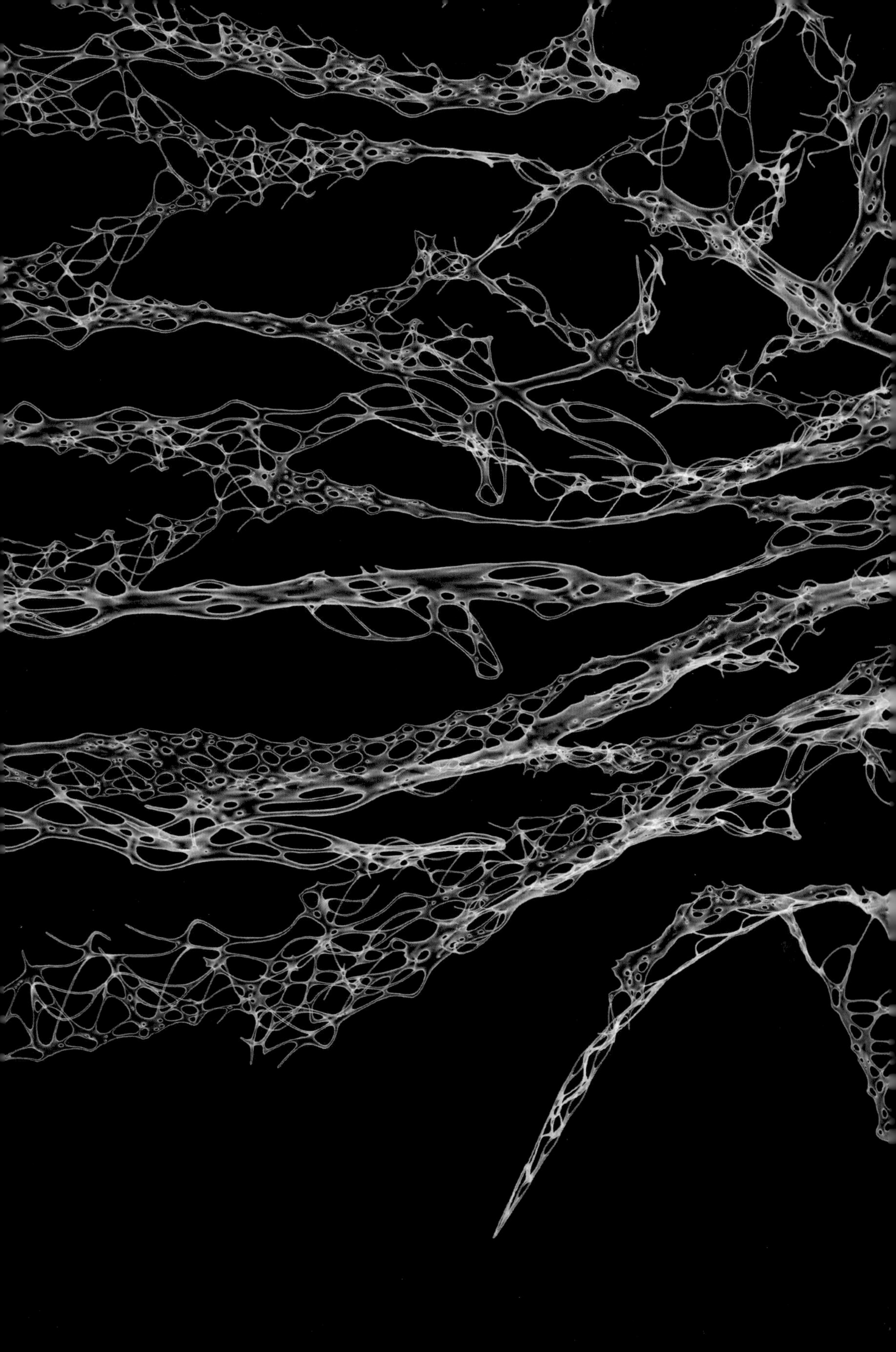

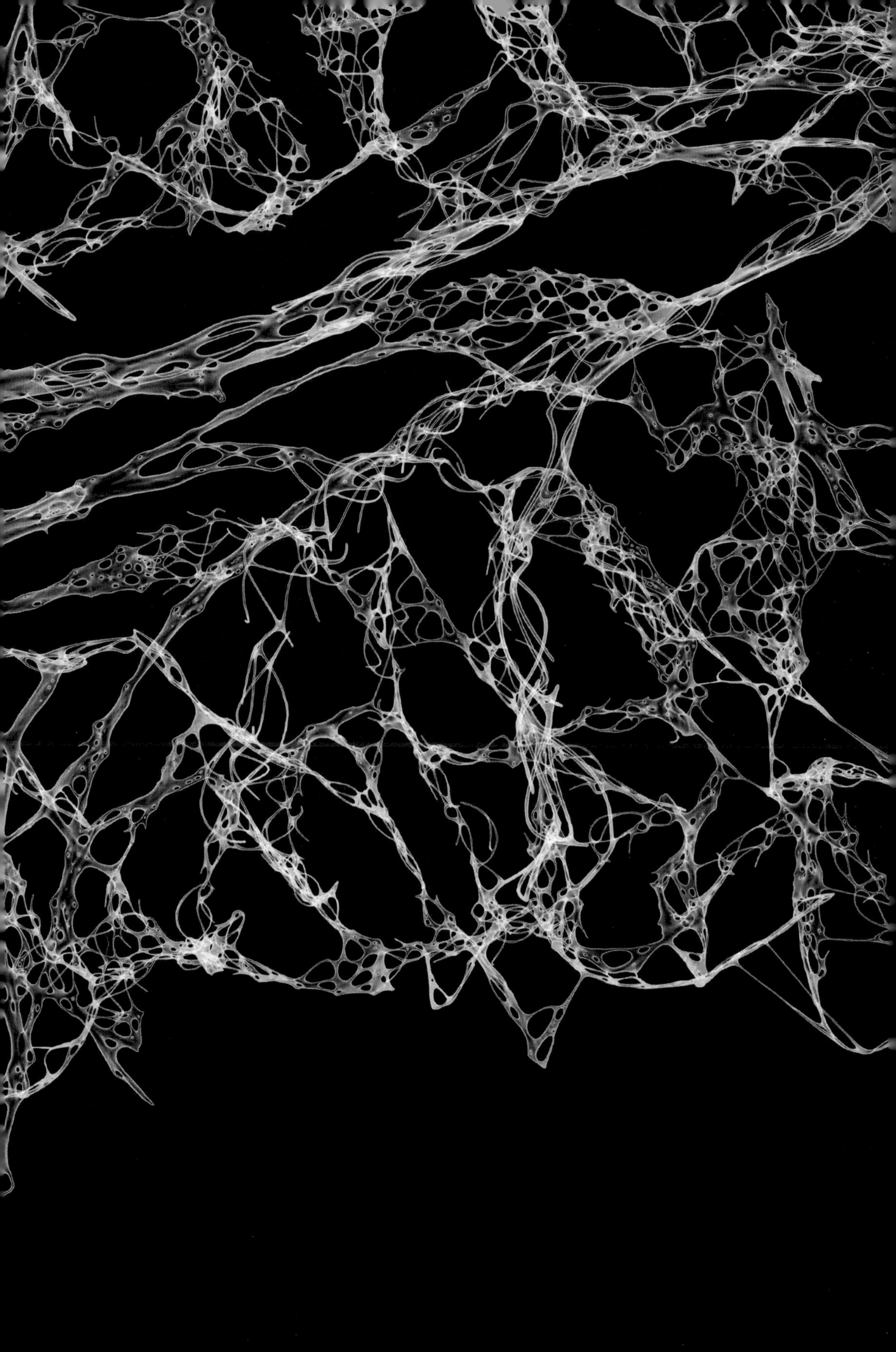

to enable the digital behavior to operate within the realm of the material's physical constraints. Similarly, fabrication constraints are encoded as behaviors within the specific geometry of the rod-based bodies of the Brass Swarm installation[3]. In these processes, the material or fabrication behaviors are not the driver of the emergent order; instead, they condition what is possible.

The intricate skeletons of agentBodies have a tendency to create woven, knitted or lace-like formations. These intricate assemblages are capable of catastrophic shifts from one condition to another, within a continuous whole. These shifts are not simply a change in degree, as is the case with linear parametric variation, but an emergent change in the characteristics of the assemblage. The agentBody studies for the Aalto University project[4] demonstrate a shift from a knitted to a woven character. The individual bodies pass in and out of legibility, expressing moments of periodicity that reveal the individual bodies before blending back into continuous interwoven strands. The legibility of the individual body is highly dependent on the surfacing of its skeleton. The Aalto University project was isosurfaced as a continuous field, which blurs the individual body into a geometric continuous whole, while the bodies of the Composite Swarm installation were cast as discrete elements that are woven together.

This design strategy inextricably links the agent and the body, creating a strong relationship between macro-scale behavior of the agents and micro-scale articulation of their networked bodies. The body forms the tectonics of the project, while its host agent is able to engage in the larger scale processes of formation, such as generating form or spatial topology. Sever-

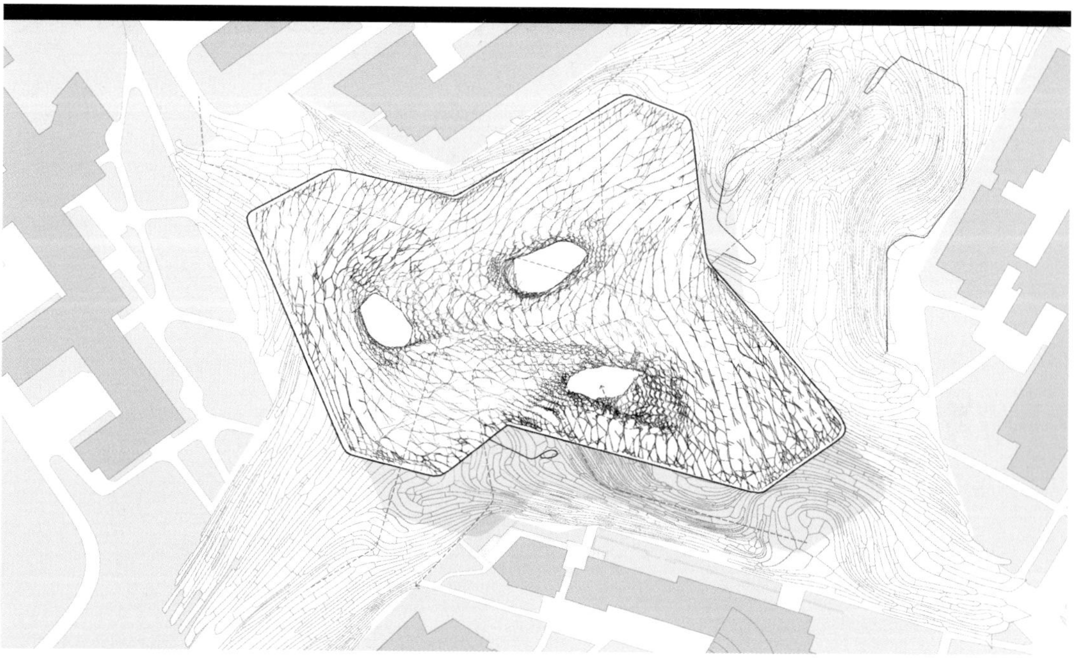

Aalto University, 2012.
Roof plan.

al recent agentBody projects, including the NGV Pavilion, RMIT Mace[5], and Brass Swarm, employ the *manifold swarm* strategy[6] to generate surface topology, while the agentBodies generate the articulation. This combination of generative approaches creates a synthetic relationship between form, structure, articulation and ornament—an ambition central to our work.

The linear and subservient hierarchy between a body and its host agent is uncharacteristic of Behavioral Formation, which inherently operates through non-linear relationships. This anomalous situation is created by prioritizing the legibility of emergent order. When the generative strategies of articulation and form create a feedback of mutual influence, the process becomes highly chaotic; and, while elsewhere an argument is posited in this publication for volatility, the risk in this case is the erosion of the legibility of the emergent order created by the individual systems. This brings into question the relative importance of the legibility of complex order and the level of actual complexity generated through self-organization.

1 Typically in the AgentBody projects, the skeleton is skinned through an isosurfacing technique, which easily enables changes in topology.

2 These two projects are described in later sections, under their relevant headings.

3 See project description in the AgentBody Prototypes section.

4 See Catalog of Projects.

5 Each of these projects are described in later sections.

6 See next strategy section.

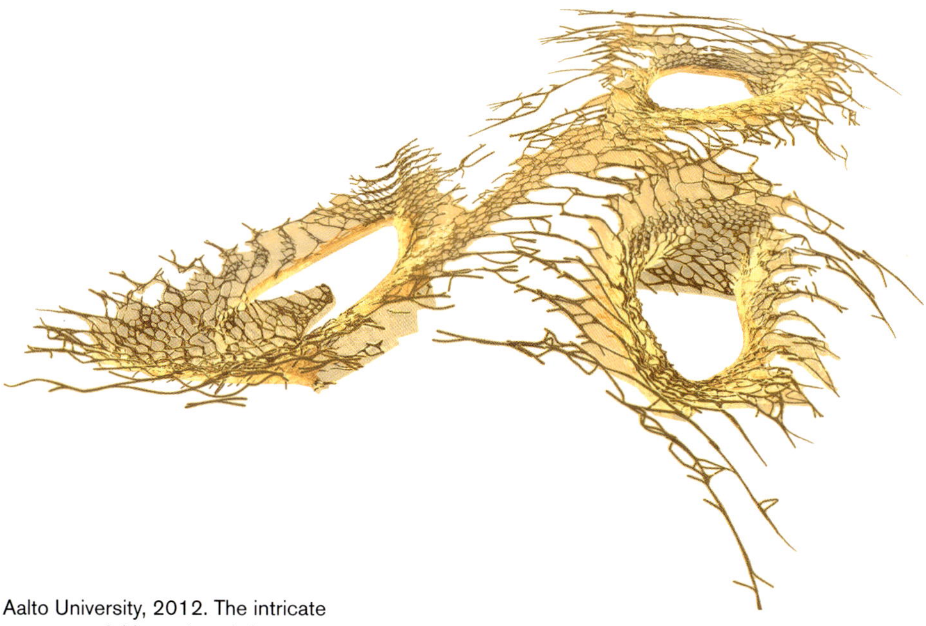

Aalto University, 2012. The intricate geometry of this roof study is generated through the interaction of agentBodies.

PROJECT

BABIY YAR MEMORIAL

Aerial perspective.

Babiy Yar Memorial is posited as an immersive space of remembrance. The project was designed as a response to a competition brief for a holocaust memorial and museum at Babiy Yar in Kiev. Our intention was to contrast a highly intricate bronze memorial space within a monolithic stone museum. Normative architectural articulation and scale were intentionally eschewed, so that the project is read as an abstract object.

In contrast to many of our projects—in which we attempt to dissolve hierarchies and dichotomies in favor of the negotiation of a synthetic whole, in this project we consciously set up a series of contradictions and juxtapositions. Top-down design intention and emergent bottom-up processes are demonstrated in their most isolated, and perhaps pure, forms in this project. The monolithic form of the museum was directly modeled, while the bronze memorial space was created through a highly volatile algorithm that operated largely in isolation from architectural concerns. The stone monolithic exterior and the

Bronze memorial space.
Following Pages: Perspective.

interior bronze memorial space provide a context for each other, rather than interacting to create a synthesis.

Through our projects we generally attempt to encode architectural roles (structure, ornament or enclosure) within the algorithm. However, as the memorial space was largely free of architectural constraints, we focused our design intention on generating intricate characteristics and exploring their affectual capacities—a purer expression of the emergent qualities of the algorithmic process.

This is an inverted monument: designed as a bronze space carved from within a stone monolith. The cast bronze memorial—rich in intricate detail—was intended to produce an intense experience and to evoke a visceral response. While we did not intend it to be referential, the detailed articulation of the bronze surface has been interpreted variously as flames or melting bodies. We designed the space and its articulation through a self-sca-

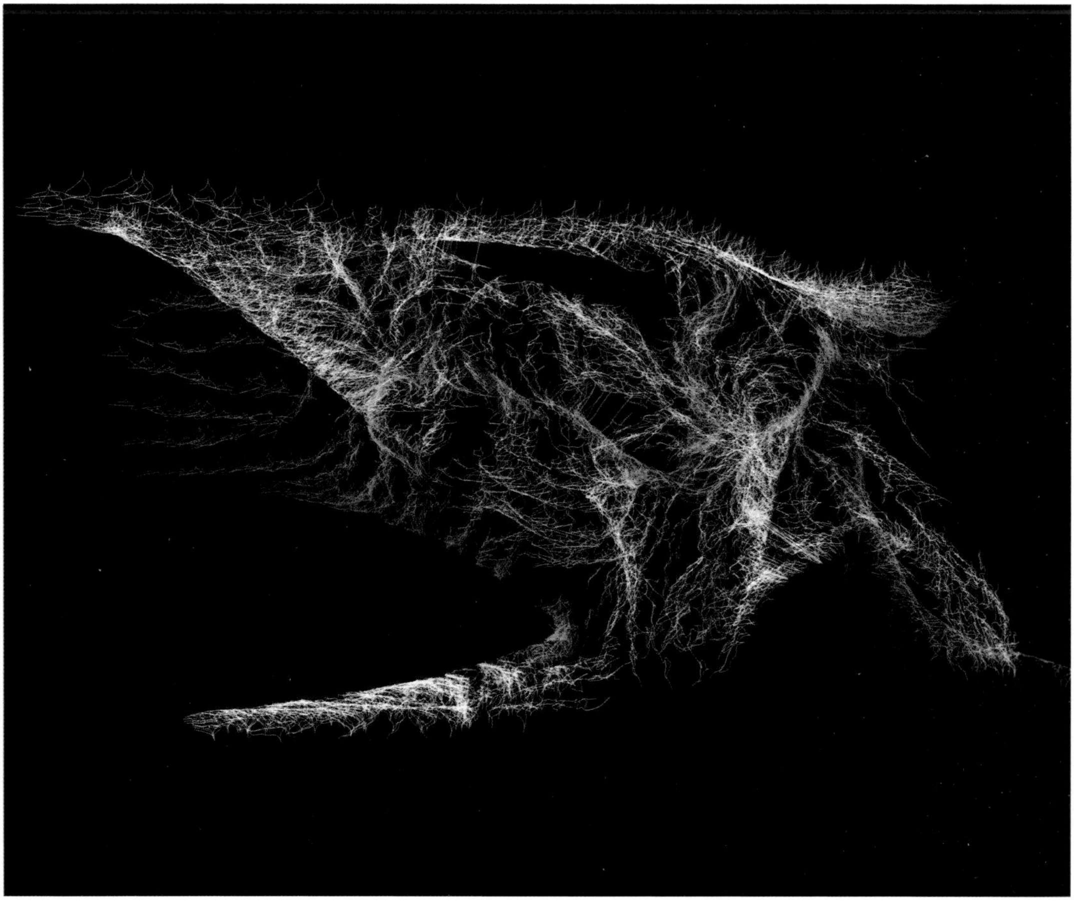

Diagram of the agentBodies that were generated through the design of the bronze memorial space.

ling *agentBodies* strategy, with the uniform surfacing blending the scales into a complex whole.

We sought a deliberate tension or conflict between various aspects of this project. The emergent field condition of the landscape is juxtaposed with the explicit object of the museum. The undifferentiated surface of the monolith is contrasted with the highly articulated bronze memorial space. This monolithic form of the museum is rendered as solid stone; however, it touches the ground lightly and is cantilevered as if suspended. Instead of subdividing the surface of the monolithic form to create the panel divisions, we intersected the form with a three-dimensional fractal grid to reinforce the reading of the form as a mass rather than surface. This grid was a ready-made geometry left over from the podium of our Taipei Performing Arts Centre[1]. The intersection of this grid with the irregular form of the museum etched a strange but ordered pattern of volumes,

The landscape, designed through a stigmergic behavioral algorithm, is a field of varying intensities.

rather than two-dimensional shapes, in the façade.

In opposition to the intricate memorial space, the exhibition spaces are deliberately calm and reflective. The glow of the opaque glass ceilings renders the spaces flat and uniform. The one disturbance to this interior space is the cast concrete wall of the memorial, which we intended to be an ominous presence, alluding to the memorial space without articulating it.

The landscape is a field of varying intensities to be traversed by the visitor: a meandering path, rather than a clear direction. The design of the landscape is a negotiation between a field that we drew directly and a multi-agent algorithm that navigates and responds to this field of influence. A figural quality emerged from this interaction of direct, top-down intention and the emergent operation of the algorithm.

1 See Catalog of Projects.

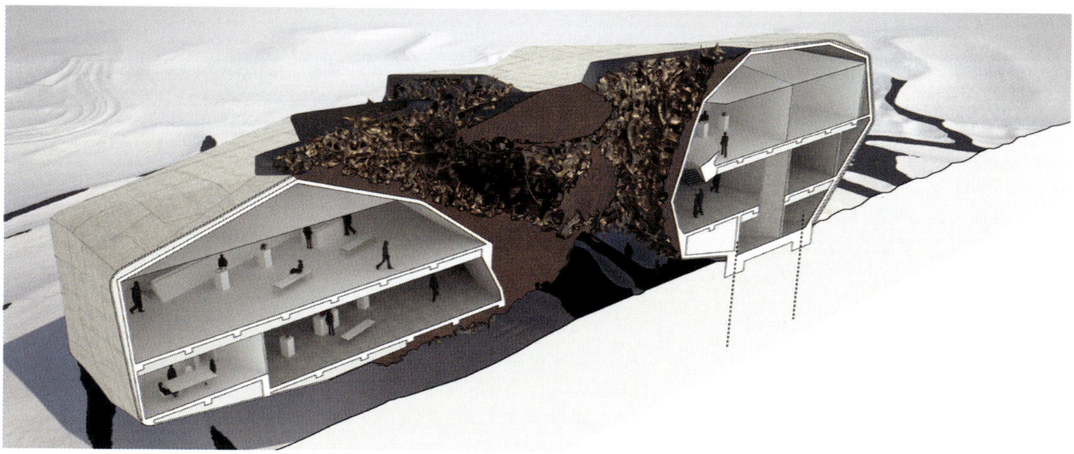

Above: The bronze memorial space is designed to appear as though it is carved from the monolithic stone museum.

Below: The contrast between the intricate memorial space and the reflective exhibition space is evident in section.

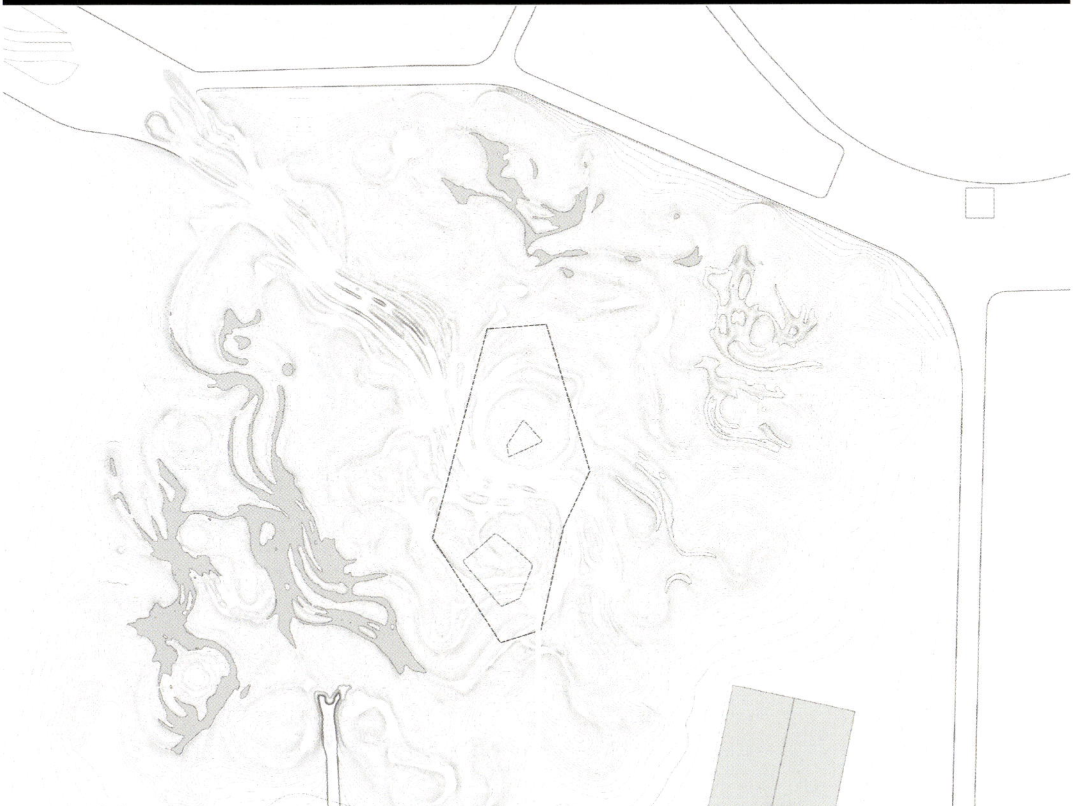

Above: Model photo.
Below: Landscape plan.

STRATEGY

MANIFOLD SWARMS

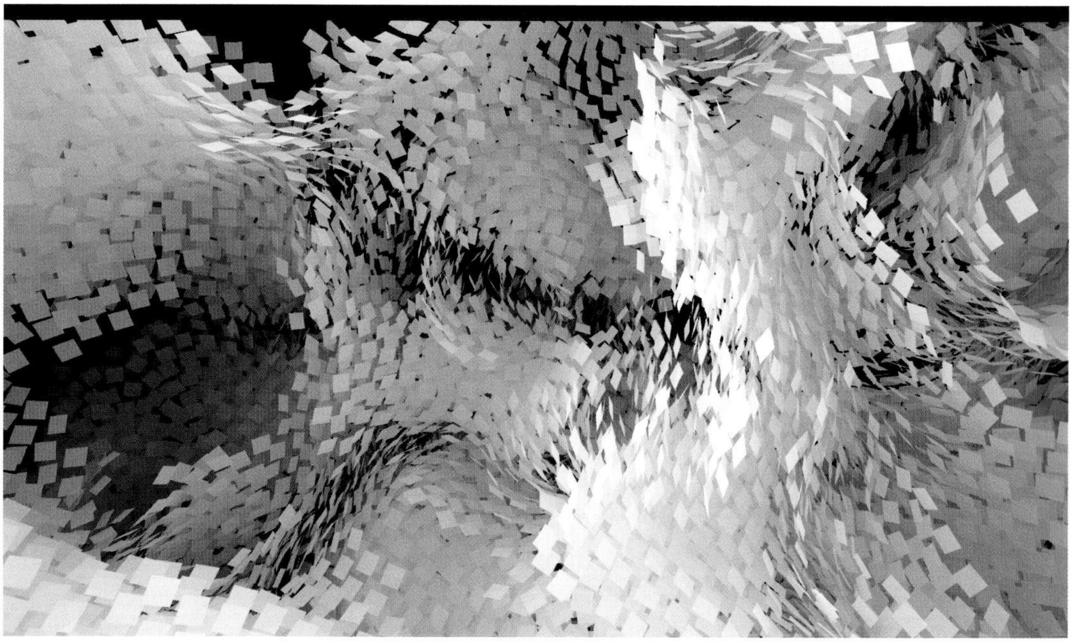

Nine Elms Retroactive Form Study
2017-2018. A manifold swarm of
plane-based agents.

Manifold swarms is a multi-agent strategy for the generation of emergent surface topology. This approach embodies a shift in our research from the generation of surface articulation and form, to the generation of spatial topology. Manifold swarms enables a behavioral approach to fundamentally engage in the design of architectural space and to establish non-linear algorithmic relationships between form, space, and articulation.

Multi-agent algorithms typically define the agent's location, direction, and relationship to a population of agents—or its environment—within Cartesian space. This algorithmic swarm logic has an inherent bias towards forming point-clouds rather than surfaces. This bias or apparent limitation has the tendency to push multi-agent design processes to operate at the extremes of scale (that of urbanism and ornament): situations in which the agents are constrained to a known surface such as a landscape or façade. The instances in which multi-agent algorithms are applied to the generation of form are typically through the creation of point-clouds or strands which get wrapped in surface as a secondary procedure.[1] As these agents have no capacity to analyze the secondary surface they are forming, and little (if any) design intent relating to surface, the generation of topology is limited to the wrapping of a volume rather than the emergence of a manifold surface. Volume and surface are very different ways of conceptualizing space and form. Working exclusively with volume and its surface wrapping[2] limits the feedback across the scales of form and articulation, as surface is extracted from the system rather than being an active participant within the design process.

Nine Elms Bridge, 2015. The behavior of the agents shifts across the bridge, with the most complex manifold topologies being generated in the tower and at the landings.

In attempting to overcome this resistance to surface and the topological ignorance of swarm systems, the manifold swarms strategy was developed for the generation of manifold topological surfaces. This strategy is based on encoding an orientation coordinate system into the agent, which is divorced from the agent's description of its location, velocity, and acceleration. This vector orientation system enables a population of agents to communicate and align their orientation coordinates to self-organize as a surface of best fit. Through this self-organization of implied surface normals, a coherent manifold surface topology emerges from disordered clouds of agents.

The manifold swarms strategy begins either with a cloud of agents that re-forms into a coherent topology, or with a starting surface designed as a direct input into this generative process. In designing the Flinders Street Station project,[3] we adopted the latter approach to define particular conditions, such as the link to the water and the form of the towers. This relationship between the starting surface and emergent process is not dissimilar to that used in the Taipei Performing Arts Centre. The towers and certain edge conditions were fixed, while the remaining surface re-formed through the manifold swarms strategy. This self-organizing process is most evident in the vortices that draw the roof/plaza surface into a more complex surface topology, providing natural light and ventilation to the station below. At its most extreme (in the columns of the manifold), the surface delaminates, creating intricate spatial and topological conditions. This emergent topology shifts between surface, network, strand, and lattice, and creates a synthesis of topology and tectonics.

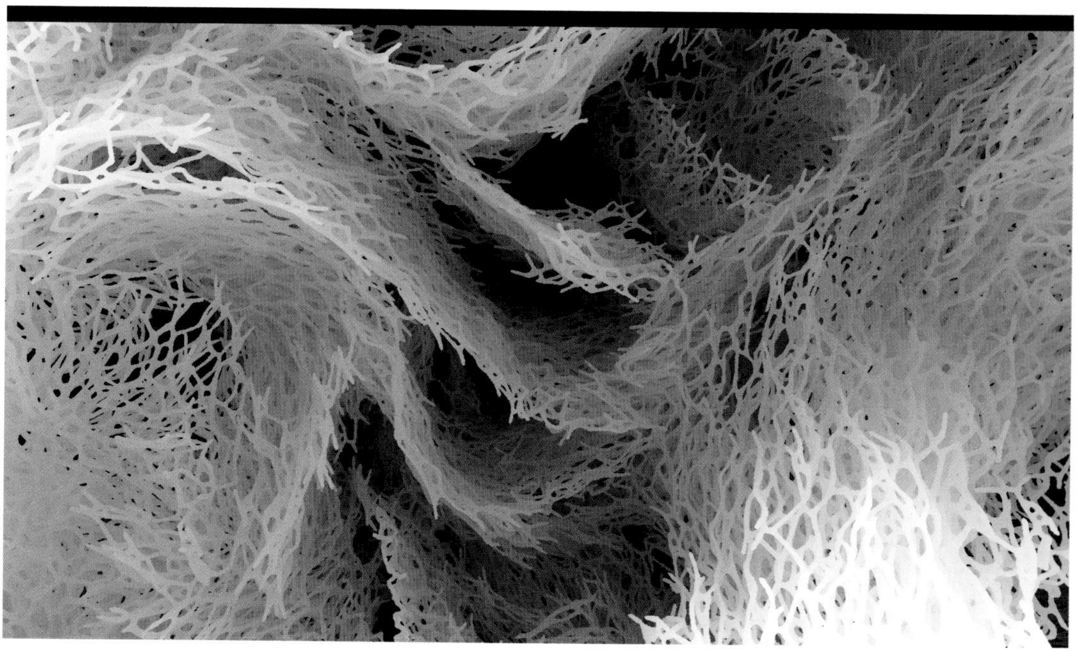

Nine Elms: Retroactive Form Study, 2017–2018. The flaking and delaminating geometry of the project is created through manifold swarm behavior.

This relatively recent manifold swarm strategy has enabled the exploration of highly generative approaches to surface topology, and is an attempt to resist the sequential application of algorithmic articulation to explicitly modeled form.[4] The correlation of form and articulation is important to the wider ambitions of our design research to conceptualize architecture as matter that negotiates design intention or behaviors, rather than as the assembly of discrete elements.[5] The automation of this feedback within the manifold swarms strategy enables a potentially seamless relationship between the generative algorithms that operate at the scale of surface topology and the algorithmic articulation of these surfaces.[6] The manifold swarms approach to surface topology operates in a highly volatile manner, with a capacity to generate a range of surface characteristics, including the flaking or delaminating surfaces of the NGV Pavilion, the near minimal surfaces of the Laminar Bodies installation[7], and the thick turbulent mass of the RMIT Mace.

The algorithmic emergence of manifold topology is of particular interest when it is allied with *agentBodies* to create a system in which the agents that form the topology also generate the tectonics of that surface. These combined processes were initially developed through the New Taipei Museum[8], Aalto University, and Flinders Street Station projects as an approach to intrinsically combine spatial division, surface, structure, and ornament into a unified process of formation–creating an irreducible whole. The interaction of these two strategies has since become the basis for many of our more recent projects such as the agentBody Prototypes and the Nine Elms Bridge.[9]

Nine Elms Bridge, 2015.

Manifold swarms create surface and spatial topology from behaviors that are specifically designed to generate surfaces, as opposed to the sequential operation of surfacing a generative scaffold (such as lines or point-clouds). This distinction is important both conceptually and from the standpoint of surface character. The secondary extraction of surface from a generative scaffold—such as a swarm of points or lines—necessarily relies on the geometric logic of the secondary extraction algorithm and, as a consequence, expresses that algorithm's formal tendencies. Often in these circumstances, it is the indexical formal characteristics of the surface extraction algorithm that dominates the emergent characteristics of the formation of the points or lines. Conversely, manifold swarms embed spatial and formal design intention within a process that generates intricate emergent characteristics.

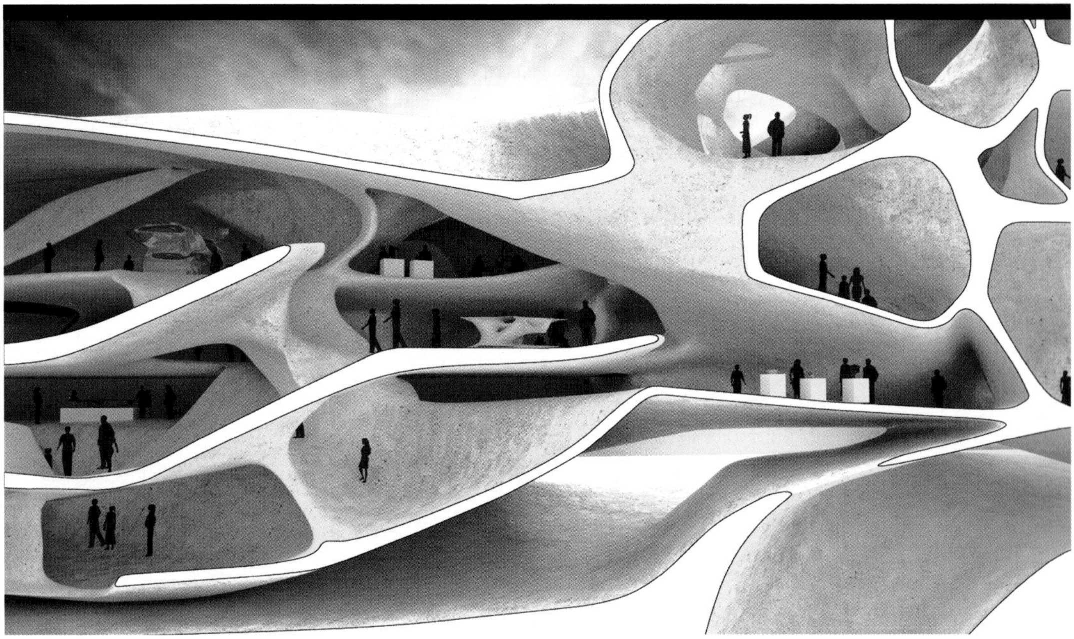

New Taipei Museum, 2011. Complex surface topology, generated through manifold swarm behavior, is evident in the section of the project.

1 As this field of multi-agent algorithmic architectural design is relatively young, stating that something is 'typical' generally refers to observations I have made when examining the experiments of my students, and from a small but growing number of architects who are adopting swarm algorithms.

2 Typically, this wrapping involves an isosurfacing algorithm or similar mesh reconstruction tool.

3 See Catalogue of Projects.

4 This linear application is discussed further in the strategy Strange Feedback.

5 This is discussed in greater detail in the Introduction and in the Behavioral Methodologies essay.

6 The other strategy that establishes a non-linear relationship between form and articulation is *strange feedback*. While strange feedback processes enable this negotiation, the manual nature of the feedback limits the number of iterations and any systemic relationship between surface and articulation. The shortcut to intuition that is so useful to strange feedback is also its conservative limitation. The projects developed with a process of strange feedback avoid the purity and indexicality of more systemic algorithmic approaches, but they carry instead certain formal tropes and biases.

7 The Laminar Bodies installation is discussed in the AgentBody Prototypes section.

8 See Catalog of Projects.

9 See Catalog of Projects.

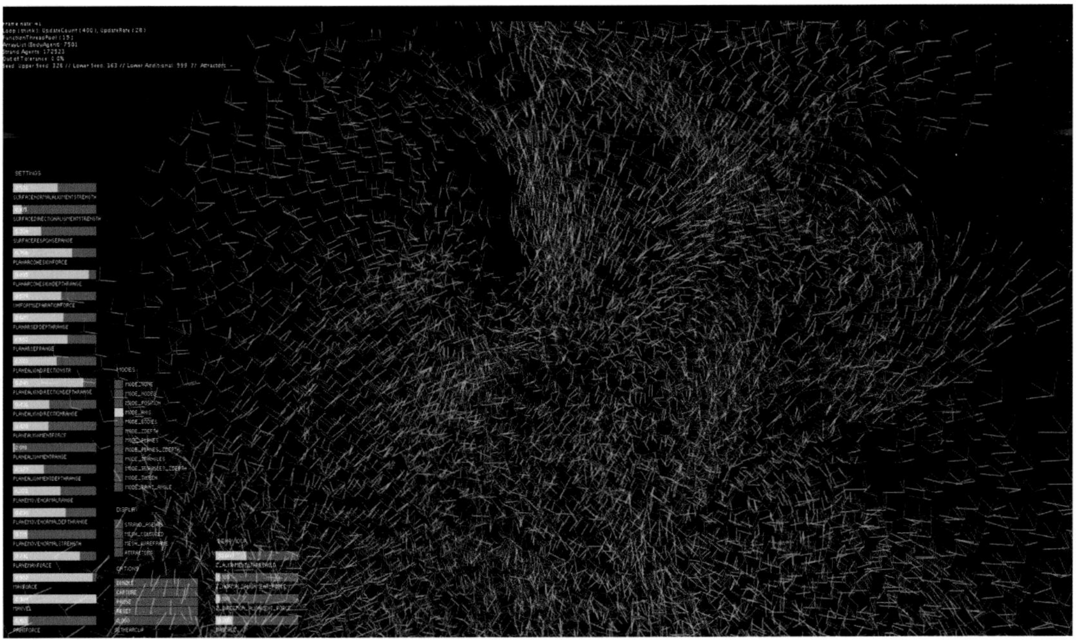

Algorithmic generative process–indicating the orientation of the manifold swarm agents.

PROJECT

RMIT MACE

Detail of the agentBody titanium printed geometry.

The design of the RMIT Mace draws upon the intricate and ornamental characteristics of historical mace and reinterprets these through behavioral processes of design. The form of the mace is defined by a fibrous mass, fabricated with titanium sintering to create a highly complex yet lightweight structure. Mass defined by the accretion of fibrous elements creates an alternative reading of form from that of surface, volume or lattice, one that is rich with intricate detail and strange characteristics.

The mace, designed in collaboration with Scott Mayson, balances highly volatile algorithmic processes with direct digital modeling. The form of the mace is characterized by deep labyrinths and unfurling mass generated by a *manifold swarm / agentBodies* algorithm. The behaviors of this algorithm were developed to generate a thickness to its topology and create a mass rather than a constant manifold surface. The interaction between this generative algorithm and a directly modeled outer volume tempers the turbulent na-

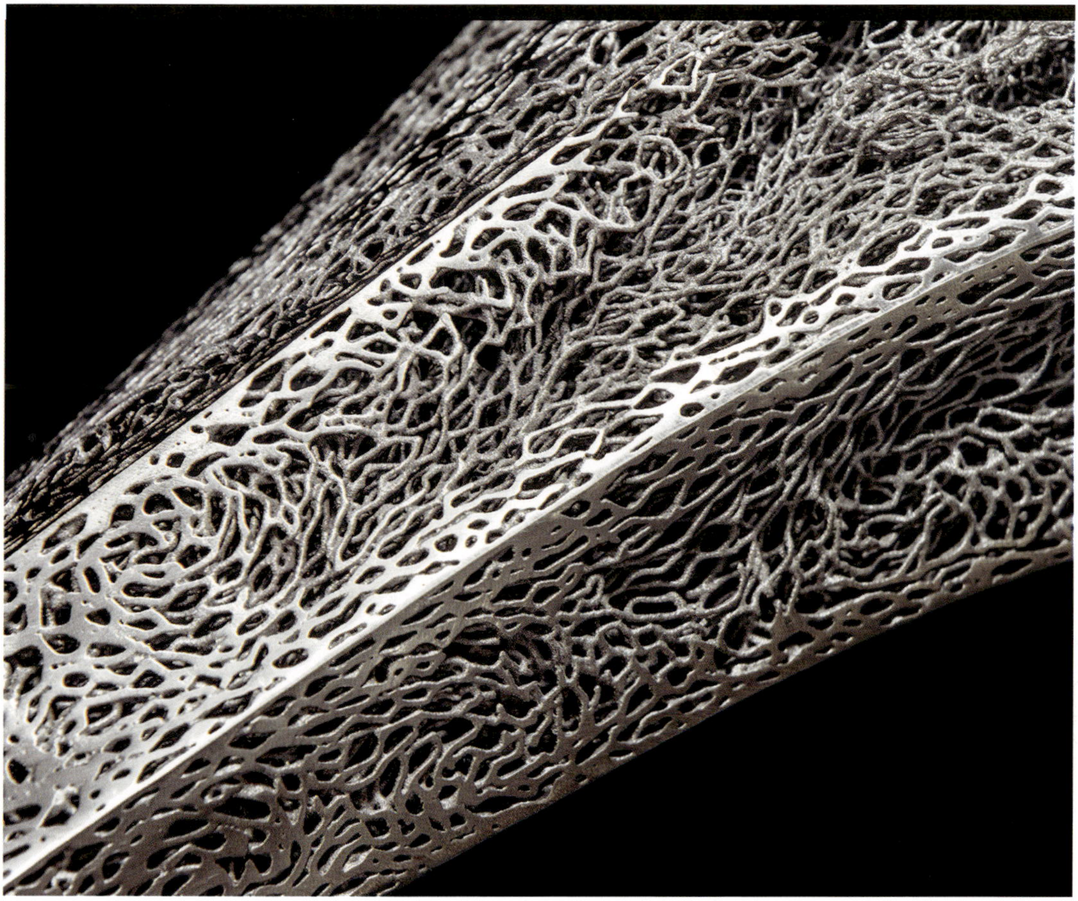

Detail of the mace shaft. The geometry shifts character from the head of the mace to the shaft, where it compresses to form a surface.
Following Pages: Rendered studies.

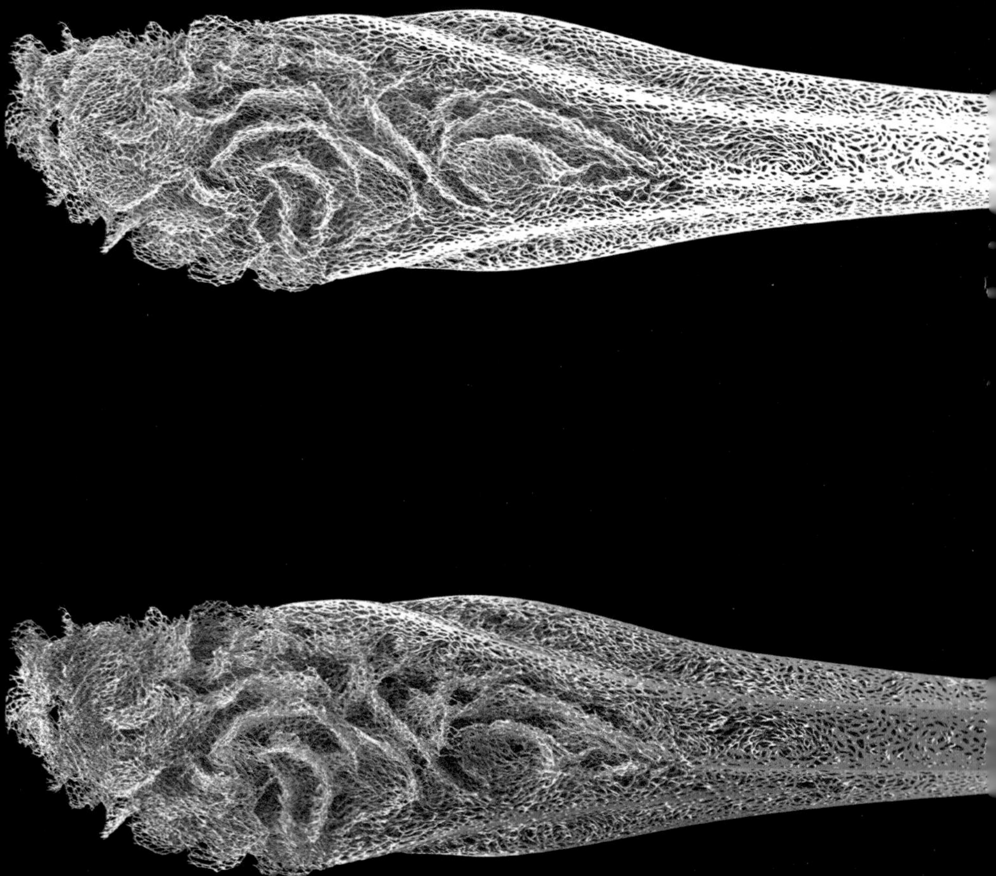

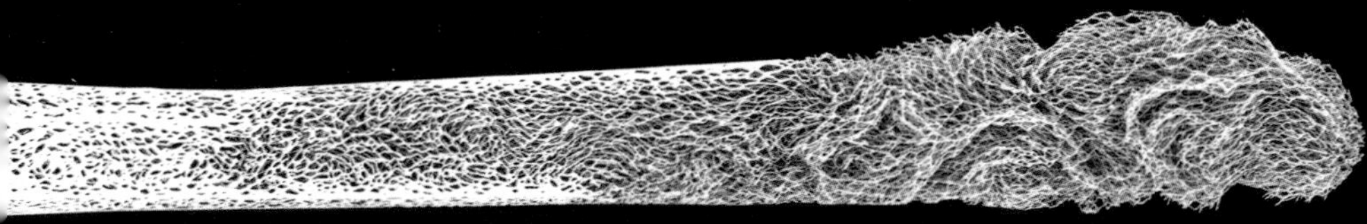

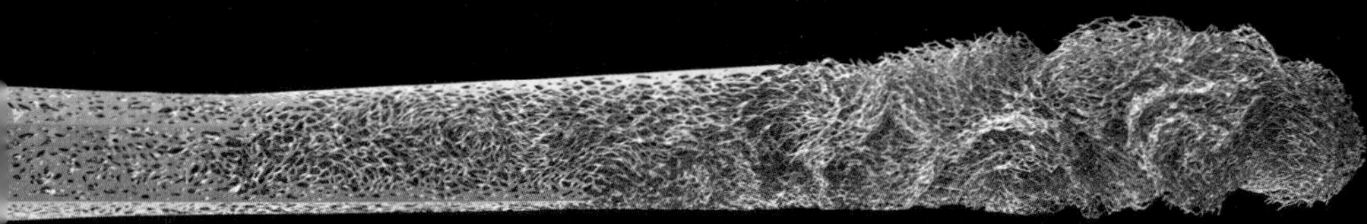

ture of the process, compressing the agentBodies to the surface of the volume where they form the shaft of the mace. This flattening to surface amplifies the ornamental qualities of the agentBodies through the local suppression of spatial complexity.

In creating highly intricate geometry, the limitation on scale was less determined by computational or fabrication limits than by the limit of legibility. Below a certain threshold of scale, the reading of the generative formation becomes that of texture. The ambition of this project, like many of the projects here, was to relate the formal characteristics created through the localized algorithmic process to the larger form of the project. The explicitly modeled, creased edges of the shaft, which wrap up into the generative ends of the mace, were an attempt to mediate the reading of scale in the project between that of the silhouette and the local formation of the bodies.

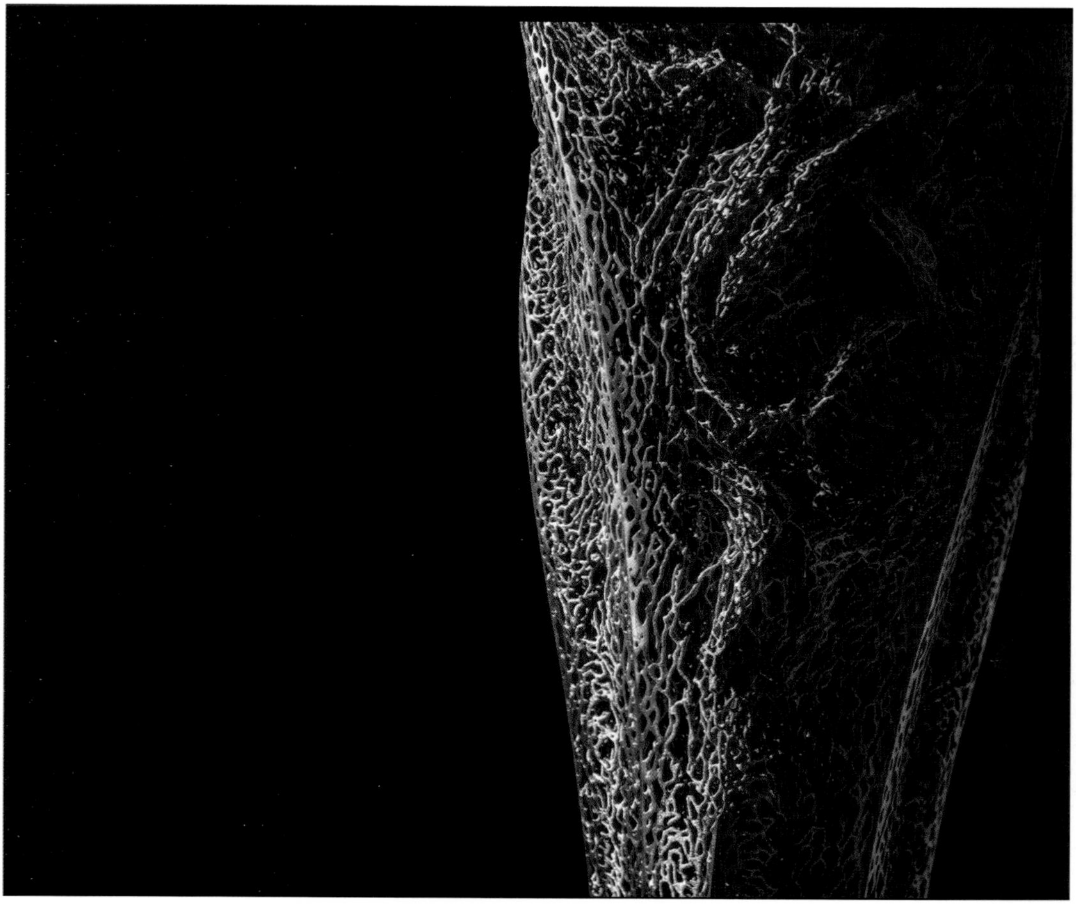

Detail of the ornamental mace head.

A direct deposition process (selective laser melting or SLM), enabled the highly intricate geometry of the mace to be fabricated in titanium. This 3D printing technique permits considerable geometric freedom and control over the position of material. However, it has specific limitations regarding the angle of cantilever and bridging distances. The degree of intricacy generated through the high population algorithms prohibited manual adjustments to the model, and necessitated a systemic approach to addressing these limitations. Our response was to develop generative behaviors that kept the geometry largely within these limitations, while a secondary algorithm steps through the generative geometry and removes non-compliant parts and reconnects those that require additional support. This close integration of generative design and fabrication processes undermines the pure traits associated with either process; instead, the characteristics generated are a negotiation between the two.

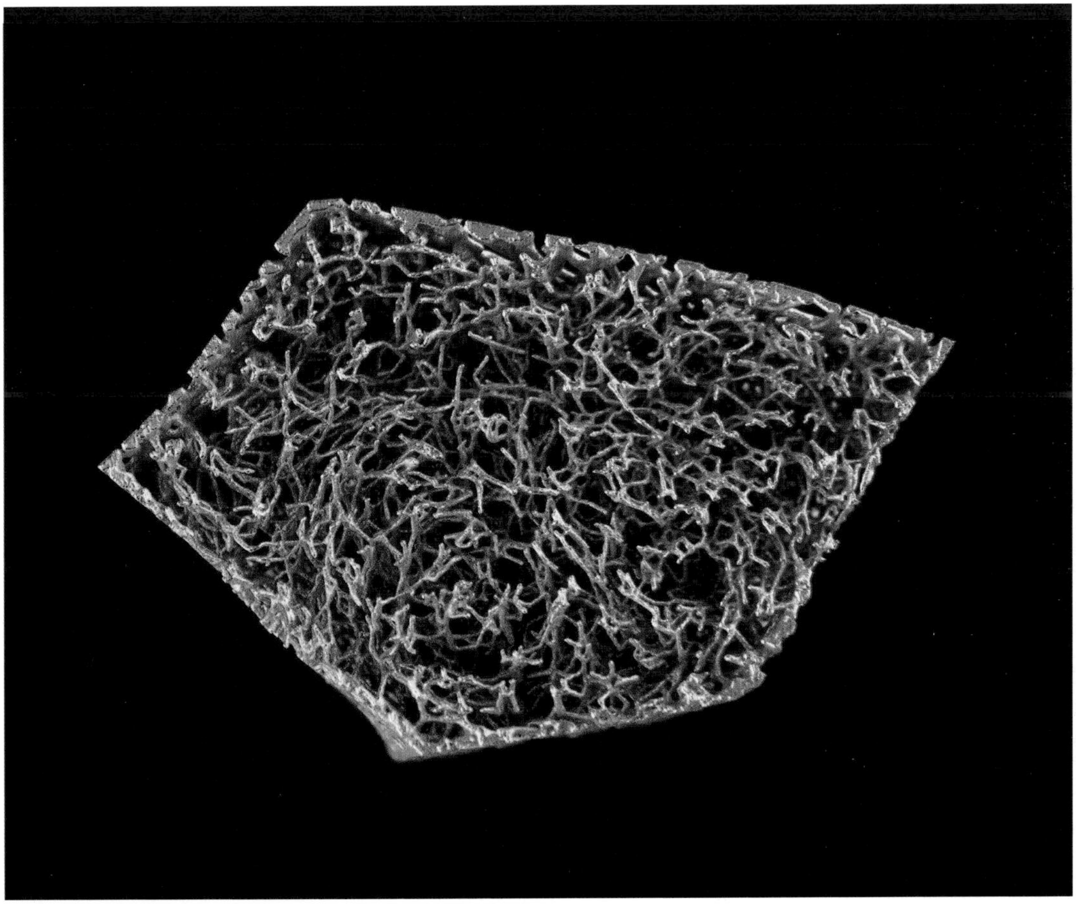

A section through the shaft of the mace reveals fibrous, lattice-like geometry within the thin surface of the shaft.

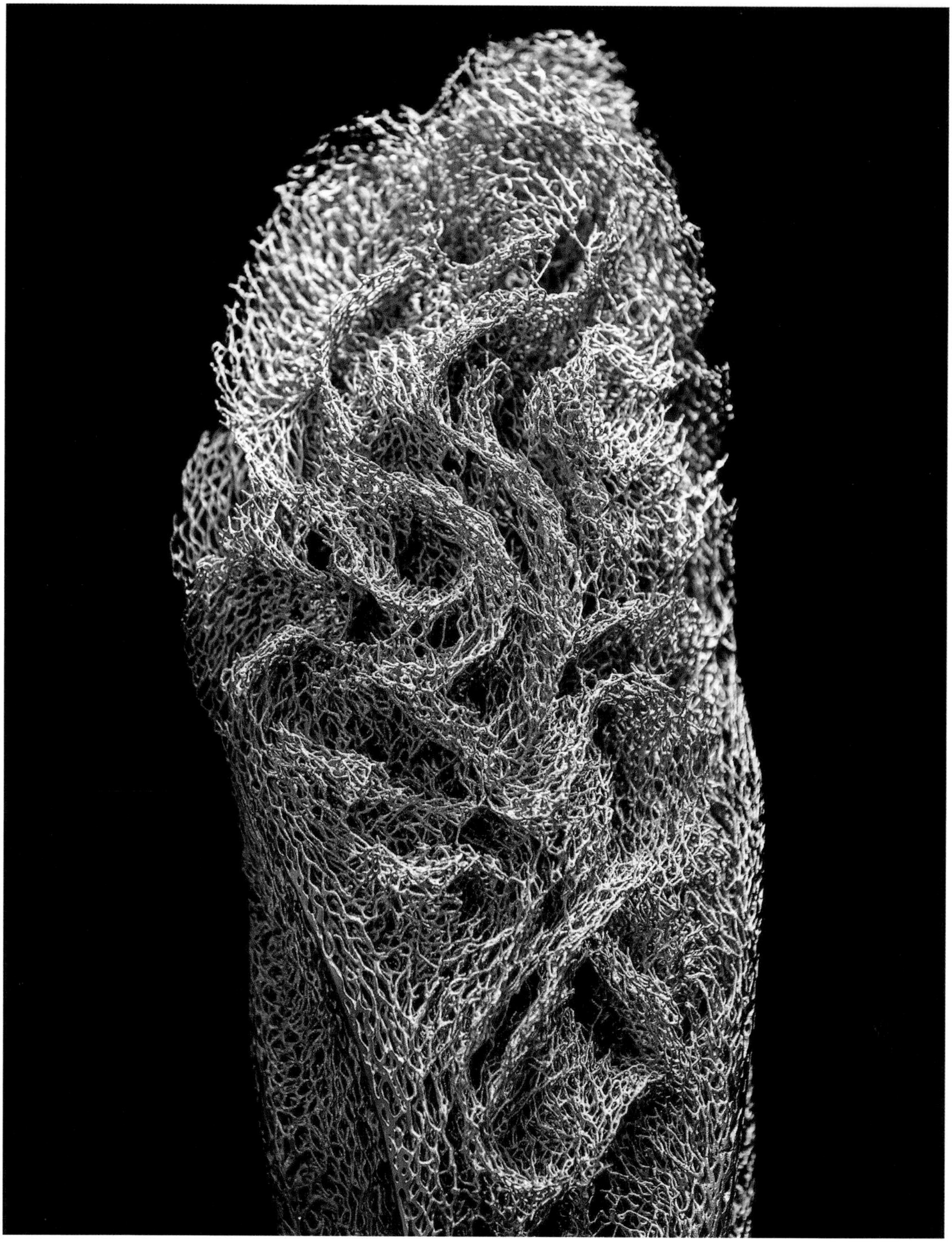

Detail of the head of the mace.

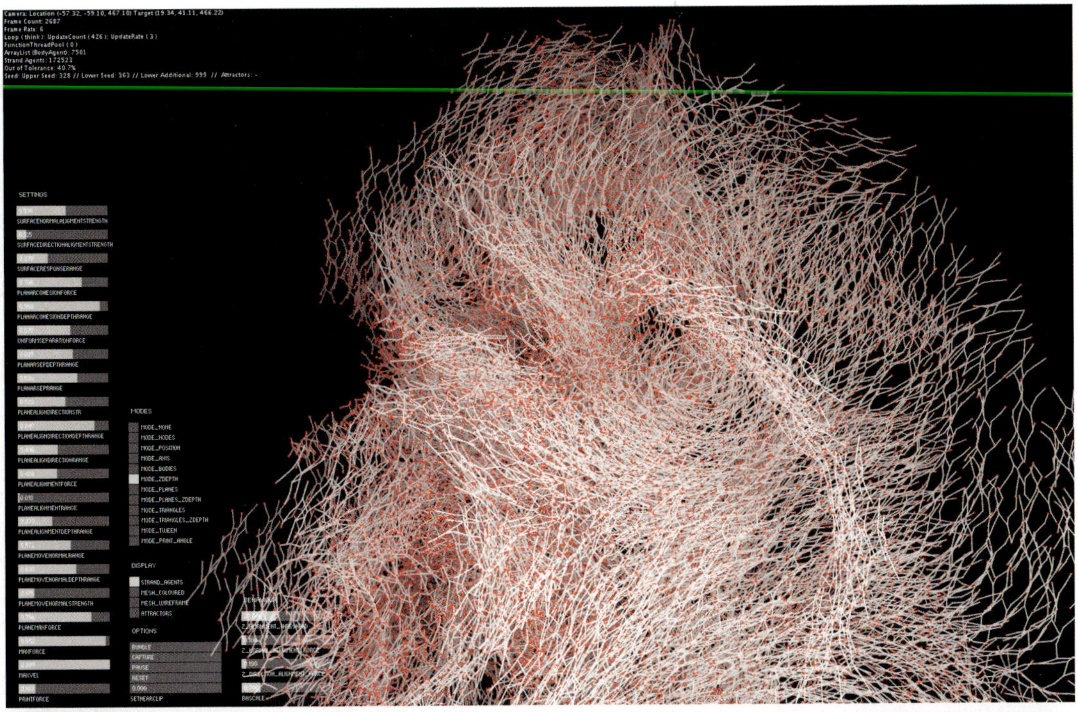

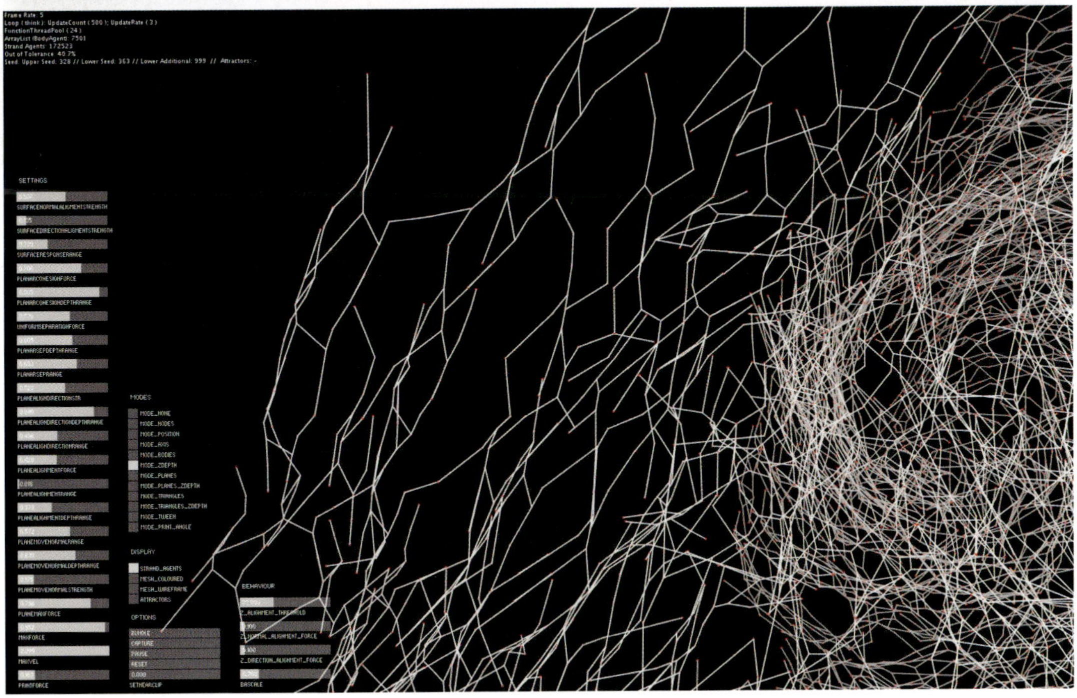

Above: Algorithmic generative process—highlighting the individual agents in the agentBody network.

Below: Algorithmic generative process—at the micro-scale, it is the interaction of the agents' limbs that create a tectonic logic.

STRATEGY

BEHAVIORAL COMPOSITES

The intricate and highly differentiated architecture designed through behavioral processes of formation is incompatible with contemporary construction techniques. This conflict is procedural rather than geometric. The self-organizing and synthesizing behavior of complex systems is at odds with the contemporary norms of construction involving the assembly of discrete parts that perform individual architectonic roles. As our work has shifted from a purely digital domain to physical materialization, it has been necessary to extend our behavioral strategies from design into construction. We have focused on the integration of tectonic and material approaches that maintain fine-grain differentiation of geometry, directionality, density, translucency and structural behavior within a continuous body of material.

Fiber composites have become a key aspect in our development of procedural fabrication approaches that parallel behavioral design processes.[1] Composites are a negotiation of two or more different materials to make a synthetic whole that behaves differently to the sum of the material parts. Composites are interdependent and complex; they offer a material parallel for the synthetic outcomes of behavioral processes of negotiation. Our initial exploration of this concept involved a literal translation of algorithmic fibrous strands to individual fibers within a composite. As this research has matured, the logic of compositing both materials and geometries has evolved its own direction and fed back into the development of algorithmic design processes.

Fibrous House prototype, 2012.
This prototype was designed to explore the expressive capacities of composite fiber fabrication.

An argument, and indeed motivation, for fiber composite construction is frequently premised on the desire for efficiency and structural performance.[2] In contrast, the argument posited here is based on the capacity of composite materials to negotiate between competing design behaviors within a continuous whole, as well as our interest in their expressive capacity. Within the contemporary discourse of experimental architecture, there has been a revived interest in fiber composite construction over the last decade, although its application in architecture dates back to at least the Monsanto House of the Future in 1957. This renewed interest leverages the capacity of fiber composites for complex geometry and structural performance.[3]

Behavioral composites align the fabrication logic of fiber composites with the computational capacity to encode agency within fine-grain geometry. Encoding agency within individual fibers, and designing through their interactions at the micro-scale, enables the generation of intricate and emergent patterns within fiber composite surfaces.[4] This reification of emergent characteristics is our primary motivation in developing the behavioral composites strategy; we consider structural performance and material behavior as secondary concerns that condition, rather than generate, the design.

Our early behavioral composite experiments, which drew on the fibrous assemblages algorithms, created both structural networks and ornamental characteristics within composite surfaces.[5] These small-scale studies of the interrelationship of pattern and surface became the basis from which to develop a full-scale prototype for the Fibrous House project.[6] The

Fibrous composite study, 2011. This prototype, developed through a workshop at the University of Technology Sydney, explored the fibrous character of strands within composite fiber surfaces.

fabrication of this prototype was focused less on accurately translating the digital model into the physical prototype, than on reifying its behavioral qualities and fibrous characteristics in material. The Fibrous House was designed through an iterative feedback loop between material experiments and digital generative processes. The prototype was fabricated through both CNC forming and manual craftsmanship. Molds for the surfaces were CNC milled, while the fibers were manually placed in accordance with the behavioral rules that operated within the generative algorithm. The intention was to use these procedures of bundling and aligning to reproduce the algorithmic character, rather than the exact pattern, of the digital model. This process follows the procedural operation of the agents in the deposition of the fibers: a physical parallel of the digital generative process.

The Fibrous House prototype was built largely through manual operations while anticipating the possibilities of robotic composite fabrication. Exploring this architecture through prototypes that are fabricated in less automated processes is useful, but the ambitions of this work will ultimately be realized through robotic approaches. Several such techniques have been explored and developed through our research, including composite taping and fiber-winding. The shift to robotic techniques in this research is not driven by a desire to achieve the seamless perfection and smooth surfaces of the current generation of fiber-placement technology used within the aerospace and yachting industries,[7] but by a desire to procedurally construct the intricate and intense characteristics of our architecture at a large scale.

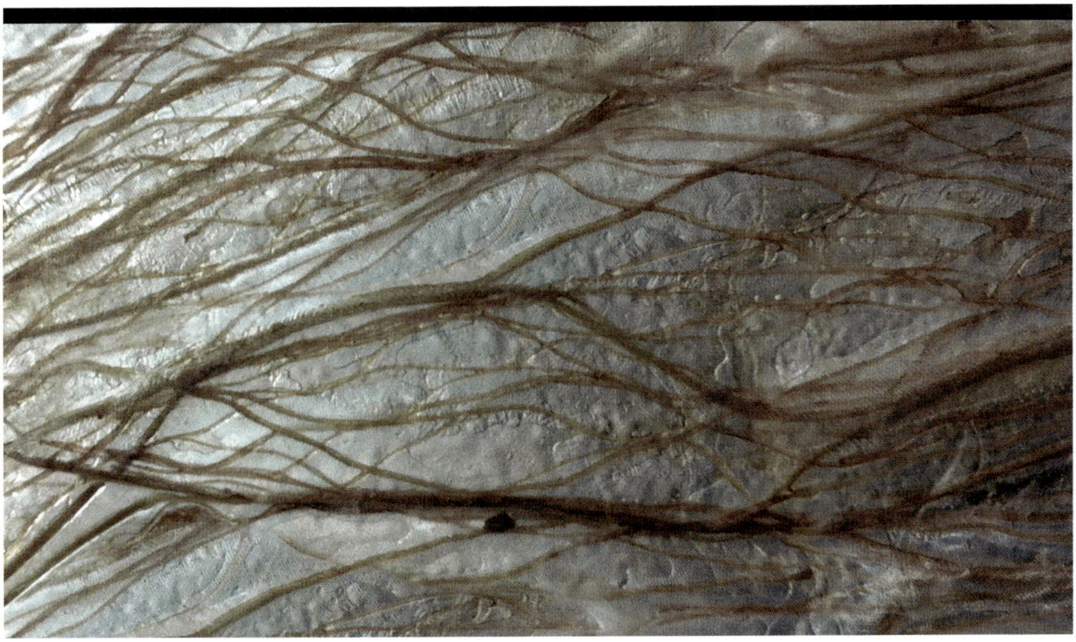

Fibrous House composite study, 2012. This prototype explored the relationship of computational and composite strands.

Through our research, we have developed a closer interaction between generative behaviors and fabrication operations by encoding design behaviors directly into the robotic fabrication process (which is discussed in detail in the *stigmergic robotics* strategy). This is an argument to compress design and fabrication into a single behavioral operation, one premised on stigmergic feedback between the form and the instrument of formation.

A recent series of projects–including the Composite Wing, Composite Swarm and RMIT Meeting Pavilion[8]–were developed from a composite of geometries, rather than purely from a composite of materials. These projects were designed through agentBody algorithms as opposed to the strand-based approach of the earlier fiber composite projects described here. In these projects, agentBodies are embedded as core material within fiber composite surfaces, where it is the algorithmically generated core that negotiates the structural and expressive behaviors of the project, rather than embedding agency within the fibers themselves. The core material of the agentBodies is structurally benign; however, their thickness generates the necessary structural depth and surface corrugation to significantly strengthen the fiber composite surface. This alternative approach to linking the digital behavior of the agent directly to the tectonics and fabrication of the composite surface offers a fabrication process aligned with the procedural logic of the algorithm.

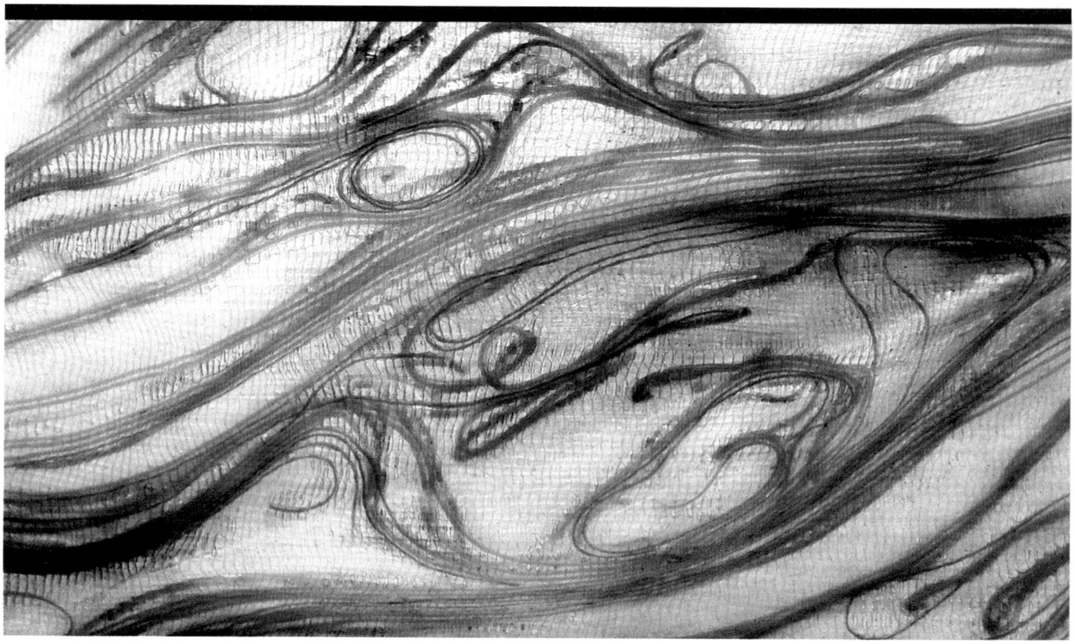

Ornamental behavioral composite prototype, 2012. This prototype, developed through a workshop at Aalto University ADD, was an exploration of the micro-scale ornamental patterns possible within composite fiber fabrication.

1 Fiber composites comprise polymer resin and fibrous material such as glass, carbon, aramid, or basalt. These composites, including fiberglass and carbon fiber, are typically used in high-end manufacturing.

2 Mike Silver discusses the potential for architectural appropriation of the aerospace industry's high-performance composite fabrication techniques in Log23 (Michael Silver 2011. "Many From One". Log23, pp. 30-33).

3 Notable projects that demonstrate this renewed adoption of fiber composites include: RV Room (Greg Lynn), Cantilever (Tom Wiscombe), League of Shadows (PATTERNS) and ICD Pavilion 2012 and 2013-14 (Achim Menges).

4 The effects of high-population agent models are discussed in more detail in the Behavioral Methodologies section.

5 Undertaken with students at Tongji University (2010), Texas A&M (2012), and Aalto University AAD (2013).

6 The Fibrous House was designed in collaboration with architecture students at Texas A&M in 2012: see Catalog of Projects.

7 For example, fifty percent of the Boeing 787 is fabricated from advanced plastic composites, using robotically controlled tape fiber-placement.

8 See RMIT Meeting Pavilion section.

Composite fiber surface prototype, 2013. This prototype, developed with students at RMIT University (Judith Widauer, Johanna Grassl), explored the relationship of structure and pattern through composite fibers.

PROJECT

COMPOSITE SWARM

Composite Swarm installed at the RMIT Design Hub, Melbourne.

The Composite Swarm installation is an architectural prototype: an experiment in compressing spatial topology, surface, structure and ornament into a single interdependent composite. The project developed out of our aspiration to physically realize the tectonic approach we established in the Aalto University and Flinders Street Station competitions, through a fiber composite fabrication method.

The geometrically unique *agentBodies* of the Aalto University and Flinders Street Station projects—the differentiation of which was created through their generative process—presents a significant problem for fabrication. We addressed this within the Composite Swarm project through the development of repeating, but flexible, bodies. Three standard body types were designed, and cast from flexible polyurethane foam, which are capable of bending and weaving, but not stretching, into complex configurations. Their material properties and constraints were encoded within the algorithmic agentBody, so their

The interconnected agentBodies create structural rigidity through increased structural depth of the skin and its surface corrugation.

digital behavior was limited to what is physically possible. This represents one of our first attempts to encode material behavior into a digital behavioral process of design.

The installation is a geometric composite of surface and agentBody network. The fiberglass surface and the foam bodies are independently too flexible to be self-supporting; however, the interaction of the two geometries creates a rigid composite. The bodies create a network of small corrugations that provide structural depth to the skin, while the fiberglass surface provides rigidity to the bodies. The structural strength of the surface is generated by a combination of this network of corrugations and the double curvature of the manifold surface, which enables the 2500mm high prototype to maintain a surface thickness of only 0.85mm. The selection of fiberglass was driven as much by its structural capacity as it was by the expressive possibilities and the translucency of the material.

A single algorithmic process was used to design the surface, structure, and ornamental

The polyurethane agentBodies are positioned by hand, based on the recesses milled into the mold surface.

The mold was coated in resin prior to the composite fiber lamination process.

qualities of the Composite Swarm, intrinsically relating these aspects of the project to create an irreducible assemblage. The composite surface is the result of the computational negotiation of these architectural behaviors. Manifold swarm behaviors generated the emergent spatial topology and curvature of the overall form, while the more localized agentBody behaviors created a network that is simultaneously structural and ornamental. The interconnectedness generated by this behavior establishes continuous lines of structural corrugations, while the geometry of the bodies creates an expressive ornamental character.

The topological nature of the *manifold swarms* strategy focuses the generative process on spatial conditions in the absence of behavior relating specifically to form and silhouette. The relatively small size and topological simplicity of the Composite Swarm installation foregrounded the silhouette and was the catalyst for a process of negotiation between al-

The glass fiber and polyurethane bodies were laminated into a thin skin through a vacuum infusion process.

gorithmic procedures and top-down decisions. Through this process we explicitly modeled the edge conditions of the wings and legs, which remained static in the algorithmic process, so that only the mid-section of the project would re-form its surface topology. This process of negotiation created both a strong silhouette and emergent spatial conditions.

The generative formation of the project draws on the agentBodies and manifold swarms strategies.

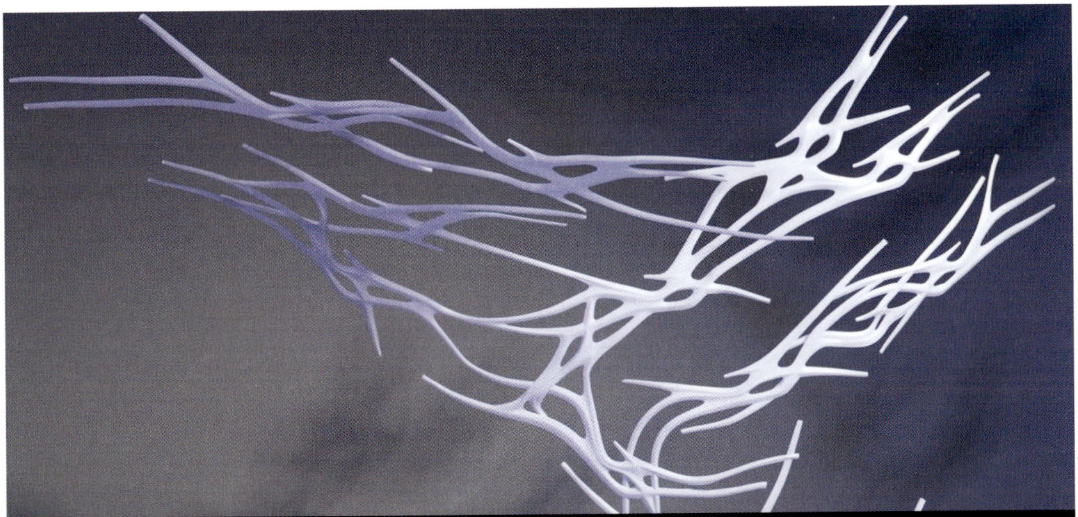

Above: Network of interconnected agentBodies.

Below: The agentBodies were designed to be laminated within a thin skin of composite fiber.

PROJECT

COMPOSITE WING

Composite Wing is an experiment in the implications of large-scale fiber composite construction of *agentBody* geometries. The installation evolved from a series of projects that embed intricate networks of veins within thin, translucent fiber composite surfaces. The design of these networks—through the interaction of agentBodies—negotiates structural and ornamental design intentions in the generation of emergent patterns. The project was commissioned as an exhibition design for the Design Museum's touring exhibition *The Future is Here*, which was co-curated in Melbourne by the RMIT Design Hub. The project comprises three wing-like surfaces composed to form a central space, with the wings also extending to create display surfaces.

This project extended the algorithmic design and fabrication logic of its immediate predecessor, the Composite Swarm installation. While the surface of the previous project

Installation photos.

measured only $7m^2$, Composite Wing is $66m^2$ and, as such, required a reconsideration of the predominantly craft-based fabrication approach of Composite Swarm. One crucial aspect of this was to leverage the efficiencies gained through re-useable molds. The five double-curvature parts that make up the Composite Wing were laminated from the same mold, each with unique profile trims that enabled the parts to assemble into a non-modular form that resists a simple reading of repetition. This reliance on a single mold shifted the design of form from the generative *manifold swarm* strategy employed in the Composite Swarm project to a focus on explicit composition.

In rationalizing the surface to a single mold, significant areas of flat surface were required to enable the parts to rotate in-plane, giving adequate design freedom in the way the panels were interconnected. The repeated underlying surface created an internally

The small-scale agentBodies were fabricated through the robotic extrusion of silicon onto a fine mesh.

consistent formal language, and it placed greater importance on the edge profile of these comparatively simple surfaces. Consequently, rather than the meandering edge of the Composite Swarm, the edge became explicitly drawn and the silhouette became more intentional. This edge characteristic was continued into the design of strongly articulated bodies defined by a sharp triangular profile. As the topology of the project became less important, it placed greater emphasis on both the silhouette and the formal gesture. A formal language of hard-edged, blunt wings developed from the interaction of the constraints of this construction logic and an aesthetic concern for increasingly robust geometries. The specificity of this language and its particular characteristics are distinct from our previous projects that evolved primarily through algorithmic processes.

The project gains its structural strength through the location and pattern of two scales of

The five curved composite parts were laminated on a single mold.

agentBodies that operate as a structural network embedded within the surface. The larger bodies were milled from high-density foam and respond to the primary structural forces. The smaller scale bodies, which address issues of local stiffening, were extruded from silicon through a robotic deposition process. These bodies were laminated within a fiberglass surface using boat-building techniques. The structural resolution of the project was premised on feedback between the structural analysis of the underlying surface and the behavior of the agentBodies algorithm. Through this process, the agentBodies respond to the structural analysis by aligning their limbs locally to the direction of the bending moments and scale their depth based on the magnitude of the bending force. This strategy enables the surface to remain only a few millimeters thick while spanning and cantilevering considerable distances.

Installation of the composite parts.

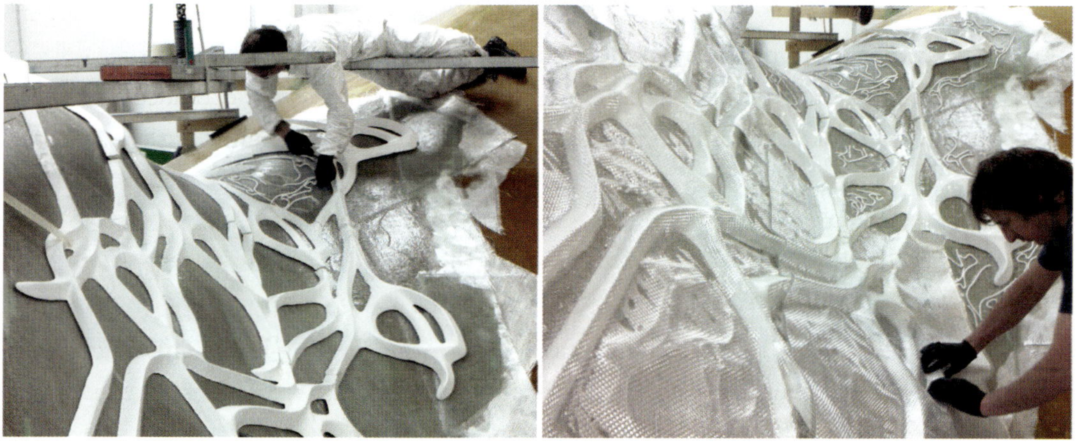

Above: The large foam and small silicon agentBodies were positioned on the mold during the lamination.

Below: Installation of the composite parts.

Composite Wing installed
at the Shanghai Biennale.

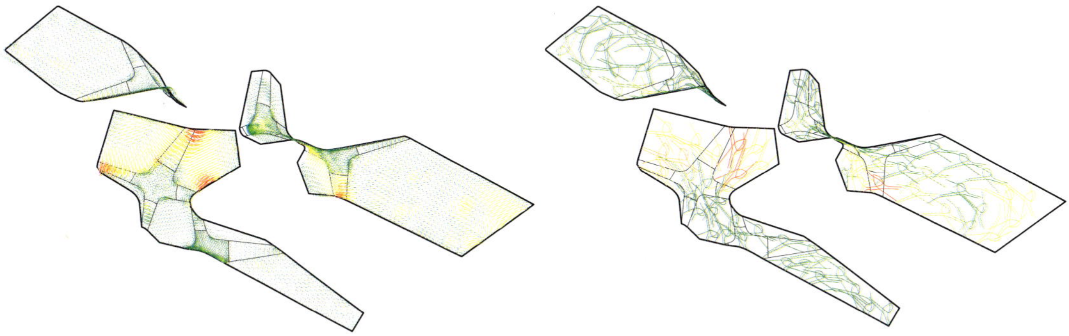

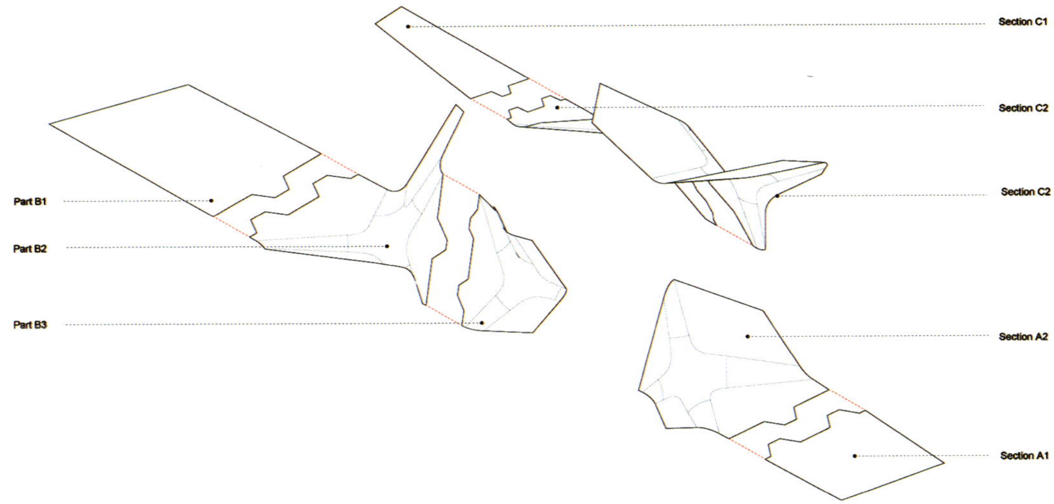

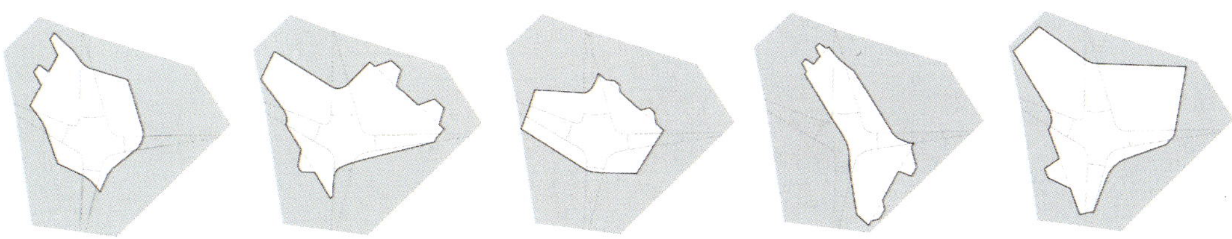

Above: The agentBodies respond to the structural analysis of the underlying surface, by orientating their limbs in the direction of the bending moments.

Middle: Composite Wing comprises eight parts, five of which are based on identical surface curvature.
Below: Mold and part diagram.

PROJECT

RMIT MEETING PAVILION

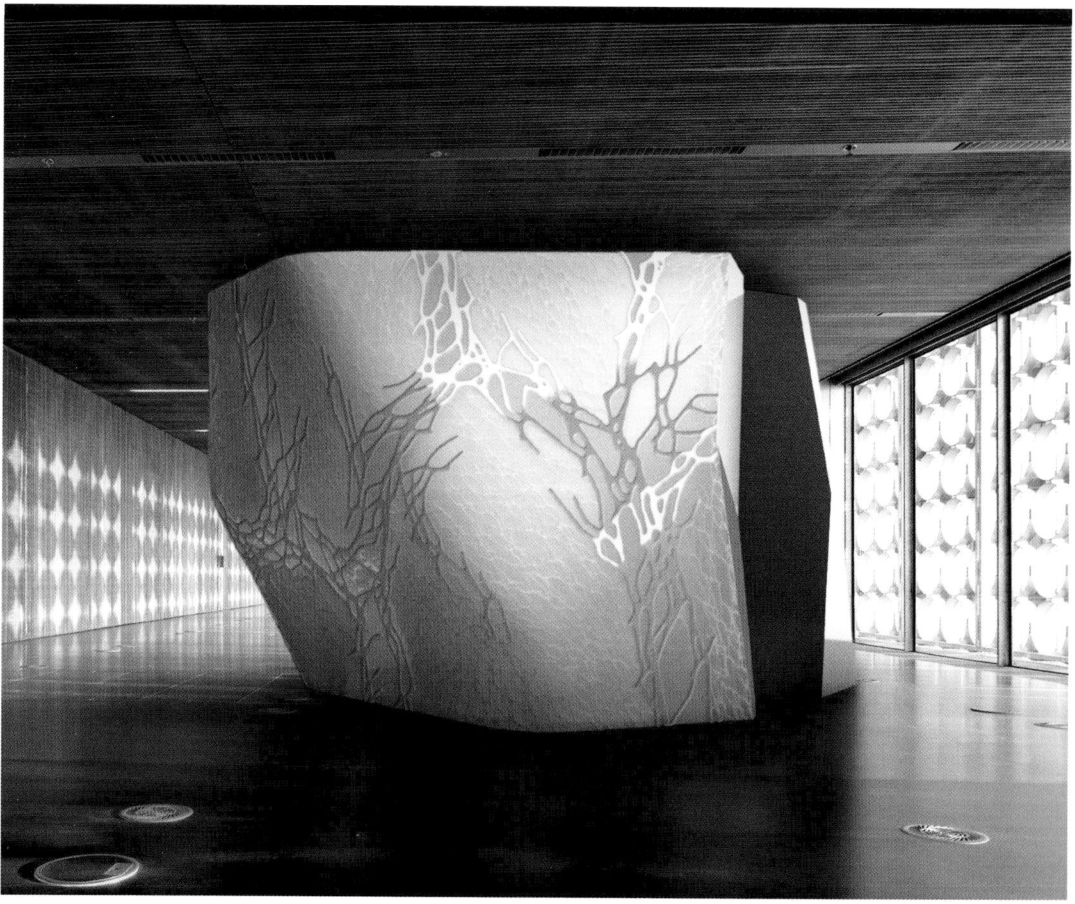

The RMIT Meeting Pavilion contrasts mute form with intricate articulation. The geological, or boulder-like, form of the pavilion operates as a foil to a highly intricate structural skeleton and ornately carved interior. The mute form is both a response to the necessity for repeating formwork and an attempt to focus the complexity of the project at the level of surface.

A metallic gold-coated composite skeleton is embedded within the translucent fiberglass skin of the pavilion's mute form.[1] This skeleton operates both as an ornamental and a structural network that has an ambiguous relationship to the form of the pavilion. The skeleton neither reinforces nor arbitrarily wraps the form; instead, a coherent, non-indexical relationship was established between the two. The *agentBody* algorithm that generated the skeleton negotiated between the requirements of structure, panel division, and ornamental concerns. The primary element of the skeleton is embedded within the skin, while additional elements stitch the panels together, forming a mechanical jointing sys-

Perspectives.

tem. In an attempt to alleviate the fabrication difficulties caused by the milled bodies in the Composite Wing, the skeleton was fabricated from flat sheet composite, with backing foam creating the necessary structural depth.

The mute formal language of the pavilion was partially driven by the constraints of designing with repeated parts. The skin was fabricated from twelve self-supporting structural panels, half of which are curved. Similar to the strategy of the Composite Wing project, the curved panels were all laminated from a single mold. This repetition creates a consistent formal language and necessitates a compositional design approach that leverages the repeated surface curvature without retaining legible repetition. The blurring of legibility is exaggerated by the independence of the skeleton from the repeating curvature.

A folded surface cuts through the smooth exterior skin to form the pavilion's entrance and reveal its carved interior. The entrance is intentionally a third logic: neither part of the in-

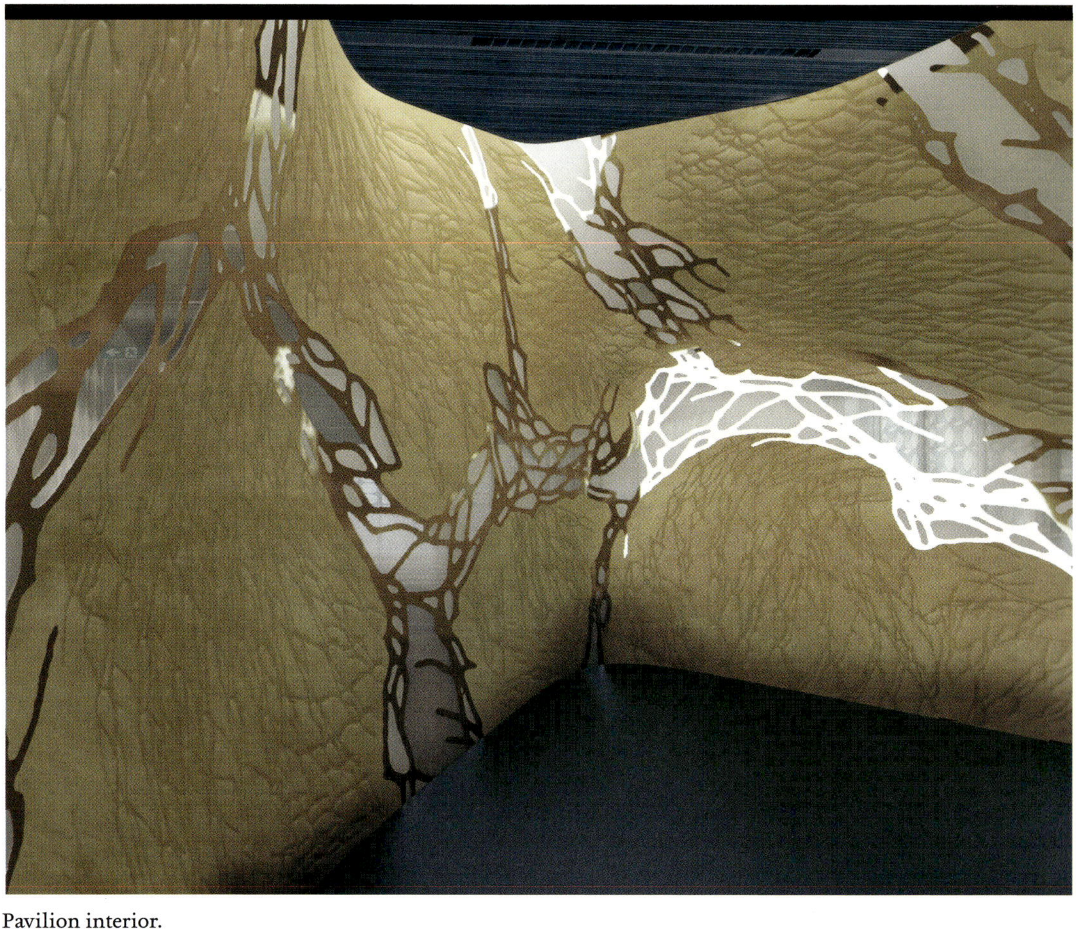

Pavilion interior.

terior nor the exterior skin. Instead, the entrance becomes an object in itself, or perhaps the trace of an object—one that is cut, or booleaned, through the shell of the pavilion.

We intended the interior to be rich with detail—almost luxurious. The velvet-like gold surface that lines the pavilion articulates a deeply carved, intricate interior. This detailed surface was carved from foam through thousands of scooping operations with a robotic hot-blade tool. The iterative passes of the tool created a combination of smooth surfaces and edges caused by the intersection of the tool paths. This surface detail was designed through a feedback between behavioral algorithms and painterly operations. The interaction between these emergent procedures and direct gestural operations created a hybrid surface character that resists an indexical trace to either process.[2]

1 This skeleton further develops the composite research of the Composite Skeleton prototype: see the following Project description, AgentBody Prototypes.

2 This feedback process is discussed in greater detail in the Painterly Formation Strategy section.

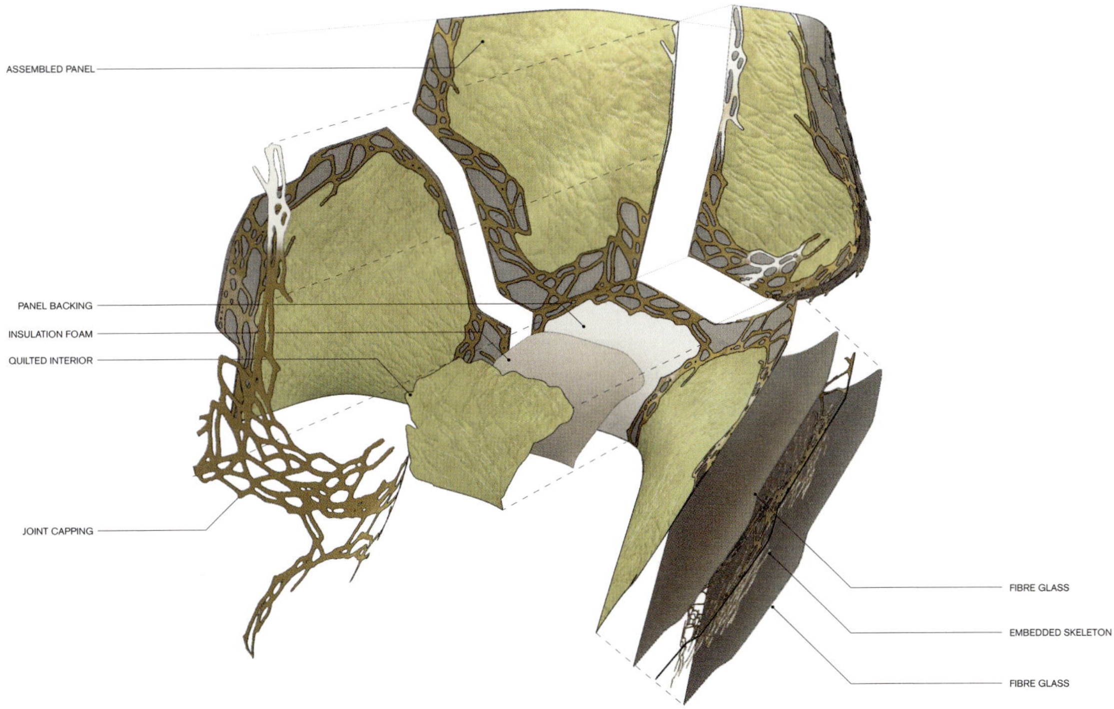

Exploded chunk diagram, which illustrates the layers that comprise the composite panels.

PROJECT

AGENTBODY PROTOTYPES

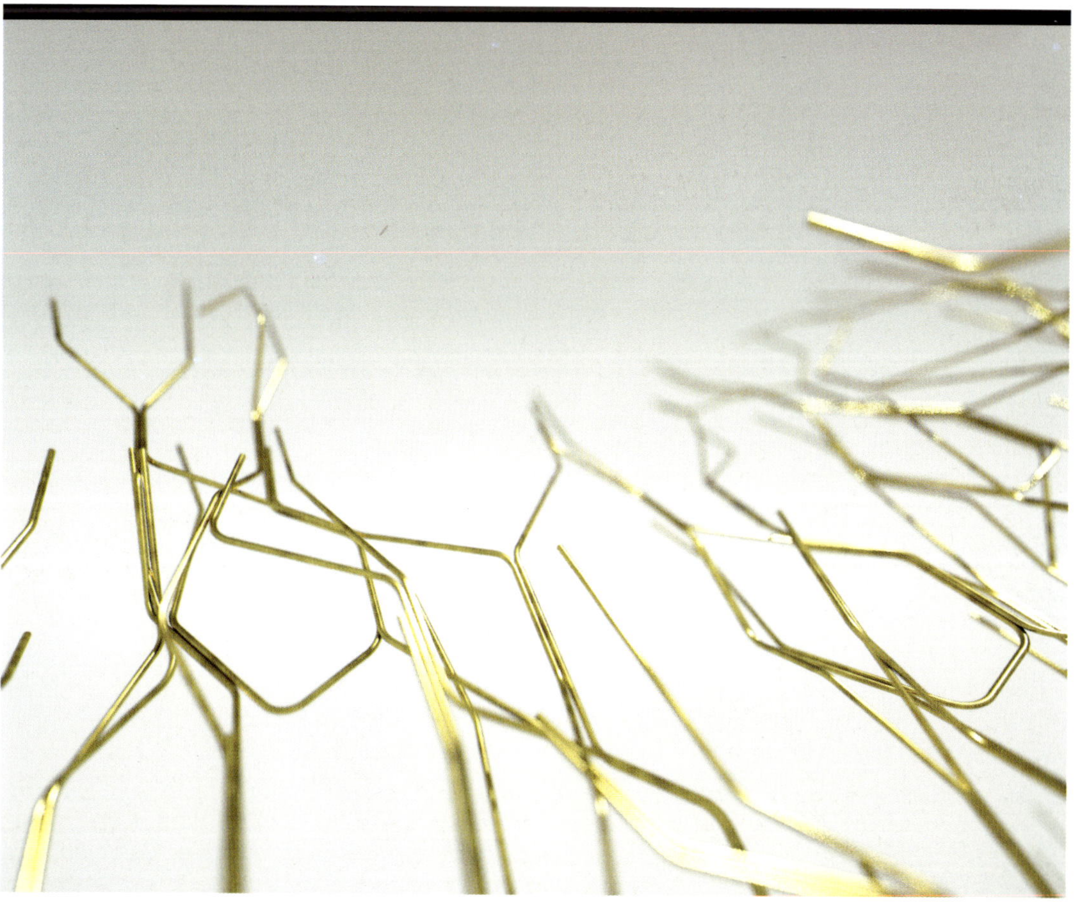

Brass Swarm, 2014. Detail.

Architectural design and construction processes evolve through mutual feedback. To construct the complex geometries created through behavioral design processes, procedural fabrication approaches are needed that respond to the generative principles of the design process rather than simply attempting to fabricate the resultant geometries. The application of conventional fabrication approaches to the non-standard geometries that emerged from architecture's digital turn reduced the pliant and supple digital surfaces to stage sets—propped up by normative framing, ribs, or egg-crate approaches.[1] The *behavioral composites* strategy was our first attempt to develop a procedural fabrication approach that mirrored the encoded agency of fibrous assemblages. However, an alternative approach was needed to construct the complex geometry of *agentBody* projects, one that related the logic of fabrication to the algorithmic structure and behavior of the agentBodies. The compression of surface, structure and ornament into a single irreducible assemblage, which is fundamental to the agentBody projects, required rethinking of the normative construction processes.

Brass Swarm, 2014. Installed at the Shanghai Biennale.

Beginning with the Composite Swarm installation in 2013, we developed a series of seven prototypical projects over the subsequent three years that explored variations on four fabrication approaches: composite lamination of foam bodies, double curvature surface from flat sheet bodies, spatial lattices of bent rod bodies, and bodies cast within a permanent formwork skin. These prototypes developed as a sequence of experiments that evolved through iteratively making and testing, in order to create increasingly feasible approaches to reifying complex geometry, while also opening up a new series of problems and experiments. This was a process of learning from failure, and iteratively developing increasingly robust fabrication processes.

The development and application of robotic and digital fabrication techniques have enabled the complex digital geometries of these prototypes to be realized within material. However, it is the interaction of these techniques with algorithmic design processes that

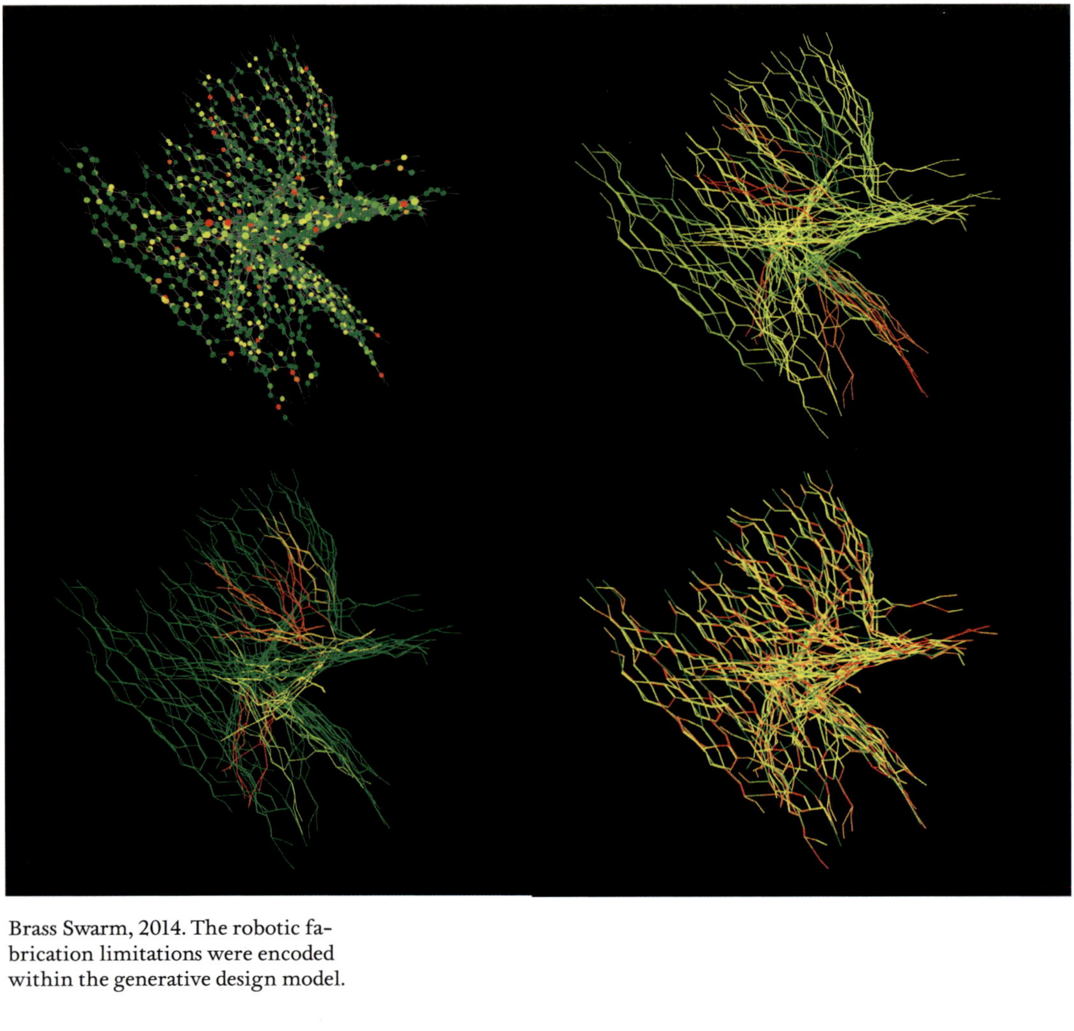

Brass Swarm, 2014. The robotic fabrication limitations were encoded within the generative design model.

creates the specific characteristics and qualities of these projects that exceed those of the digital. In these prototypes, a new set of formal characteristics—which are neither exclusively indexical to digital or material behavior—are created through this non-linear interrelationship of material behavior, robotic fabrication, and computation.

A physical body was developed for the Composite Swarm project that mirrored the logic and range of behavior of the generative algorithm. The flex and bend of the foam body were similar to the behavior of the algorithmic body, while the limited stretch of the physical body was encoded back into the generative algorithm. With the exception of the exacting requirement to flatten the agentBodies to the composite surface, this process enabled a close relationship between the digital and physical processes of formation. However, it became evident that the excessive material, machine time and hand finishing involved in constructing a mold for the entire surface of the prototype made this a non-viable approach

Brass Swarm, 2014. The 270 unique brass rods were bent through the interaction of two industrial robots.

to building-scale construction. The large-scale viability was also diminished by the composite fabrication process, which involved hand-layup of fiberglass and the manual positioning and bending of the pre-cast bodies, both of which require a level of design understanding or expertise. The shift to a more industrial scale in the Composite Wing project partly mitigated these issues. However, it was the limitation of working with a mold in these two composite projects that acted as a catalyst for the development of the subsequent agentBody prototypes.

BRASS SWARM AND DADA PAVILION

In the Brass Swarm and DADA Pavilion prototypes, the agentBodies were conceived of as swarms of bent metal rods. These two prototypes demonstrated an approach to building a thick, spatially complex network of bodies that, unlike the previous composite projects, are not limited to a surface. The Brass Swarm was developed as an installation for the Shanghai

Laminar Bodies, 2015. Installed at Adam Art Gallery, Wellington.

Biennale (January 2015), and was followed by the DADA Pavilion at Tongji University (July 2015) that tested the structural capacity of this approach.

Of all the agentBody prototypes, these two projects have the tightest interrelationship of fabrication and generative approaches. A multi-robot rod-bending technique was developed for these projects, the constraints of which informed the generative algorithm, and integrally linked the pragmatics of construction with the volatility of the behavioral design process. The Brass Swarm prototype was fabricated from 270 unique bent rods. This technique, which utilizes two Kuka industrial robotic arms, is constrained by factors such as a minimum length between bends,[2] a maximum bend angle, and the relative direction of subsequent bends. These limitations were explored through empirical tests, and then encoded as behaviors within the multi-agent algorithm. Algorithmically, these robotic behaviors interacted with a broader set of design behaviors intended to drive the formation of pattern and geometry.

Laminar Bodies, 2015. The installation is assembled from hundreds of flat-sheet, steel, laser cut parts.

The capacity to scale up from a prototype to a larger architectural project is critical to our research. The scalability of the population and size of the individual bodies using this bent rod approach was tested through a doubling of the scale of the Brass Swarm in the DADA Pavilion. This second prototype was fabricated with correspondingly scaled robots.[3] A further increase in scale has been speculatively proposed through the design for the Nine Elms Bridge competition.[4]

LAMINAR AND BLURRED BODIES

With the Laminar Bodies and Blurred Bodies prototypes, our research focus turned again to surface: through the development of a technique for creating complex curved surfaces from flat bodies. The curvature of the surface is created during the lamination of flat-sheet, laser-cut steel components through their specific geometry and pattern of connection.

Laminar Bodies, 2015. The steel parts are riveted together to generate the overall surface curvature.

This fabrication strategy is significantly different, conceptually and technically, from contemporary approaches to unrolling complex curvature surfaces.[5] Rather than being designed as a surface that is subdivided into developable strips, these surfaces emerge from the interaction of the flat bodies that comprise their fabrication system, and thus create a procedural relationship between the process of generative design and fabrication.

Unlike the depth created by the lattice of the Brass Swarm, in these two prototypes the agentBodies flatten to create surface. This local flatness of the geometry limits the structural depth, necessitating the creation of structural strength through surface curvature. Consequently, a multi-agent algorithm was developed to generate surfaces with a high degree of double curvature from a *manifold swarm* of agentBodies. As with the other prototypes, the fabrication constraints (such as minimum surface curvature) were encoded within the algorithmic design process.

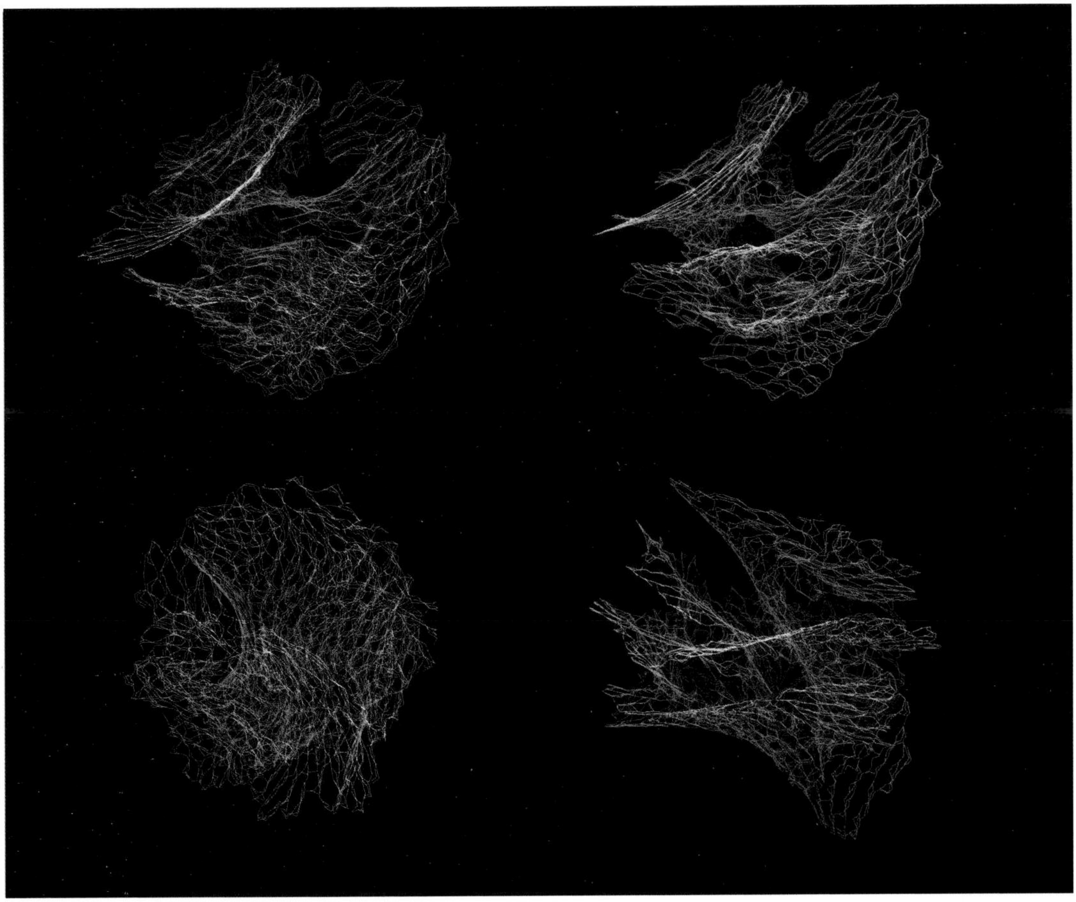

Blurred Bodies, 2015. AgentBody generative iterations.

COMPOSITE SKELETON

The procedural fabrication strategy of creating double curvature skeleton surfaces from flat sheets that we developed in the Laminar Bodies prototype opened up an opportunity to eliminate the problem of the mold in fiber composite lamination. Central to the Composite Skeleton prototype is an innovative process we developed in which a composite skin is laminated directly onto a skeleton though a vacuum infusion technique. In this process, the skeleton is laser cut from rigid sheets of fiber composite, which are then assembled to generate a double curvature surface in a similar manner to the Laminar Bodies prototype. Unlike the Composite Swarm and Composite Wing projects that generate their structural strength through the depth of the skeleton, this strategy relies on structural stiffness generated through surface curvature and the material strength of the skeleton. Fabricating a skeleton from composites, such as carbon fiber, generates considerable strength, while the fiberglass membrane resists the in-plane shear forces and creates a continuous skin overcoming a limitation of the Laminar Bodies prototype.

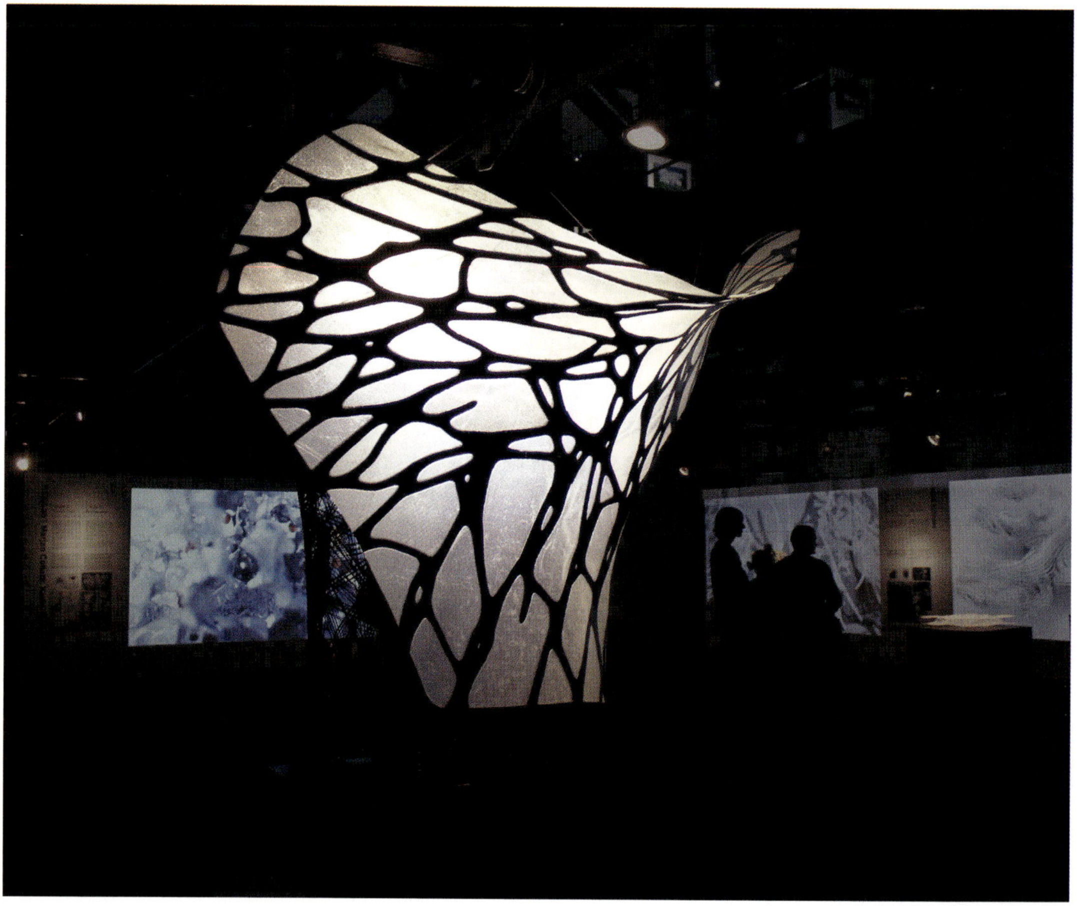

Composite Skeleton, 2015. Installed at the Tallinn Architecture Biennale, Estonia.

This prototype was an opportunity to revisit the problem of joints between composite panels. The Composite Swarm project avoided mechanical joints by laminating the complete prototype onto a single mold, which sets logistical limits on the size of a project. A system of overlapping tabs was developed for the Composite Wing project; however, these were external to the logic of the skeleton and broke the continuity of the surface pattern and geometry. In contrast, a connection logic that extended the geometry of the skeleton was developed to mechanically join the three parts of the Composite Skeleton prototype. These capping strips conceal the joints and create an additional level of detail that is consistent with, and reinforces, the algorithmically generated skeleton.

The result is a composite surface that removes the prohibitive costs of one-off molds and leverages the assembly logic of the skeleton to privilege complex curvature. This strategy opens up a highly unusual architectural condition—one in which the most economical geometries to create are double curvature surfaces.

Composite Skeleton, 2015.

SACRIFICIAL SKIN

The prototypes discussed above can be categorized as either privileging surface (Laminar Bodies and Composite Skeleton), or forgoing surface to create topologically complex networks (Brass Swarm and DADA Pavilion). The most recent prototype, Sacrificial Skin, is an attempt to bring together topologically complex networks of bodies and surface through an approach to sacrificial or permanent formwork. This inverts the logic of the previous prototypes, in which skins were laminated onto the skeleton, by casting the bodies within the skin. This strategy leverages large-scale, robotic, polymer printing and fiber-reinforced concrete to open up a broad spectrum of formal possibilities.

Sacrificial Skin exploits the intricate geometric capacity of 3D printing and the fabrication efficiencies of more traditional cast-in-place concrete. The intention of this line of research is to print thin skins of buildings, within which structural and thermal mass is cast.

Sacrificial Skins, Hawthorn Public Art Installation, 2016. Perspective.

As such, only a small percentage of the building mass is printed, while still enabling geometric complexity and intricacy. Although 3D printing technologies are developing rapidly, the extrusion of material is significantly slower than the pouring of liquid within a cast, and this strategy therefore utilizes the relative advantages of both operations. Systems such as mechanical ducting and joints can also be printed within the skin to produce complete prefabricated building components.

This iterative series of prototypes are premised on the importance of establishing a construction logic that parallels the generative process and situates material and fabrication as integral to algorithmic design. The agentBodies approach enables the structure and logic of the body to be designed into the algorithm, which simulates the body's physical material behavior and fabrication constraints. Through this approach, material and fabrication logic are encoded within the generative design algorithm, significantly influencing the character of the project. These prototypes demonstrate a series of iterations through this process in

Sacrificial Skins, Hawthorn Public Art Installation, 2016. Detail.

SECOND EMPIRE
CAFÉ
BY EPICURE

which fabrication and design evolve together through mutual feedback.

An important difference exists between utilizing robotics to fabricate digital forms and generating digital forms through the constraints and limitations of robotics. By engaging the parameters of robotic fabrication early in the generative process, the robotic tools enter a feedback with digital processes, where each is developed in response to the other. This methodology expands the architect's role not only into the methods of fabrication, but, more importantly, through the implications of this on design.

Each of these prototypes attempts to address specific problems or aspects of the translation of the digital into material. Together, they are intended to establish a platform from which larger scale architectural applications can be explored. While sculptural in nature, these projects are fundamentally architectural prototypes. They are part of an on-going exploration into the synthesis of surface, structure and ornament through complex systems.

1 Examples of the construction of digitally generated surfaces from conventional fabrication processes include projects such as Lars Spuybroek's Son-O-House (2004) and Kas Oosterhuis's Salt Water Pavilion (1997).

2 The interest in using robotics in these two prototypes is less for their capacity for rod bending (as specific CNC rod bending machines are used in industry) than for their capacity for assembly. The robotic bending of the rods for the Brass Swarm prototype was a rapid process, taking a single day; however, the prototype was assembled and welded by hand, involving five people over five days. Evidently, the relevant problem is one of assembly rather than fabrication. The intention is to extend this research so that a single collaborative robot cell is able to bend, place and weld the rods.

3 The Brass Swarm prototype was fabricated from 900mm long brass rods, while the DADA Pavilion was fabricated from 1800mm long aluminum rods.

4 See Catalog of Projects.

5 Marc Fornes's pioneering work, such as the Labrys Frisae installation at Art Basil Miami, exemplifies the capacity to unroll complex surfaces into strips through mesh walking algorithms.

Sacrificial Skins, Hawthorn Public Art Installation, 2016. 3D printed sacrificial formwork prototypes reinforced with cast concrete.

PROJECT

NGV PAVILION

The fibrous mass that defines this pavilion for the National Gallery of Victoria (NGV) negotiates a boulder-like silhouette and intricate filigree. This fibrous tectonic was developed through the self-organizational processes of *agentBody* algorithms and a direct deposition robotic fabrication approach. The pavilion was designed in parallel with the Sacrificial Skin research project,[1] which explored the formal possibilities and architectural implications of polymer 3D printed permanent formwork skins.

The design of this pavilion was an attempt to shift away from the formal logic of flow, evident within many of our projects, towards a more robust formal expression. This extension of the geological forms of the Babiy Yar and Malibu House projects[2] was an attempt to create a strong silhouette in response to nebulous forms generated through the *manifold swarms* strategy—an issue that is common amongst many generative processes. Rather than being conceived of as a field, the pavilion was designed with a concern for its objecthood and silhouette.

A sacrificial formwork strategy was proposed to create an intricate network of concrete structural members cast within a 3D printed, translucent skin.

Through the design process, we established a synthetic relationship between generative techniques and explicit modeling in an attempt to dissolve the distinction between the two.[3] Behaviors were designed for a swarm of agentBodies to fill boulder-like virtual volumes, while creating frayed edges and delaminating into surfaces. Unlike the Babiy Yar project where a highly intricate space is distinct from, and carved within, a mute mass, the NGV pavilion creates a synthesis of the two. Through this project, we were exploring the relationship between volume, surface and network: the form hovers between these conditions without privileging one over the other. The filigree created through this process—and its intricate pattern of shadows—is positioned as a foil to the adjacent monolithic bluestone building of the National Gallery of Victoria.

The geometric character of the agentBodies was designed in response to the hard silhouette of the project's underlying geological form. Three body types were designed that res-

The manifold surface delaminates into a more complex fibrous network below the outer surface.

pond to their relative location on the pavilion. The bodies closer to the edge of the form flatten to create a clearer reading of surface, while those within the mass of the pavilion have greater depth. The deep three-dimensionality of the resulting mass creates a very different reading to the surface-based approach employed in the composite agentBody prototypes.

The shifting of the fibrous mass between surface and lattice is made possible through a fabrication process involving robotic printed polymer sacrificial formwork. In contrast to the agentBody prototypes, which are skinned with composite surface, we developed a fabrication process in which the bodies are cast within a 3D printed skin. This inversion of logic enables the swarm of agentBodies to be cast as a highly interconnected network of fiber-reinforced concrete structural members.

1 Described in the preceding section, AgentBody Prototypes.

2 See Babiy Yar Project section and the Catalog of Projects.

3 This process is discussed in greater depth in the Strange Feedback strategy.

Perspectives.

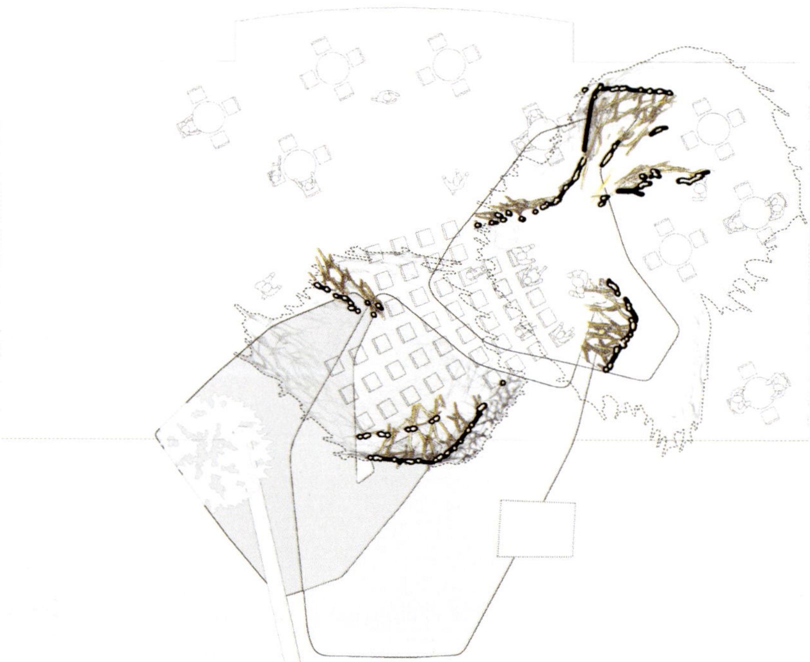

Above: Section.

Below: Plan.

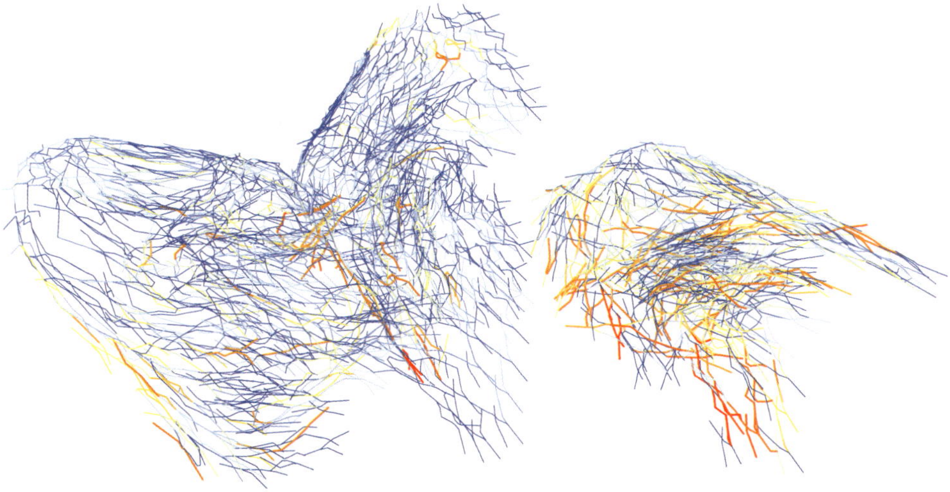

Above: Diagram of structural forces.

Below: The volatile behavioral algorithm is conditioned by the explicit model of the exterior shells.

PROJECT

STRIATED POLYMERS

The recent evolution of our robotic fabrication research has led to strategies for integrating the logic of direct deposition processes within behavioral design methodologies. Large-scale, 3D printed, sacrificial formwork has been an effective strategy to realize the *agentBody*[1] geometries of the NGV Pavilion[2] and Sacrificial Skin[3] projects. However, this approach evolved primarily from a computational agentBody tectonic, rather than a fabrication approach. More recently, we have developed an alternative behavioral methodology that seeks to fundamentally incorporate the logic and limitations of large-scale polymer 3D printing within the generative design process. These printing limitations, such as maximum overhang or draft angles, are intrinsic to the nature of the surface that is being printed. Consequently, an algorithmic approach was developed that directly encodes behaviors into surfaces, with the design agents embedded within the vertices of a computational mesh. This methodology aligns the behavior of the generative algorithm closely to the logic of fabrication. Through the interaction of both design and fabrication

Fold Pavilion, 2017. This pavilion was designed through the logic of large-scale polymer 3D printing. A mesh-based algorithm was developed to manipulate surfaces within the limitations of this fabrication technique.

Following pages: SensiLab Studio, 2017. Large-scale polymer printing of a prototype panel.

KUKA

behaviors, the algorithm acts to fold, crease, and corrugate surfaces, while conditioning this geometry through the limits of fabrication.

Initially developed through the design of the Fold Pavilion,[4] this methodology has been refined through two recently built projects: SensiLab Studio and Floe. Through these projects, we have articulated an approach to 3D printed architecture premised on a surface-based tectonic strategy. To resolve this approach required the development of a logic for detailing and addressing issues relating to fire codes and structural requirements.

SensiLab Studio (2017) is a polymer 3D printed studio located within an open-plan research space. The folding, or corrugated, translucent polycarbonate walls of the studio were designed to refract intricate patterns of light and create varying transparencies. These corrugations, operating at several scales, act in unison with the interconnection of a triple skin to generate the structural integrity of the wall. This interconnected surface

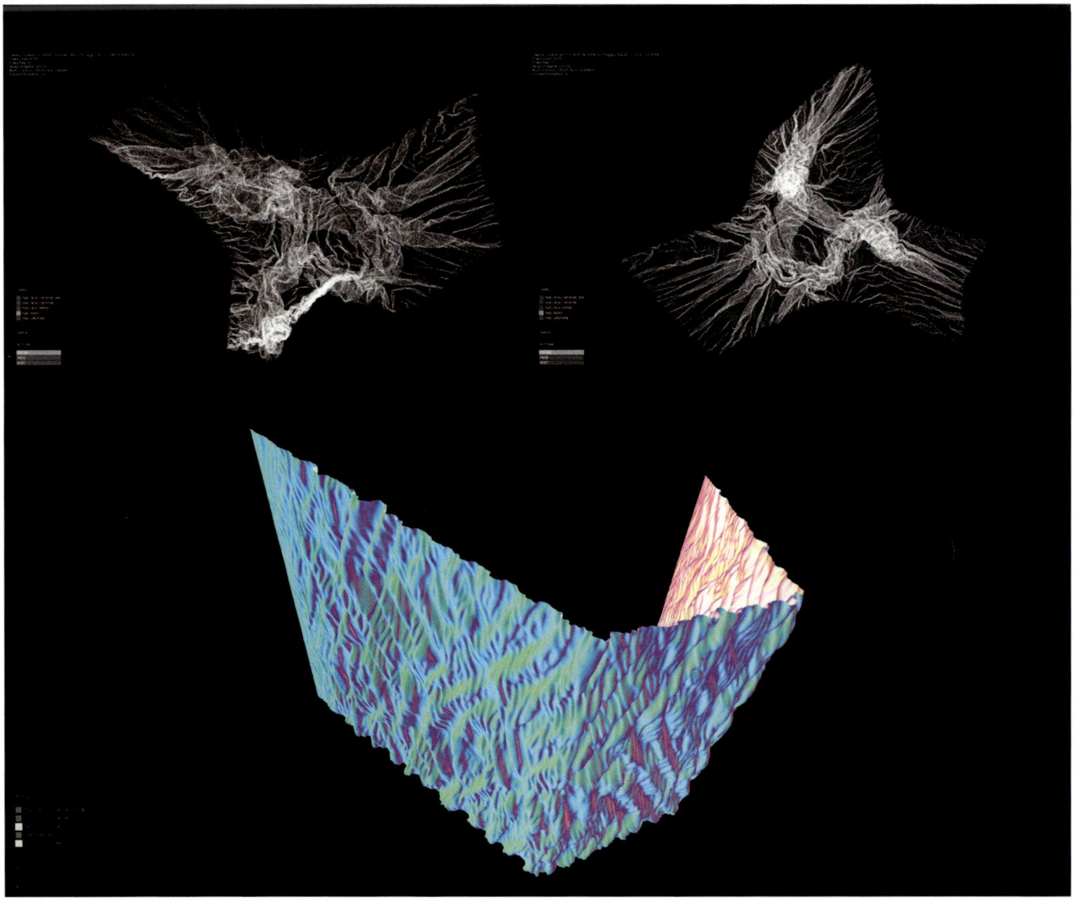

Mesh-based behavioral generative algorithms.
Above: Fold Pavilion, 2017.
Below: SensiLab Studio, 2017.

geometry, and the cavity between the layers of polycarbonate, establish the necessary structural depth and acoustic rating within the wall. The studio was printed in ten panels with integrated structural joints. This is a pioneering project for 3D polycarbonate printing, and an important step in developing an approach from experimental prototypes to addressing the complexities of permanent buildings, including building and fire codes.

Floe, commissioned by the National Gallery of Victoria for its Triennial Extra program (2018), draws on the atmospheric effects of the Antarctic landscape to create a speculative architectural installation. The project was designed in response to, and incorporating, a sound installation by Philip Samartzis, based on his recordings of Antarctica's constantly shifting ice shelves, glaciers, icebergs, and sea ice. Floe was an opportunity to investigate the application of large-scale polymer 3D printing, and its integration with other construction and structural systems. The primary element of Floe is a six-meter polymer

SensiLab Studio, 2017. Detail

Following pages: SensiLab Studio, 2017.

tower—which requires rapid assembly and disassembly—necessitating a lightweight steel structure, rather than the in-situ cast concrete system employed in the Sacrificial Skins research. This folded steel structure, designed through an agentBody strategy, interweaves through the translucent polymer skin. Unlike SensiLab Studio, which was conceived as a single surface, the polymer skin is articulated as a swarm of seventy unique, overlapping, 3D printed components.

These projects demonstrate a viable large-scale 3D printing approach to fabricating intricate geometries, and to materializing the design agenda of Behavioral Formation. While the projects are printed in polymer, this is part of our expanding research agenda to develop generative approaches for direct deposition at the building scale. As this research shifts towards a more diverse range of materials—including concrete, ceramic, metal, and biodegradable materials—it is continuing to expand this space of design possibility.

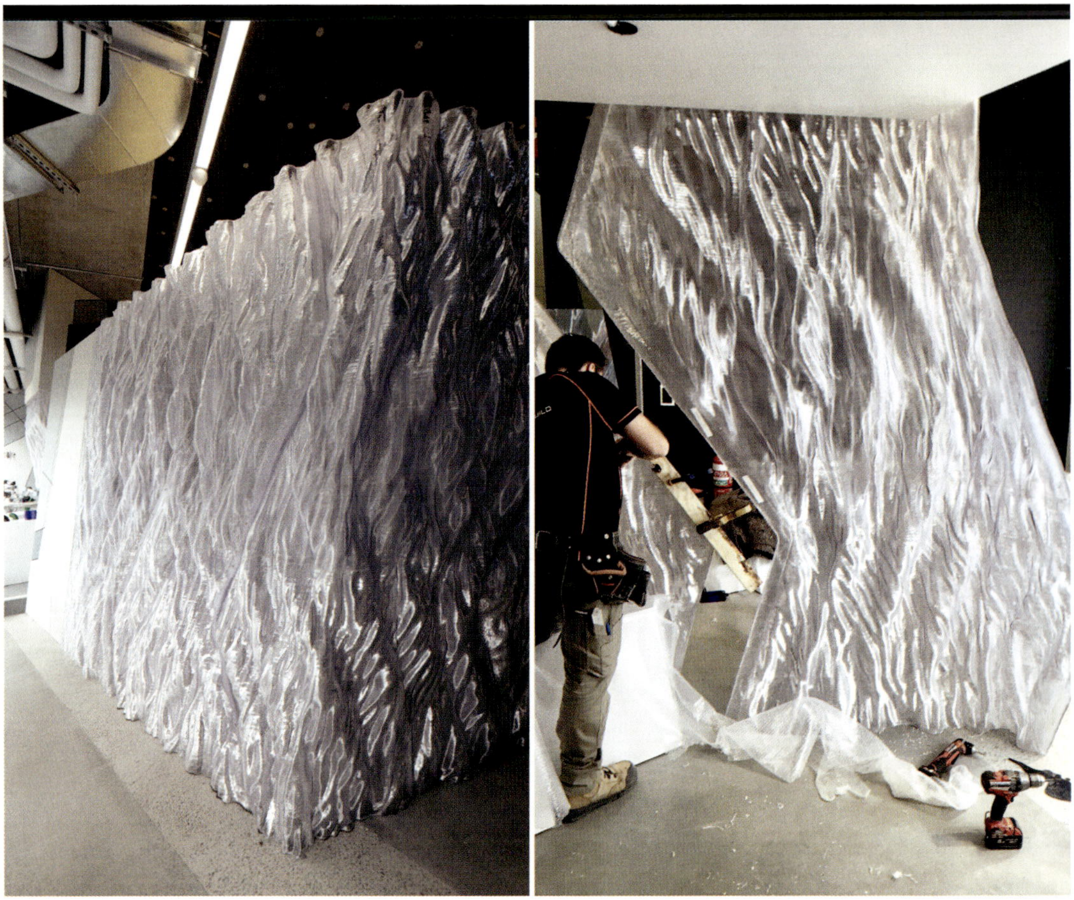

SensiLab Studio, 2017. The studio is composed of ten interlocking polymer panels, assembled on-site.

1 See AgentBodies Strategy section.

2 See NGV Pavilion Project section.

3 See AgentBody Prototypes Project section.

4 See Catalog of Projects.

Floe, 2018. Installed at the National Gallery of Victoria.

Following pages: Floe, 2018.

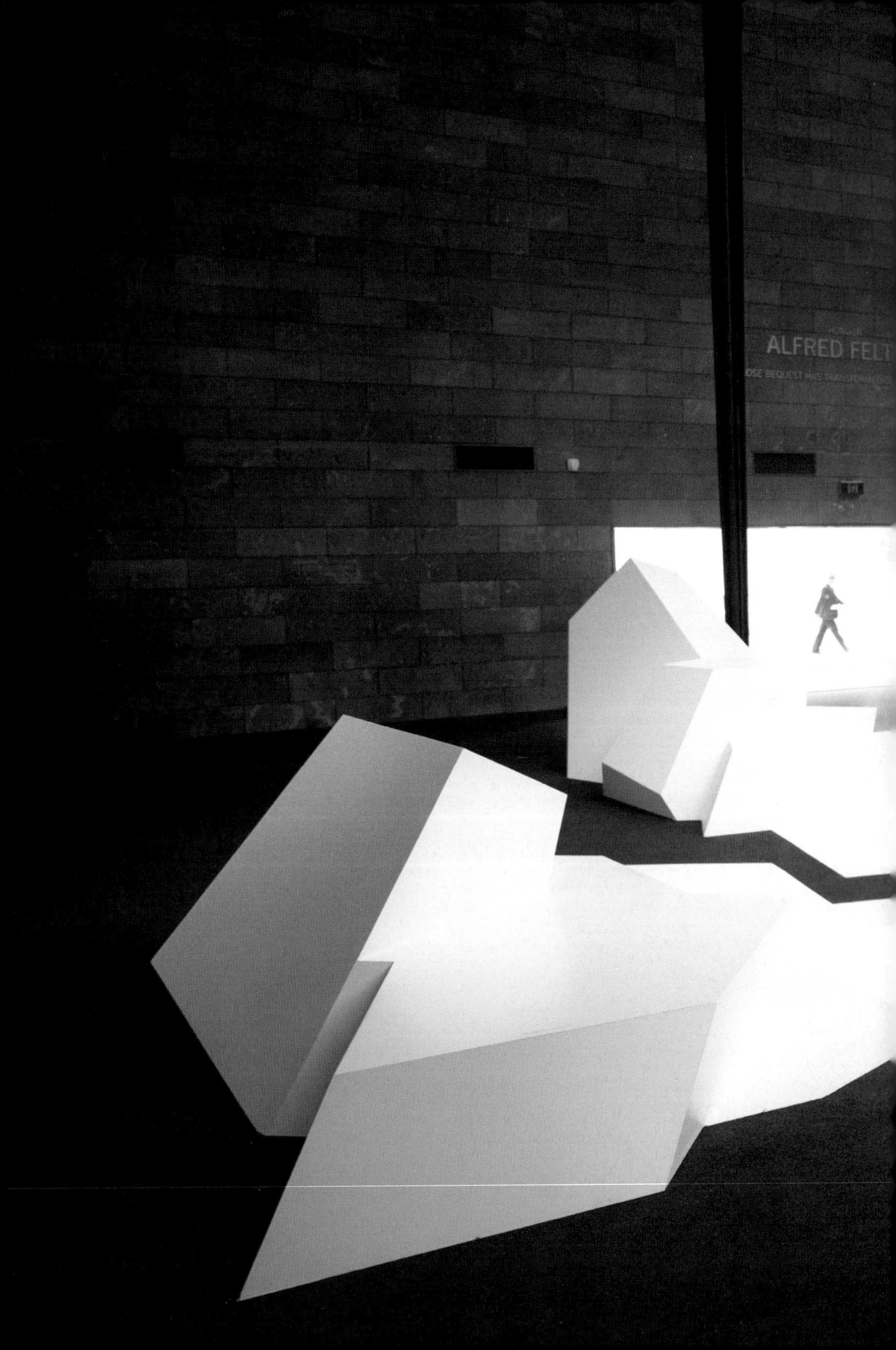

Floe, 2018. Detail.

Above: Floe, 2018. Interior view towards the Leonard French stained-glass ceiling.

Below: Floe, 2018.

ESSAY

VOLATILITY

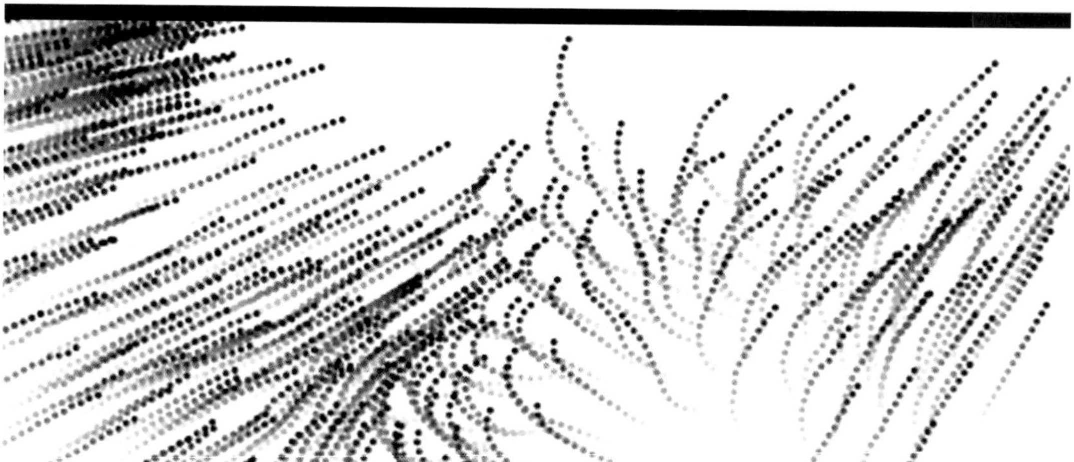

Flocking algorithm.

The volatile nature of complex systems and intensive processes of formation, those which self-organize and are capable of catastrophic change, are inherently generative. From these edge-of-chaos conditions, new forms of order emerge, generating strange behaviors, and traits—conditions potent with architectural possibility.[1]

Computation is an essential tool when working with complex systems. In architecture, however, computational methods have been adopted that privilege certainty over open-ended processes. These systems of parametric variation and optimization are complicit in the automation of design, marginalizing risk, and foregrounding stability and equilibrium. In contrast, our design research posits an argument for complex systems of formation that operate through the volatile interaction of algorithmic behaviors, and engage the speculative potential of computational processes.

The instability of a system enables the emergence of an order that is radically different from its initial conditions. Complex systems with the capacity for catastrophic change, such as Stephen Wolfram's cellular automata rule 110,[2] operate on the edge of chaos and are highly generative. Within these globally volatile conditions, new characteristics and locally stable situations emerge from a constant state of flux, resisting periodic or predictable order.

Similarly, the cusps and bifurcations of chaotic systems map catastrophic change within internally coherent systems. Manuel DeLanda discusses these states in terms of thermodynamics: "It is only in these far-from-equilibrium conditions, only in this singular zone of intensity, that difference-driven morphogenesis comes into its own, and that matter becomes an active material agent, one which does not need form to come and impose itself from the outside."[3] It is the emergent capacities of these complex systems, hovering between order and chaos, that offer significant generative potential for architecture.

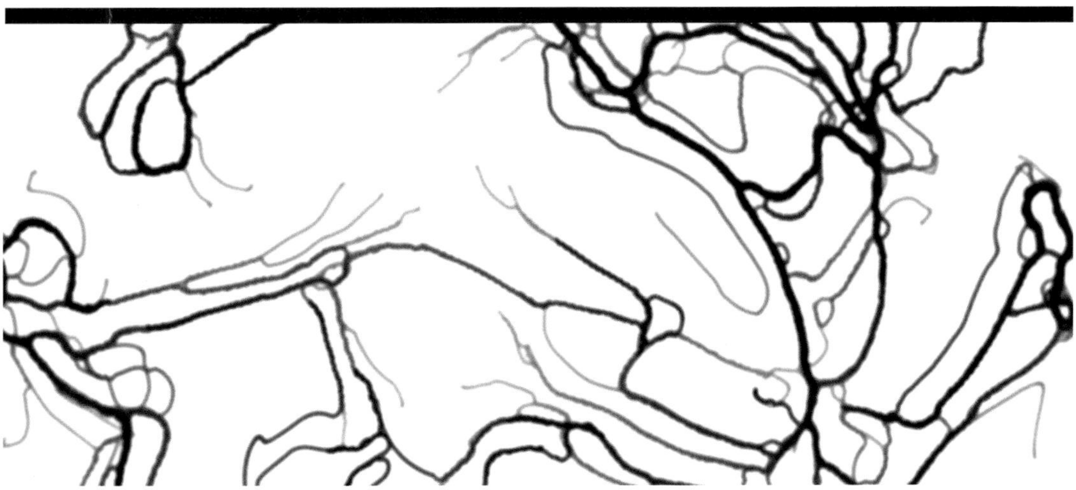

Stigmergic ant-trail algorithm.

THE STABILITY OF COMPUTATIONAL ARCHITECTURE

The underlying reliance of complex systems on iteration and feedback has rendered computation indispensable in generating and simulating complexity. Architects, however, have largely relegated computation to the service of explicit control. Within architecture, computational design can be described through several broad categories: parametric modeling, optimization, form-finding, and generative algorithms. The first three categories are inherently based on stability, or the search for equilibrium, while the latter category exposes the potential of open-ended complex systems. The necessity for risk and indeterminacy in design is not reducible to the dichotomy between linear and non-linear systems—although these are key protagonists—but is more precisely defined by the opposition of stability and volatility.

Parametric or associative modeling describes a linear relationship between a parameter and a geometric transformation, enabling the precise control and manipulation of flexible digital models.[4] It is curious, then, that parametric design has been so enthusiastically promoted as a generative tool in contemporary architecture. Generative design can be described as designing the design process rather than the object, implying an abstraction of the designer from the object. However, parametric models are structured hierarchically, having direct, cascading, causal relationships—an obvious impediment to this description of generative design. The parameters within these models—as the now ubiquitous sliders in software programs epitomize—confine the model to a known set of limits. Unlike complex systems, parametric models do not embed their history; instead, they retain a reversible and repeatable association to their parameters. A parametric model does not contain an active process, but simply a set of associations. So while parametric models enable a distribution of difference, this is not the difference that emerges from intensive processes, but rather a directly described, top-down, smooth gradient operating within a predefined range. Here, all possibility is already given within the starting condition.

Optimization routines search a discrete set of possible solutions for maximizing or minimizing a known condition such as structural or energy efficiency. The volatility of the

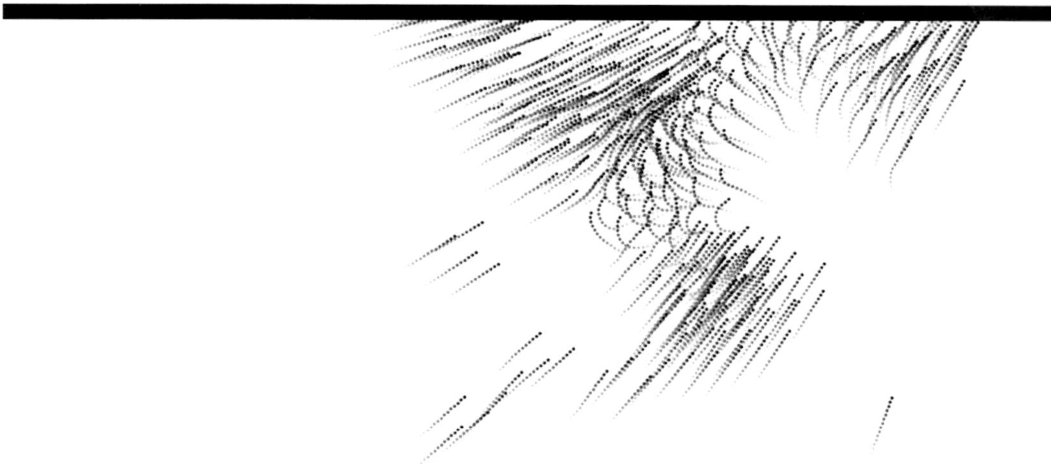

Flocking algorithm.

search algorithms that underlie optimizing processes range from incremental change to the stochastic[5] operations of particle swarm optimization or genetic algorithms. However, the internal volatility of search algorithms has little influence on the volatility of the design process, as these algorithms are searching for a predetermined optimal position. These strategies presuppose that architecture can be objectively evaluated through predetermined criteria, but these effectively impose a straightjacket on speculative design. Optimization rejects subjective evaluation in favor of a reductive approach.[6] Qualitative nuances, references, complexity, richness, and experience of architecture are beyond the capacity of numerically describable criteria. While optimization is able to engage in highly volatile generative processes, it must operate in a support role rather than being the driver of the process: conditioning volatile outcomes rather than attempting to generate them.[7]

Physics based form-finding is a non-linear approach to optimization, where each element negotiates with the adjacent elements to equalize difference, minimizing energy within the entire system until an equilibrium position is reached. The non-linear operations imply volatility, but form-finding techniques are inherently risk-averse due to the stable nature of their formal characteristics and rapid convergence to equilibrium. The speed of convergence is a property of the algorithm and the initial conditions of the model. Typically, a model's initial position is close to its form-found equilibrium, and consequently the form-finding algorithm operates as an application of a known and entirely consistent formal character. However, if the model's initial conditions are far from an equilibrium position, it effectively has to unravel itself in negotiating the imbalance of force within the model, and is inherently less stable.[8]

Regardless of its convergence, characteristics of curvature within form-finding models such as a catenary chain model, or of minimal surface within a soap-film model, are stable, immediately recognizable, known, and indexical. Their precise character is known in advance and the application of these techniques can become a matter of style or cliché. Consequently, the stable process of selecting an algorithm, rather than the algorithm's non-linear operation, has the dominant influence over architectural form and character.

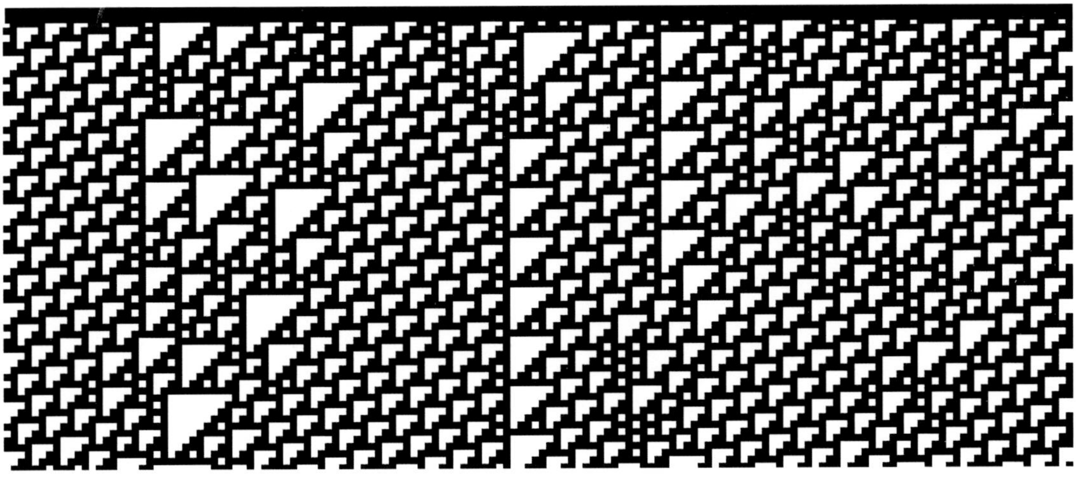

Cellular automata, rule 110.

Volatility is predicated on resisting equilibrium. This resistance emerges from the negotiation of positive and negative feedback in maintaining a dynamic condition, from which a system reorganizes and unique forms of order emerge. Given the relative speed or simplicity with which a form-finding algorithm reaches equilibrium and its stable characteristics, a volatile strategy is possible only if there is a radical topological reorganization. Without this, the computational design process is simply the application of a predefined formal character to an a priori topology, since there is only one possible outcome to a minimal energy model for a given topology. The misunderstanding of this inherent stability as a form of objectivity is an unintended disguise for the desire for certainty—a retreat from risk and the subjectivity of design.[9]

The localized operation of non-linear models is a critical determinant of their meta-stability. Non-linear form-finding models, such as Frei Otto's wet grid,[10] self-organize in a restrictively localized manner and are unable to re-form the assemblage at the level of the system. Macro-scale order does not emerge within these models. This localized self-organization is restricted to creating known formal or organizational character at the micro-scale, an act of selection rather than volatile generation.

Generative algorithms that engage recursive and self-organizing procedures are critical to the formation of complexity within computational design. While the role of generative algorithms in architecture is diverse, the architectural relevance of algorithmic design is dependent on the ability to encode architectural intent within the operation of the algorithm. Typically, generative algorithms are simply deployed as templates for architecture: abstract formal generators, operating on an appropriated logic, devoid of any recognition of the architectural problem or proposition. Likewise, the application of algorithmic processes to discrete elements, such as facades or surface pattern, limits complex systems to playing a minor role in defining architecture and confines non-linear processes within a known set of architectural hierarchies.

If computational design provides the framework within which to rethink architecture through a non-linear paradigm, then it is not enough simply to apply the image of

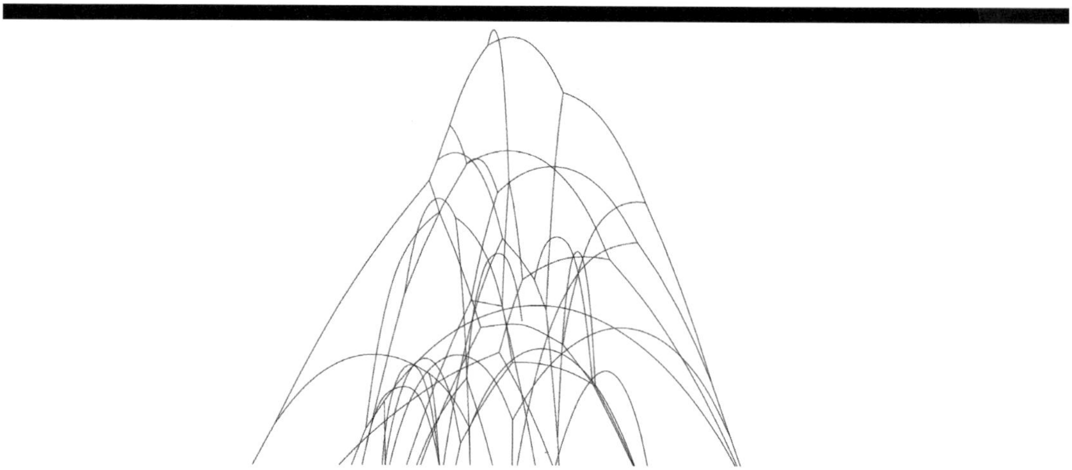

Catenary model diagram.

complexity to the body of modernity. It is perhaps this tendency that contributes to the perception of algorithmic architecture as obsessed with formal and aesthetic concerns—a perception that is antithetical to the organizational logic of complex systems. While this logic implies the potential for designing the inherently organizational aspects of architecture such as program and structure, complex systems are equally adept at engaging with form, as the emergence of form can be understood as the organization of matter.

The emergence of a strange or unknown set of characteristics requires a willingness to experiment through the design of an algorithm rather than simply its selection. Algorithms with highly indexical and stable relationships to their formal characteristics do little to advance an open-ended design process; instead, they reduce algorithmic design to an act of stylistic selection. Within the highly networked computational design culture, the adoption of the default mappings of algorithms with a known indexical character—such as voronoi, reaction diffusion, l-systems,[11] magnetic fields, or cellular automata—inherently denies volatility, and risks falling into cliché. The mimetic nature and safe connotations relating to beauty, and optimization of the algorithms extracted from biology demonstrate a prevailing conservatism within contemporary computational architecture.

The computational design methodologies outlined above can be seen either to be inherently stable or to be volatile within a predictable range: seeking a known attractor and the stability of selected characteristics. The rapid adoption within contemporary architecture of computational techniques that privilege pseudo-objective criteria, known characteristics and direct control demonstrates a prevailing desire for stability, and an unwillingness to engage with risk and the highly volatile conditions that are required for something new to emerge. But rather than advocating highly volatile systems that resist authorship or that privilege the unrepeatable accident,[12] what is needed is an alternative understanding of control and interaction between top-down and bottom-up processes.

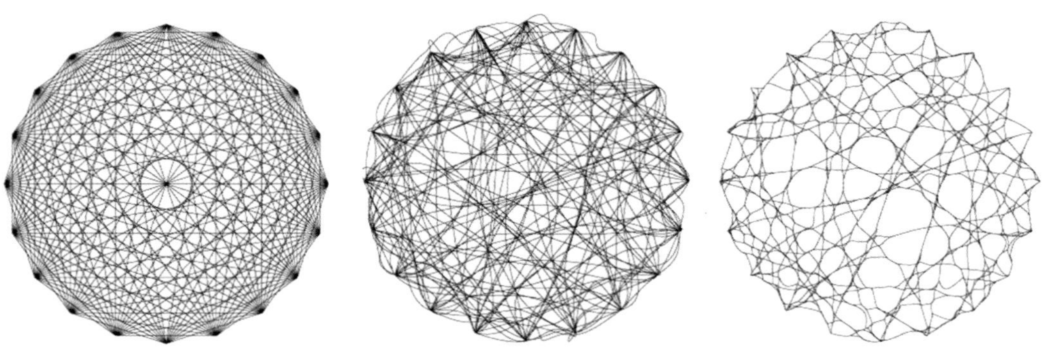

Wet grid algorithm.

VOLATILITY AND INTENTIONALITY

The volatility of a design process is dependent upon the nature of the design intent and the level of abstraction between that intent and the designed object. The nature of authorship, or intent, within generative design can be categorized as either criteria or procedure. Designing to criteria is inherently stable, as the criteria constrain the possible realm of the object. In contrast, designing through procedure is inherently speculative, as it is concerned with the conditions of operation rather than conditioning the outcome. This necessary abstraction between the design intent and object enables an emergent outcome through the interaction of design procedures.[13]

The highly volatile approach of Behavioral Formation is posited here in opposition to the inherently stable computational models that have been adopted more broadly within architecture. This methodology is not intrinsically tied to formal or organizational characteristics that are simply selected, but instead is an experimental approach that generates emergent architectural order, organization and characteristics.

Self-organization within behavioral processes of formation generates emergent characteristics in a manner not dissimilar to many of the non-linear generative algorithms that are criticized here. What differentiates Behavioral Formation is the architectural nature of the rules from which the characteristics emerge: these are loaded with specific architectural design intent. Original characteristics emerge through a design process based on architectural tendencies and behaviors rather than the adoption or misappropriation of stable characteristics and known criteria from biology or computer science. One such volatile architectural logic is the formation of emergent spatial topology posited in the *manifold swarms* strategy. This is an example of a design strategy that is less concerned with the emergence of original formal character (as it tends toward a smooth manifold surface), but instead focuses on the volatile emergence of an original topology.

In contrast to optimization algorithms, there are no a priori criteria constraining Behavioral Formation. Instead, a subjective design sensibility emerges from orchestrating the interaction of many micro-decisions and intentions. While design intent might be prescriptive at the

Reaction diffusion algorithm.

level of the agent, these processes are never stable at the macro-scale because the agent is oblivious to the emergence of the swarm. The Behavioral Formation logic of encoding agency within geometry avoids any generic mapping of known algorithms and, as such, Behavioral Formation resists the indexical nature of appropriated algorithmic techniques.

Behavioral Formation is a theoretical, conceptual and procedural approach to architecture, distinct from the architectural adaptation of multi-agent algorithms. As with all algorithms within architecture, multi-agent systems have been variously misappropriated and abused. The classic mapping of the boids algorithm as a swarm, or more recently stigmergic organization as ant-trail simulations, are at risk of being applied within architecture in a generic or clichéd manner. While the underlying operation of these algorithms are potent with possibility for the architect, as demonstrated in our design research, their unaltered adoption is as limited and problematic as any appropriated algorithm that is applied rather than being reinvented to negotiate architectural intent.

GLOBAL IGNORANCE

Complex systems privilege local interactions over global understanding or communication at the level of the system. This *global ignorance* is necessary for the emergence of complex order and its attendant volatile behavior; however, it is problematic, as numerous architectural concerns operate at the global scale. These concerns are inherently topological. While design intention operates through the agent's adjacent connections, they do not operate with an understanding of the larger field of connectivity: the topology of the network. This limitation is most acute in the design of topologically defined systems such as enclosure, spatial topology, or structure. Consequently, one focus of our design research is the development of strategies to engage this contradiction of volatile emergent systems and the ignorance of the topological conditions they create.

Macro-topological conditions are difficult to define computationally and are perhaps most easily perceived by the designer. This observation catalyzed the development of a strategy

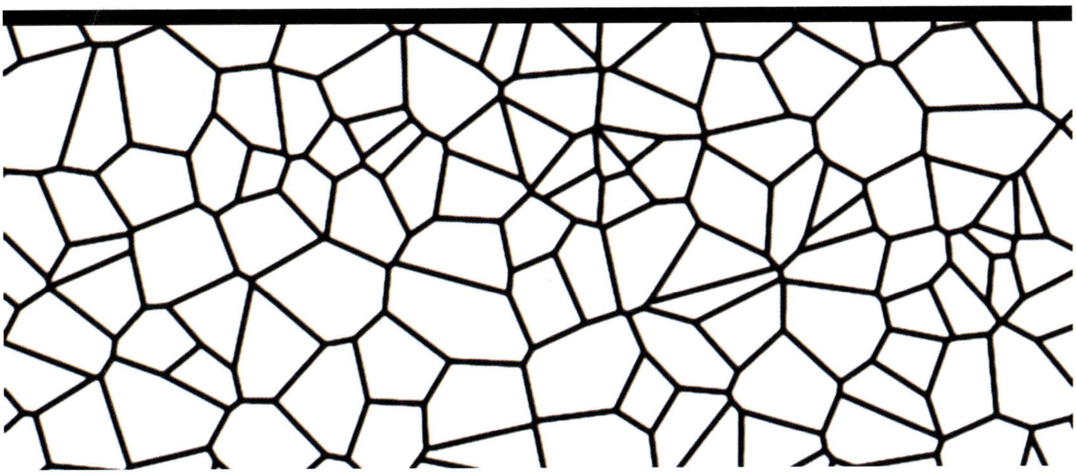

Voronoi algorithm.

of *strange feedback* between generative processes and surface modeling, which is premised on balancing the volatile behavior of the algorithm with direct formal and topological operations. In opposition to this messy manual feedback, the *agency of structure*[14] was developed as a systemic approach to the relationship of volatile emergent behavior and topology. The connectivity of an entire system must be known in order to analyze load paths, as the structural load at a given point in a system cannot be known exclusively from local analysis. Consequently, this strategy feeds information from global structural analysis to inform the local structural heuristic operations of the agents.

The inherent conflict between the local operation of Behavioral Formation and macro-architectural intent generates a series of new problems, techniques, and opportunities that enable original organizations, forms, structures, and characteristics to emerge. The internal resistance of the agency of structure and strange feedback strategies differentiate these approaches from the direct application of algorithmic processes to normative hierarchies and explicit initial conditions. It is through the constant negotiation within these processes that design intuition and heuristic approaches operate. Through this volatile struggle, algorithmic strategies become deeply embedded within architectural design.

Volatile algorithmic design methodologies can be understood as part of a broader contemporary interest in indeterminacy and non-linearity that has been emerging since the development of chaos and complexity theory. However, the argument for volatility is more than a theoretical concern; it is a fundamental concern for the importance of subjectivity and the nature of risk within design.

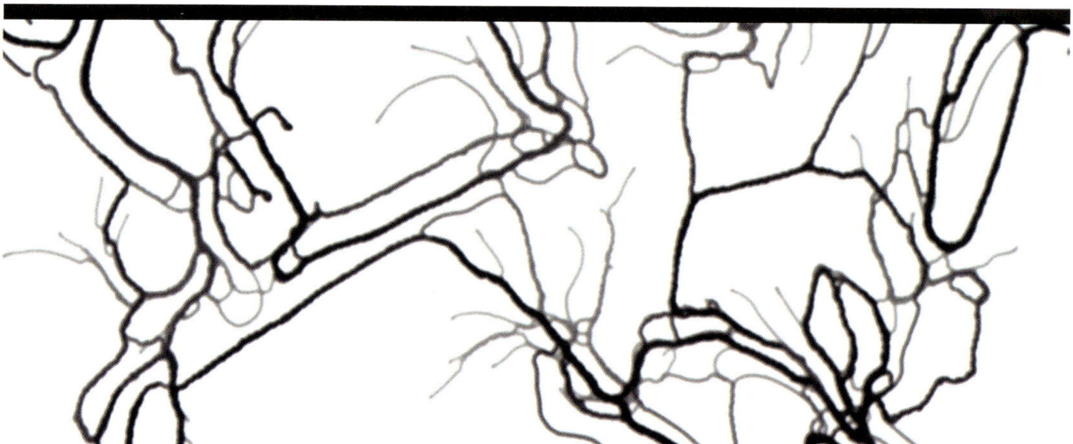

Stigmergic ant-trail algorithm.

1 A more detailed discussion of emergence and complex systems is presented in the Introduction.

2 Cellular automata rule 110 is a one-dimensional cellular automation that operates on the edge of chaos. Cellular automata is a grid of cells, each with a state (such as black or white). These states change iteratively in response to the adjacent cells.

3 Manuel DeLanda, "Deleuze, Diagrams, and the Open-ended Becoming of the World", in *Becomings: Explorations in Time, Memory, and Futures*, ed. Elizabeth Grosz (Ithaca: Cornell University Press, 1999), p. 32.

4 The term *parametric* is used in this context to describe the technique of parametric or associative modeling (see Glossary of Terms). It should be distinguished from Patrik Schumacher's concept of *parametricism*, which is an attempt to outline a broad methodological approach to architecture (Schumacher 2012).

5 See Glossary of Terms.

6 John Holland, who is credited with the development of the genetic algorithm, argues that the creative capacities of genetic algorithms are dependent upon the nature of the search criteria with respect to the evolutionary operation of a system. Holland contends that a search algorithm seeking an optimal solution is critically different from the evolutionary capacity of a genetic algorithm, since the latter is capable of volatile evolution. See interview with John Holland published in Neil Leach and Roland Snooks, eds. *Swarm Intelligence: Architectures of Multi-Agent Systems* (Tongji University Press, forthcoming). This being stated, the role of evolutionary techniques within architecture has been firmly tied to optimization.

7 Optimizing algorithms that engage multiple criteria or have an abstract relationship to the form and organization of the project are inherently less stable. Search algorithms that operate through multi-objective criteria negotiate between various necessities, generating less predictable or at least less indexical results. Structural and environmental criteria, embedded within optimization strategies, condition form but in themselves are not explicitly formal. This level of abstraction, while less directly indexical, does not ensure volatility.

8 Axel Kilian and John Ochsendorf argue that dynamic relaxation or force density algorithms typically operate through minor formal modifications in finding equilibrium situations, while particle-spring models are capable of more radical change. See Axel Kilian and John Ochsendorf, "Particle-spring Systems for Structural Form Finding", *Journal for the International Association for Shell and Spatial Structures*, no.47, (2005).

9 The conservative nature of selection in form-finding processes is particularly evident in the numerous contemporary catenary vault projects, which exhibit considerable formal similarity.

10 See Otto (1996).

11 See Glossary of Terms for *voronoi*, *reaction diffusion*, and *l-systems*.

12 Critiquing the accident within generative design strategies, Mark Burry makes an argument for the importance of repeatability within the design process. See Mark Burry, "Paramorph: Anti-Accident Methodologies", in *Architectural Design: Hypersurface Architecture II*, (London: Academy Editions, September 1999), pp. 78–83.

13 A more detailed discussion of the nature of design intent is outlined in the Introduction.

14 See the following two strategy sections on *agency of structure* and *strange feedback*.

STRATEGY

AGENCY OF STRUCTURE

The *agency of structure* is a design strategy that we developed to condition the volatile generative nature of behavioral processes of formation by encoding structural heuristics within the agent. It is a process of feedback designed to mitigate the global ignorance of multi-agent algorithms by establishing an interaction between the local operation of agents and the global evaluation of structural analysis.

The *agency of structure* operates by iteratively testing agent-based geometry, such as a network of elements or bundle of strands, using finite element structural analysis. Finite element methods analyze the complete network of structure, and return information pertaining to each individual node or agent. The behavior of the agent adapts in response to this information through heuristic structural rules. Through this strategy, agents respond to the local implication of global conditions and, in doing so, re-form the global conditions, setting up a continuous feedback loop.

Rather than generating form through structural performance, this approach conditions the behavior of generative design agents with structural information. Structural heuristics inform their behavior. This is an important conceptual difference from the contemporary fascination with the generative capacity of structural analysis and evolutionary optimization.[1]

This behavioral approach to structure can be described through strand models such as the algorithm developed for the airBaltic Terminal project.[2] In the case of excessive deflection, for example, the strands separate vertically to generate greater structural depth, create more

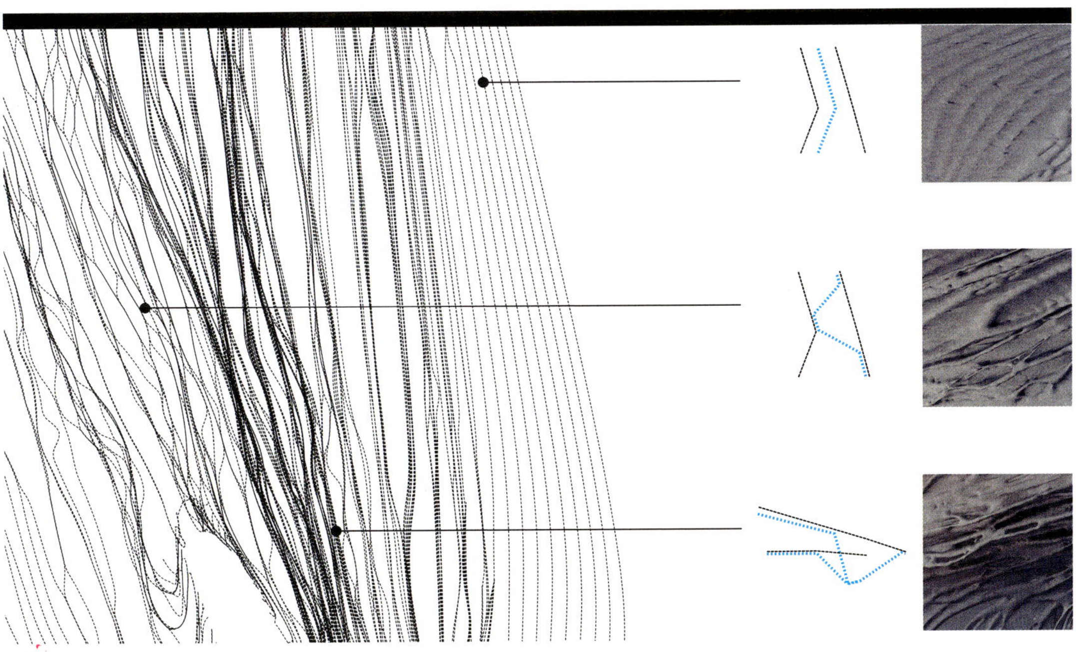

airBaltic Riga Airport, 2010. The generative process developed for the airBaltic roof was conditioned by structural heuristics encoded as behaviors within strand agents. Through this process, the agents negotiated between structural concerns and more esoteric design intentions to generate a fibrous network of beams.

strands to dissipate load, and bundle to generate greater structural rigidity. These operations integrate structure as one of the agents' many competing design behaviors. This integrated approach enables a highly volatile design process to resolve structural forces without imposing a predetermined structural schema or post-rationalizing architectural form to ensure structural integrity.

Embedding structural logic within behavioral systems is conceptually different from multi-agent systems that respond to the structural analysis of surfaces that are exterior to the network of agents. These approaches establish a linear relationship between the agents and the structural analysis. Instead, what is being posited is a self-organizing feedback loop where a network of agents heuristically reacts and re-forms their network in response to its structural analysis. This feedback creates a non-linear relationship of generative design intention and structural rationalization. The implications of the feedback between global analysis and local procedure extend to any quantifiable system of global analysis that can assign a value to its individual nodes.

This approach to encoding structural heuristics is an example of how quantifiable pragmatic concerns are encoded as behaviors to condition more volatile and esoteric design algorithms. Through this research, energy modeling,[3] material behavior,[4] and fabrication limitations[5] have all been encoded as behaviors that influence the generation of form, structure, and articulation.

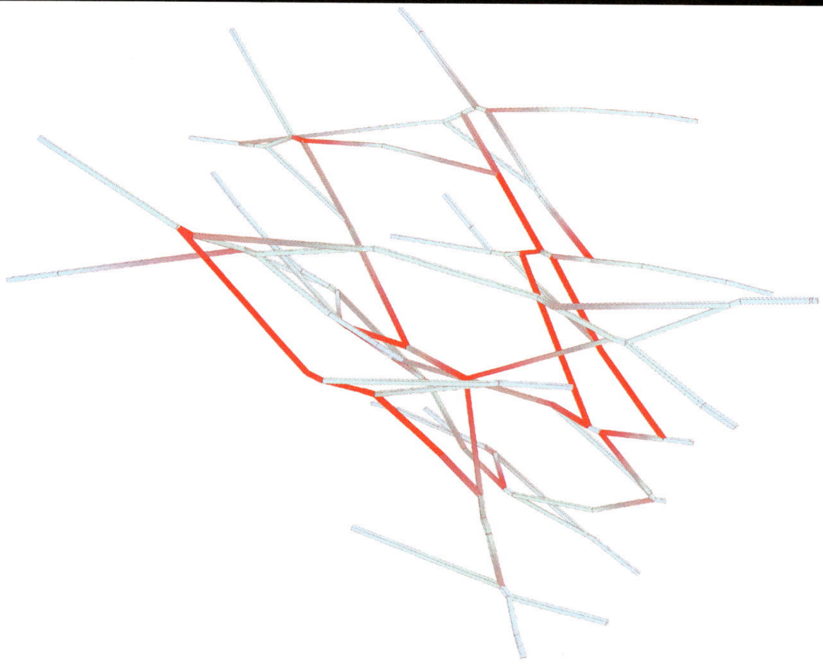

AgentBody structural study. Bending moment analysis.

Although issues of building science are, of course, necessary in realizing buildings, they are never the motivation for these projects. Integrating building science into volatile generative processes avoids any manipulation or post-rationalization of projects that would otherwise be necessary to conform to these pragmatic concerns. The conceptual importance of this strategy is the capacity of Behavioral Formation to negotiate a plethora of design influences or behaviors, including structural necessity, without establishing a hierarchy of processes. What is being argued for here is that issues of building science should condition, rather than drive, design.

1 This contemporary concern for the generative capacity of structural analysis and evolutionary optimization is evident in publications such as *The New Structuralism* (Oxman 2010), and *Performance Oriented Architecture* (Hensel 2013).

2 See Catalog of Projects.

3 The feedback of global energy analysis to agent models was a focus of the Fibrous Assemblages design research course that I directed at RMIT University in 2014.

4 An example of encoding material behavior within a generative algorithm is discussed in the Composite Swarm project, where the behavior of polyurethane foam is encoded within the agentBody logic.

5 The Brass Swarm is an example of a project that embeds the limitations of robotic bending processes within the generative algorithm. This is discussed further in the AgentBody Prototypes project section.

STRATEGY

STRANGE FEEDBACK

Taipei Performing Arts Centre, 2008.

Strange feedback is a non-linear and inconsistent strategy of negotiation between generative and direct design procedures. This strategy operates through the continuous feedback between algorithmic processes and direct digital surface modeling, an attempt to maximize and hybridize the potential of each mode of design. The output of one process becomes the input to the other in a recursive loop. This constant, but non-systemic, feedback produces a correlation between generative and direct procedures, creating new characteristics from which a synthetic or unified architectural vocabulary emerges. While algorithmic procedures are capable of generating highly emergent outcomes, the inability of multi-agent systems to sufficiently comprehend macro-scale concerns—such as spatial topology, enclosure, form, and silhouette—is mediated by explicit modeling. This interaction is both a shortcut for intuition and a mechanism for direct, subjective and non-systemic decisions.

Strange feedback, premised on the interaction of top-down and bottom-up design decisions, developed out of our broader concern for the intertwined relationship of emergence and intention. A shift is evident in our work, from the earlier projects that were exclusively focused on the development of bottom-up generative algorithms, to this more recent negotiation between explicit and generative strategies. The Taipei Performing Arts Centre was the first of our projects to examine the relationship between bottom-up multi-agent procedures and top-down modeling decisions. The roof of the project was modeled as a surface and embedded with a network of agents that self-organized with various degrees of volatility. Although

the design process engaged both generative and direct modeling, the relationship was entirely sequential: an explicit condition was modeled that subsequently re-formed algorithmically.

The Yeosu Pavilion proposal for the 2012 World Expo in South Korea,[1] a collaboration with Tom Wiscombe, advanced this relationship between top-down and bottom-up processes, placing them in a feedback loop. The project went through a constant process of negotiation: between multi-agent algorithms that created a network of strands, and direct surface modeling operations. The overall form was directly modeled as a series of ellipsoids, with the formal articulation and webbing between these volumes being designed through a process of strange feedback. The character and pattern of the veins emerged from the behavior of the algorithm, while their development into pleats and their relationship to surface were designed through direct modeling. The non-systemic feedback between these two design approaches generated a unique and non-indexical formal vocabulary.[2]

The global ignorance of multi-agent algorithms denies the agent an understanding of the overall topology of which it is a part. Given that many key architectural concerns are topological—such as enclosure, spatial division, and structure—strange feedback provides an opportunity for intuitive decisions regarding these topological concerns to interact with the algorithm's capacity for emergence. Our proposal for the National Art Museum of China[3] was designed through the strange feedback of an expressive swarm algorithm and direct surface modeling to

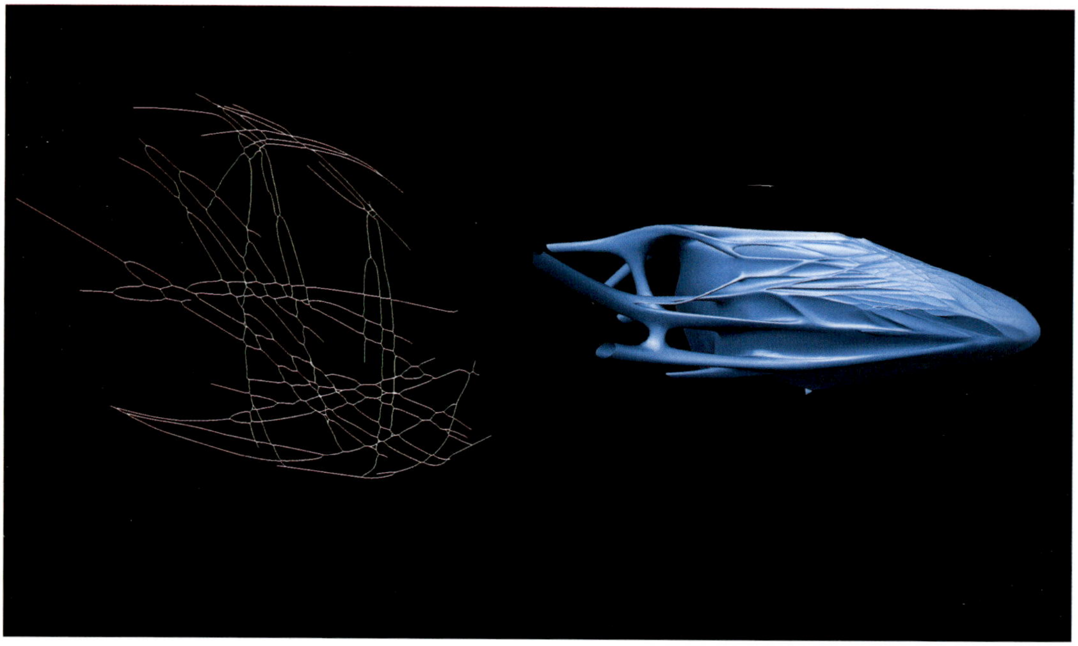

Yeosu Pavilion, 2009. The articulation of the pavilion was designed through the strange feedback of algorithmic and surface modeling techniques.

generate a synthetic relationship between form and articulation. This strategy negated the limitations of emergent surface generation and enabled the topological complexities of enclosure to be resolved.

A similar process of strange feedback in our proposal for the Kazakhstan Symbol hybridized the intricate capacity of the multi-agent algorithm with the topological control of surface modeling at the macro-scale. This interaction created an intricate turbulent form in which ornament was not applied but was inherent to its formation. This interaction suspends the reading of the project between the turbulent forces of natural systems and the cultural references of ornamentation. While the National Art Museum of China exhibits a close relationship in scale and organization between form and articulation, creating a unified object, the greater discrepancy between the two in the Kazakhstan project enabled more expressive ornamental characteristics to emerge.

This research is clearly concerned with design methodology; however, it is underpinned by the belief that any building must ultimately stand on its own qualities without the scaffolding of process. Algorithmic architecture is often a culprit in claiming validity through the value of its process rather than the value of its outcomes. Strange feedback is an attempt to counter this tendency and the dogma of algorithmic purity. Instead, algorithmic techniques are posited here as simply that: techniques. They are not essentialist or pure, but simply one facet of the design process.

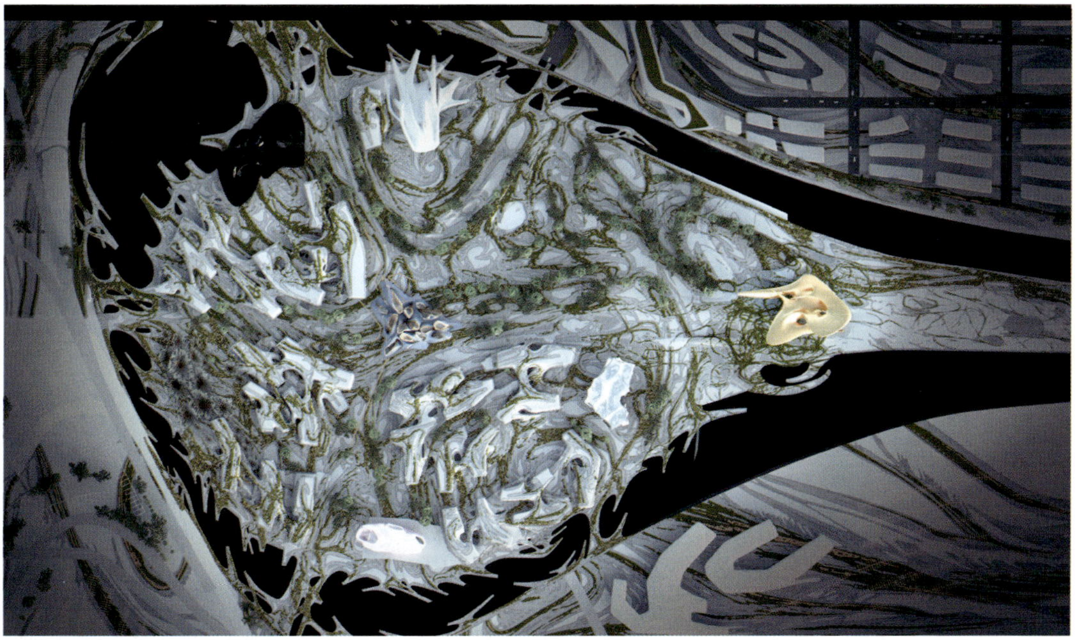

Kazakhstan Symbol, 2013. Designed as part of a larger masterplan project for the Astana 2017 World Expo.

The indexical nature of found algorithms is discussed at length in the essay, "Volatility". However, it is worth pointing out at this juncture that strange feedback plays an important role in resisting indexicality and cliché. Typically, linear algorithms are the most evidently indexical and recognizable, as their selection becomes the defining aspect of the project rather than their manipulation. As multi-agent algorithms are non-linear and highly emergent, this concern is somewhat mitigated, although the output or mapping of these algorithms can still lapse into indexical clichés. It is from the impurity of strange feedback, the interaction of intuitive design decisions, and the logic of systemic algorithms that something strange and esoteric can emerge.

1 See project, "Yeosu Pavilion".

2 A process that Tom Wiscombe refers to as 'messy computation'.

3 See project, "National Art Museum of China".

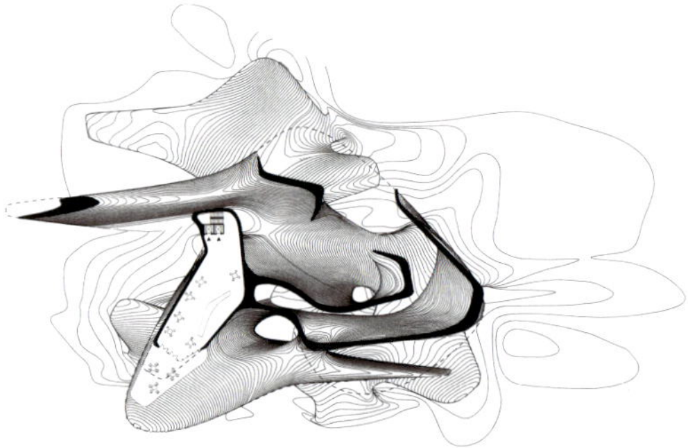

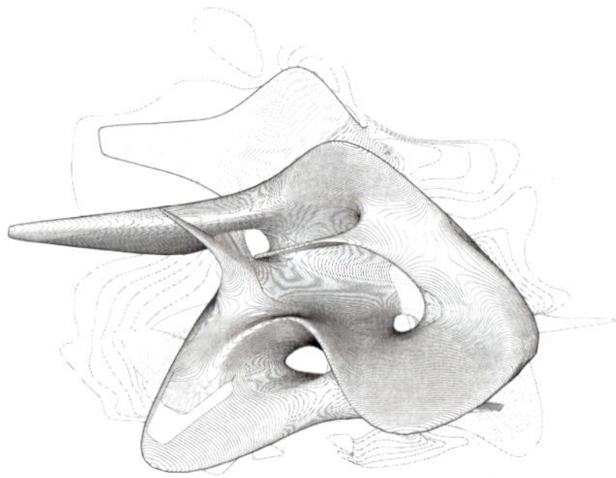

Kazakhstan Symbol, 2013.

The project was developed for an invited competition to design a national symbol for Kazakhstan, as part of the Astana 2017 World Expo. The turbulent ornamental form was designed through the negotiation of emergent processes and architectural modeling. The intention was to create a reading of form suspended between the forces of natural systems and the imposition of artificial form.

PROJECT

YEOSU PAVILION

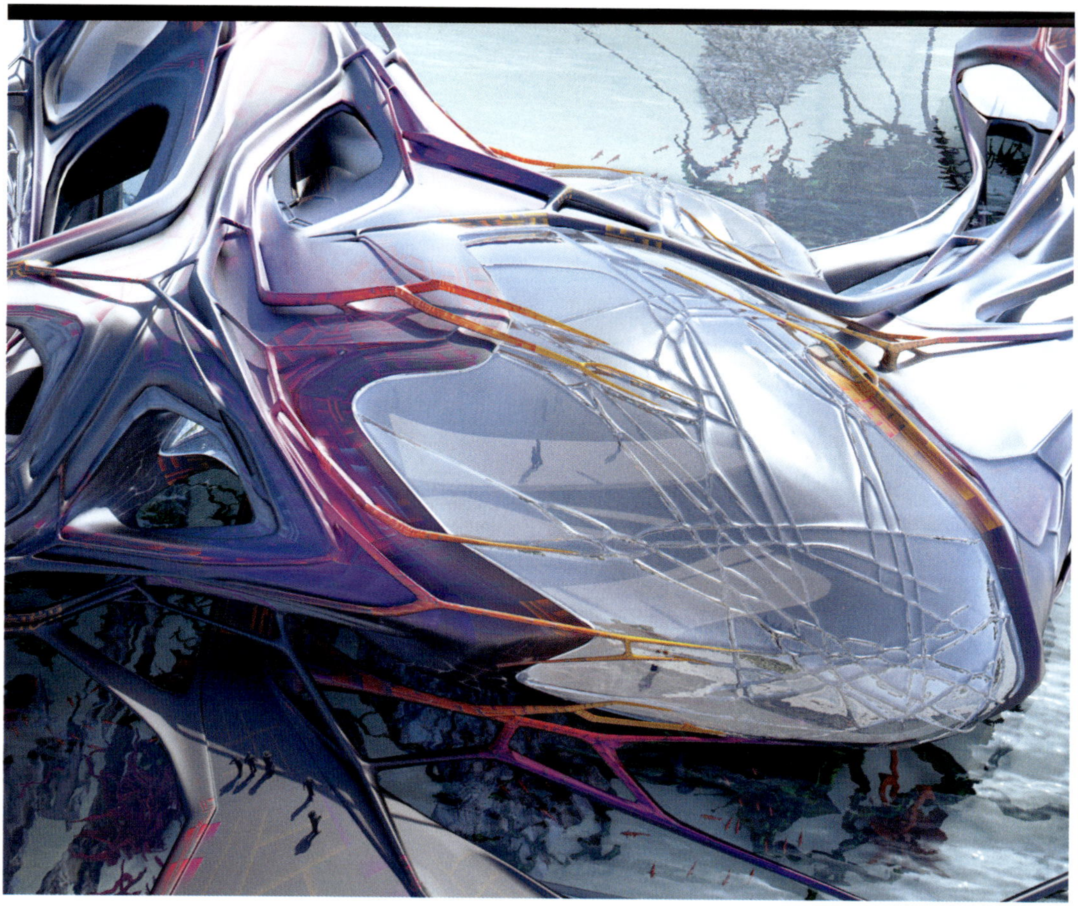

The Yeosu Pavilion, designed for the 2012 World Expo held in South Korea, responds to the Expo theme of the ocean as a living organism. The project was designed in collaboration with Tom Wiscombe, and was defined as much by the negotiation of our differing design methodologies as by our many shared sensibilities. It was through the design of this project that the process of *strange feedback* became clearly articulated. The design evolved through numerous permutations over a nine-month period before a coherent vocabulary had emerged from the relationship of direct and generative design decisions.

The design was an attempt to resist normative architectural readings and to create something otherworldly. The floating pavilion alludes to a strange biological origin, while eschewing any recognizable biological references or strategies.

The project was designed as a series of soft membrane bubbles that were joined and wrapped together by a rigid monocoque[1] shell. The explicit design of the egg-shaped bubbles

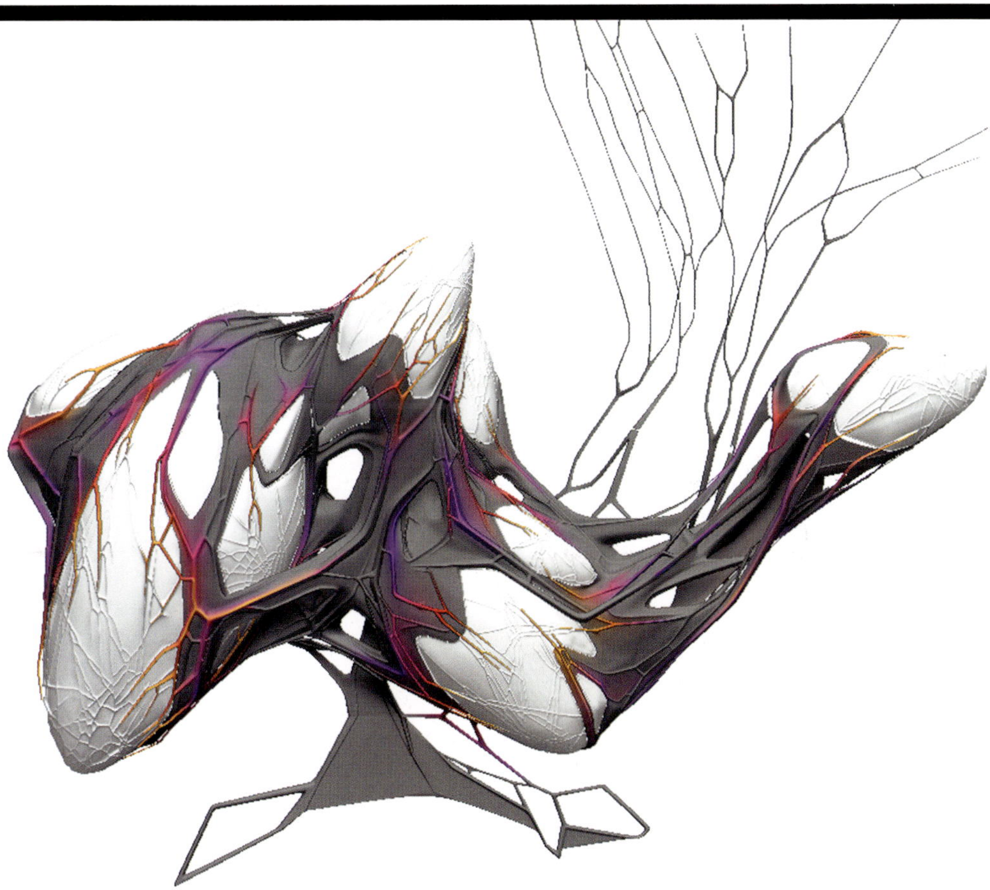

Roof plan coloration study.

remained relatively unchanged throughout the process; by contrast, the shell connecting these bubbles was volatile and subject to a strange feedback of explicit and generative procedures. The final form maintains the remnants of these explicit decisions, and establishes a balance between the purity of the bubbles and the contested characteristics of the shell.

Algorithmic processes were employed in the design of articulation and character rather than in the generation of the primary spaces or overall form. This articulation varies in intensity, creating a diversity of conditions in color, form, and character. An inconsistent coherence is created through these multiple conditions, which resists any systemic reading of the project in favor of its specificity as an object.

A polyscalar network of strands articulates the basic form of the pavilion, expressed as pleats in the surface, and armatures that extend from the surface. These take on architec-

Perspective.

tonic roles that are blurred and multiple, which we deployed in the service of formal and spatial manipulation, structure, and ornament. This uncoupling of geometry from role is amplified by the shifting scale of the strands, which resists a simple assignment of architectonic categories. The large strands tie together the soft membrane bubbles; as these reduce in scale, the tendency of the strands is to operate structurally, and at the smallest scale they act to micro-stiffen the ETFE membranes. The larger scale pleats and armatures have structural members embedded within the fiber-composite surface, while smaller pleats provide stiffening and directional strength to the surface.[2]

The ETFE transparent membranes are pressurized with air at two scales. The entire pavilion is pressurized to give some global structure to the soft membranes, and a detailed network of high-pressure air strands or conduits wraps over the membrane to stiffen the surface locally.

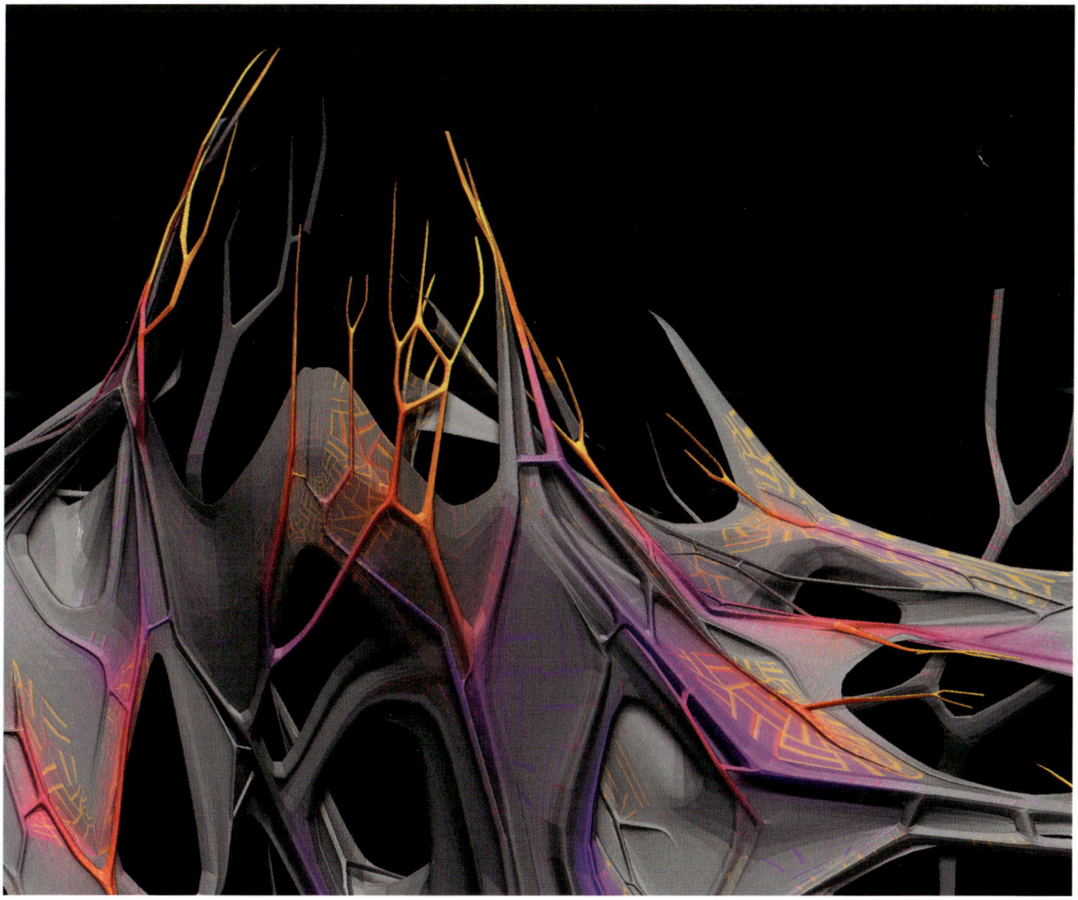

The color of the composite shell intensifies through a coherent, but non-indexical, relationship to the intricacy of the geometry. Glitches in the digital color mapping process were exploited to create the hatch pattern between the pleats.

The coloration of the project reinforces varying intensities within the geometry. As pleats and armatures reduce in scale, they shift from purple through to bright yellow. This is not an indexical condition, however. The coloration, like the changing operation of the strands, is not entirely systematic; our intention was that they should exhibit tendencies – commonalities that have emerged from the strange feedback of its design process.

1 See Glossary of Terms.

2 The structural system was developed in conjunction with Matt Melnyk from Buro Happold.

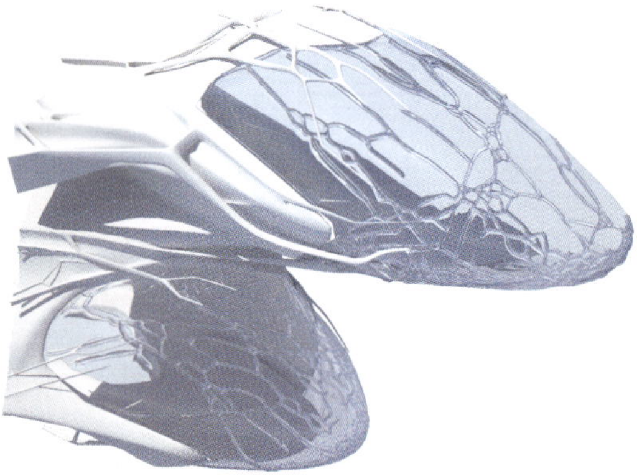

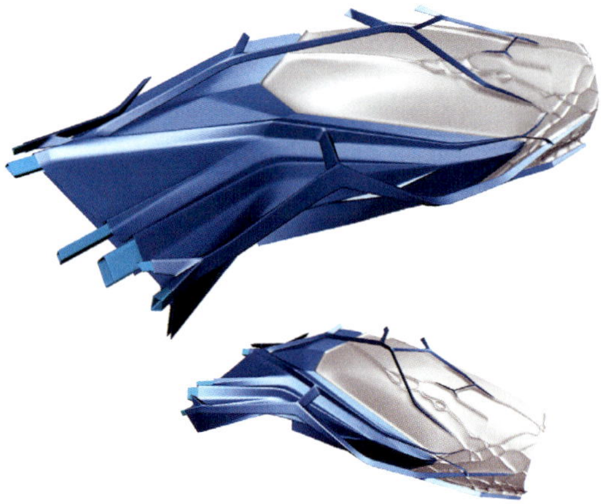

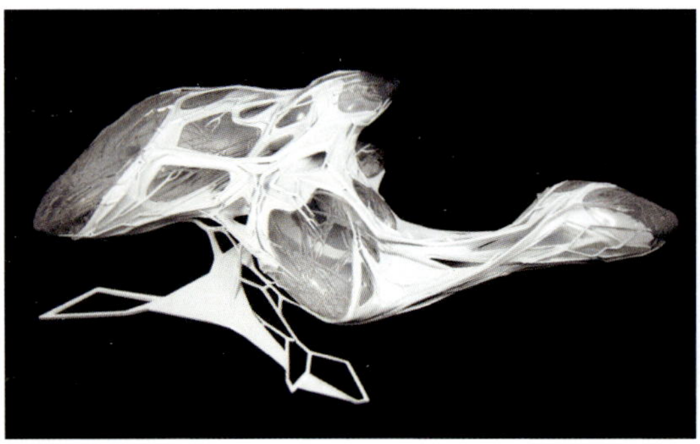

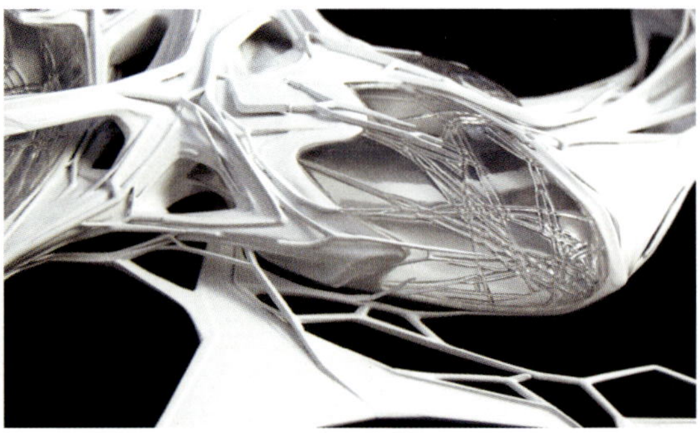

Above: The fiber-composite shell is reinforced with embedded structural beams, while the ETFE membrane is reinforced with a network of high-pressure inflated veins. The geometry of the pavilion was designed through a series of 'chunk models', which we used to develop the character and articulation of the form.
Below: Model photos.

First floor plan.

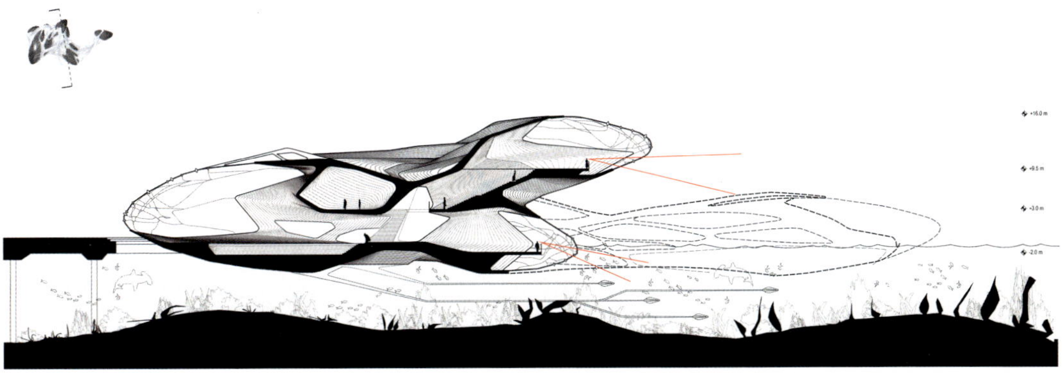

Section.

PROJECT

NATIONAL ART MUSEUM OF CHINA

Aerial perspective, detail.

The impetus for the glass cloud of the National Art Museum of China (NAMOC) arose from our ambition to design a diffuse or formless form. The project was a shortlisted competition entry for a museum on the former Beijing Olympic site, which comprises a field of monumental objects including the Birds Nest stadium and the Water Cube. Rather than designing another highly delineated object, we drew on the amorphous quality of clouds—which became a procedural influence as well as a metaphor.

Creating a figural or gestural form was the focus of the design process. This represented a shift from the emphasis of our previous projects, where we had been concerned with the negotiation of architectural roles through geometry. The cloud-like form of the museum was designed through a variation of a multi-agent swarm algorithm that we developed to mimic fluid dynamics and to create turbulent and laminar flows.

Model photo, detail.

We were attempting to design the cloud and its eroded landscape from a single algorithm, to inextricably tie the two parts of the project into a unified relationship. The cloud houses 40 percent of the building program, while the remaining program is contained within the landscape podium.

A primary intention was to bring into correlation, or develop a synthetic relationship between, the structure, articulation, and form of the cloud. Our strategy of *strange feedback* was employed to negotiate between the generative algorithm and explicit surface modeling techniques. This process raises the question of where to start: with the algorithm or with explicit modeling? Our answer was both at once. We developed two competing schemes: one that started with the volatile turbulent algorithm, while the other focused on modeling cloud-like forms. Neither strategy won out; instead, they both converged,

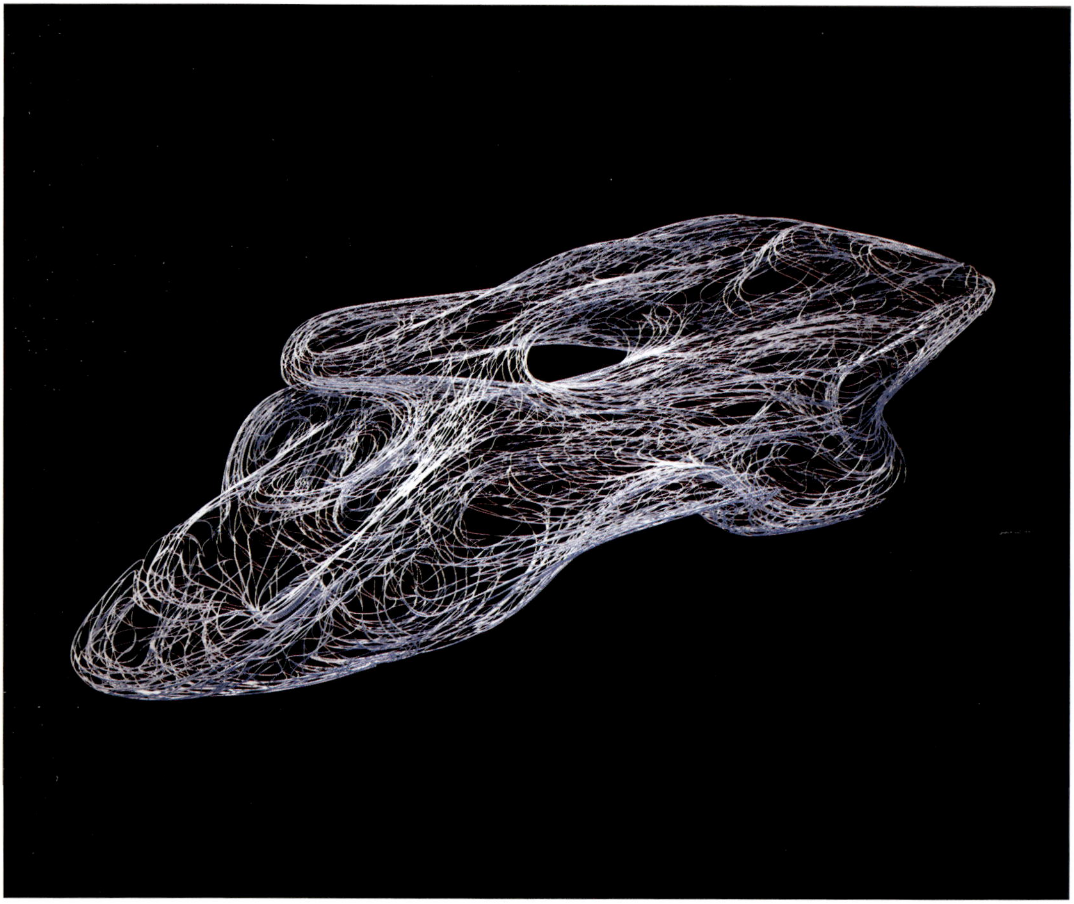

Cloud skin study. An expressive structural network creates the primary articulation of the cloud.

with each informing the other. This feedback continued throughout our design process as the output from one technique became the input to the other: a messy process of feedback that slowly created a correlation of form, structure, and articulation.

The result is a surface that appears thick—as a volume or mass of turbulence—rather than a thin membrane. This implied mass is partly the result of the correlation of surface articulation and form, where the two are evidently part of a unified process of formation. The same algorithm was used in the generation of the form and distribution of the shingles, enabling the articulation and form to be created simultaneously as an inseparable whole. The shingles are identical, but their fixing allows a variable overlap and rotation to achieve the fluid articulation of the form. This glass cloud blurs the reading of the suspended masses within.

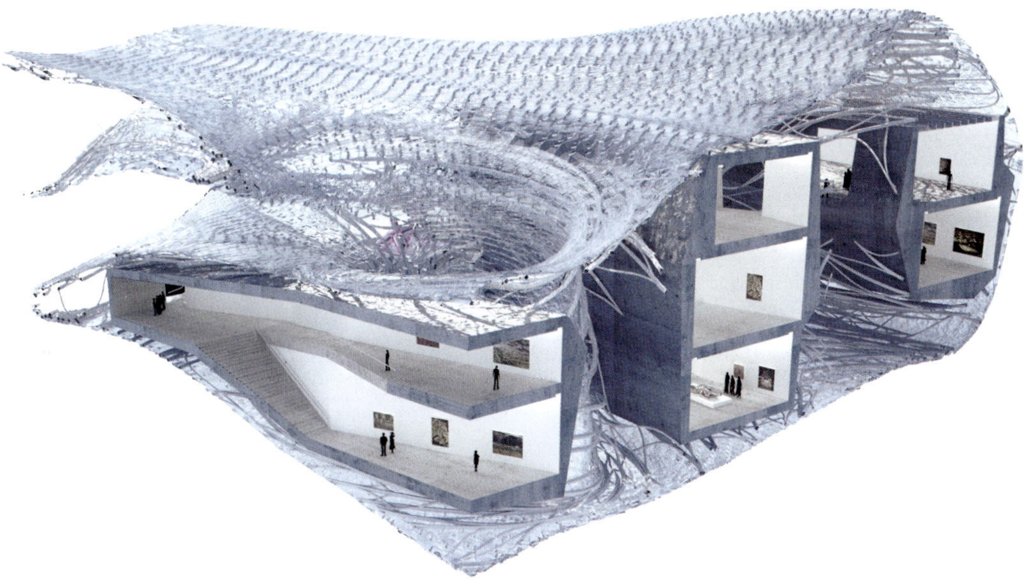

The primary gallery spaces are contained within monolithic beams, surrounded by a series of more informal exhibition spaces.

These interstitial spaces are wrapped by the structure and skin of the glass cloud.

The cloud is internally organized through the relationship of stacked gallery beams and the delaminating substructure of the cloud. The delamination of the substructure operates in a sculptural and spatial role as it thickens to envelop the beams. The interstitial space created between these elements is devoted to circulation and informal exhibition areas, mainly for large sculptural pieces. The structure, which was generated from the same algorithm as the cloud, was designed to be deliberately expressive, to reinforce the turbulent character of the cloud and produce ornamental qualities.

Atrium interior.

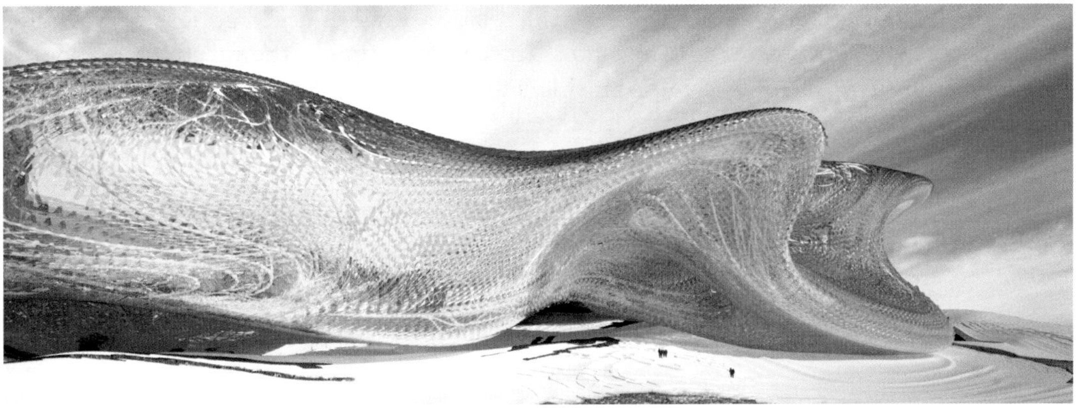

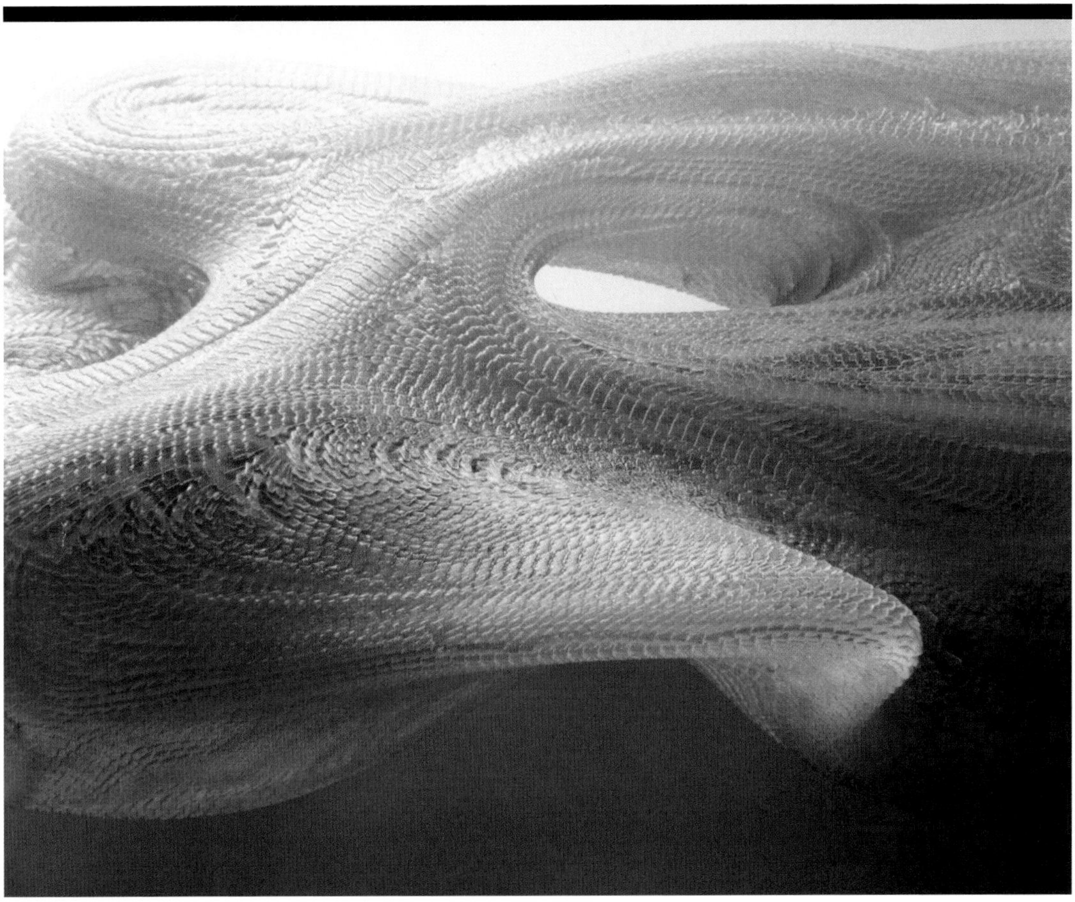

Above: Perspective.
Below: Model photo, detail.

ESSAY

STRANGE SPECIFICITY

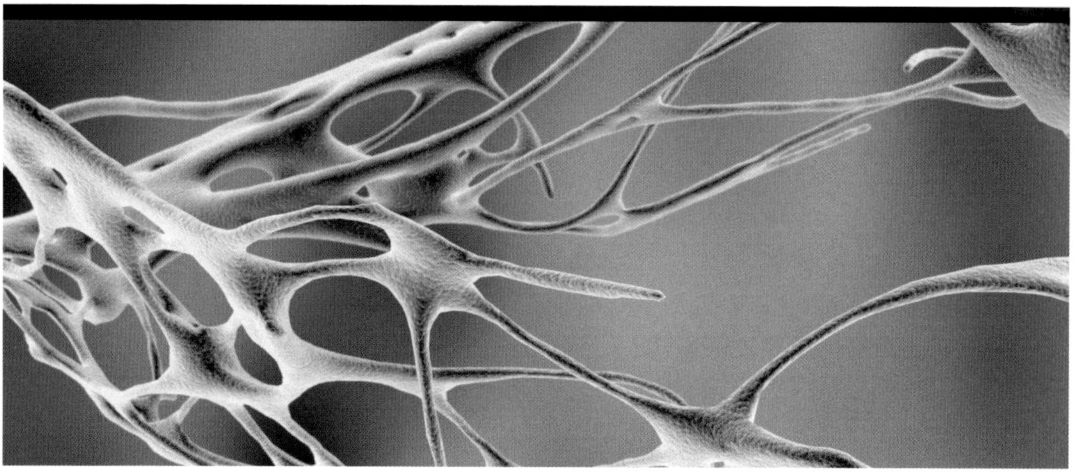

Swarm Matter, 2009. Detail of the intertwined agentBodies.

The projects posited here exceed, and are not reducible to, their concepts and processes. Strange new qualities emerge from the interaction between explicit decisions and generative processes, which exceed the individual capacity or sum of those approaches. This architecture is intrinsically tied to the emergent capacity of non-linear algorithms. However, unlike many examples of contemporary algorithmic architecture, it is neither indexical nor an automated approach, and it does not defer authority to nature, engineering, optimization, or any essentialist notion of form-finding. Instead, it relies on qualitative evaluation that is inherently subjective and draws on intuition.[1] Within processes of Behavioral Formation, intention is embedded within the generative algorithm as behaviors that interact with qualitative judgments and direct architectural decisions.

The primary concern of this research has shifted over the past eighteen years: from articulating a methodological and theoretical basis for the architecture of swarm intelligence, to a concern for the strange specificity of the architecture of Behavioral Formation. This is a shift from a purist understanding of the wider intellectual and cultural milieu of emergence, to a concern for the interaction of self-organization and subjective architectural decisions. Swarm intelligence provides an abstract, procedural logic for generative design, but is devoid of architectural intention or specificity.

In exceeding their strategies, these projects have contributed to the creation of an idiosyncratic architectural language. Not a vocabulary that references its process of formation, although it is highly contingent upon this, but rather one of strange specificity that is teased out of the volatile interaction of intention and emergence.

TOWARDS STRANGENESS

The strange qualities that are created through Behavioral Formation are intended to resist immediate evaluation. Phenomena that can be evaluated immediately, such as beauty, sit within the sphere of one's known judgments, whereas strangeness exceeds this scope of previous judgments. In this sense, strangeness relates to, but is not reducible to, the novel.[2]

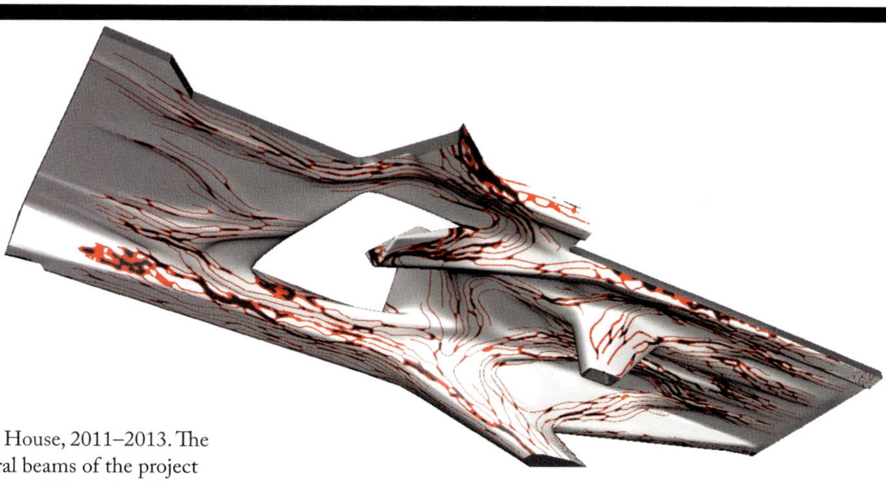

Malibu House, 2011–2013. The structural beams of the project are organized through a fibrous assemblages algorithm.

Strangeness is dependent on partial recognition—a distorted familiarity.[3] It is a discernible characteristic; one that can be understood as an emergent qualitative phenomenon. When the Swarm Matter project was being designed in 2009, for instance, it did not adhere to the contemporary computational design tropes of smooth continuous surfaces, parametric gradients, or the interest in digital Baroque ornament. The project instead had a new set of behaviors and characteristics: intricate, complex patterns that blur the recognition between emergent order and a field of anomalies. Something idiosyncratic and strange had emerged. The specificity that is created through the generation of strangeness is more resilient than strangeness itself—which has a tendency to normalize via familiarity—but the specific qualities remain.

NOT NATURE

Frédéric Migayrou and Marie-Ange Brayer articulated the prevailing interest in natural systems and a synthesis of architecture and biology, through their *Naturalising Architectures* ArchiLab exhibition at the FRAC Collection, Orléans, in 2013. The Babiy Yar, NAMOC and Swarm Matter projects were exhibited in the exhibition alongside the work of a group of contemporaries,[4] many of whom share an interest in complex systems, but articulate a very different relationship to natural systems. While multi-agent algorithms can be used to simulate the flocking of birds or the schooling of fish, they can equally be used to model financial markets and as optimization routines. These algorithms are ideologically neutral, albeit rich with tendencies. The approach posited here is not concerned with the algorithmic logic of nature, but with emergent, self-organizing processes that generate complex systems. This is an interest in the operation of these systems, not in any particular instance of their rules—be they biological or social.

There are, nevertheless, aesthetic relationships to nature in Behavioral Formation, which may arise from a shared procedural logic of complex systems. However, what separates this research from architects concerned with biomimetics is the explicit role of the architect's intention within the algorithm, rather than deferring authority to nature. This research is concerned

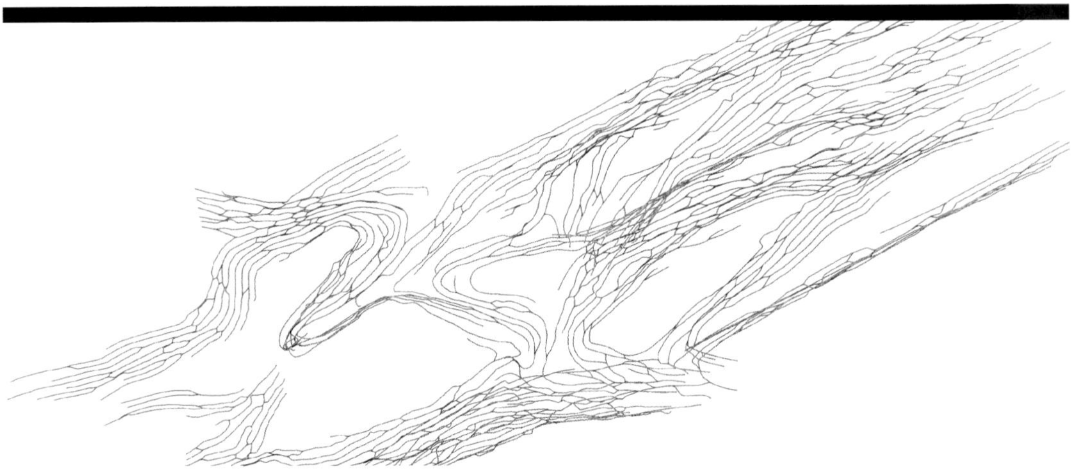

Malibu House, 2011–2013. Structural beam network.

with the design of strange formal and tectonic characteristics, rather than retreating into the known forms of nature inherent in biomimetics. The architecture posited here is a consciously directed human activity; it is cultural, driven by intention rather than evolutionary pressures. It is argued here that architecture needs to emerge from processes in which architectural decisions self-organize, in order to produce work that is contingent on, but not indexical to, its process.

INTENTION AND THE EMERGENCE OF CHARACTER

The relationship of emergence and architectural intention, explored through this body of work, is premised on a qualitative understanding of emergence. If emergent phenomena are qualitatively discernible patterns arising from complex systems,[5] then their intrumentalization is dependent on our ability to discern or recognize this order, which cannot be described mathematically.[6] The volatile and generative capacities of non-linear algorithmic design processes are inherently speculative, while the architect's role in teasing out the emergent phenomena is a subjective process. This is an argument for the role of intention and strategy rather than autopoietic processes;[7] architectural design is not equivalent to the autonomous processes of formation in the physical world.

The qualitative effects that are teased out of these emergent processes can be described in three categories: recurring characteristics, complex order, and affectual capacities. Recurring characteristics are those that consistently emerge from a process, while other descriptions such as topology or dimension remain more volatile. These characteristics, which resist being drawn or modeled, are generated at the local scale from the internally consistent operation of the algorithm. This is evident, for example, in the particular curvature and bundling of the fibrous ceiling pattern of the Malibu House, the shell of Fibrous Tower 2, or the agentBody tectonics of the Aalto University Architecture School.[8] This specific fibrous characteristic develops from the local behavior of the algorithm, rather than being a pattern generated by the complexity of a whole system. These characteristics are often layered, intricate, porous, differentiated, knitted, or woven.

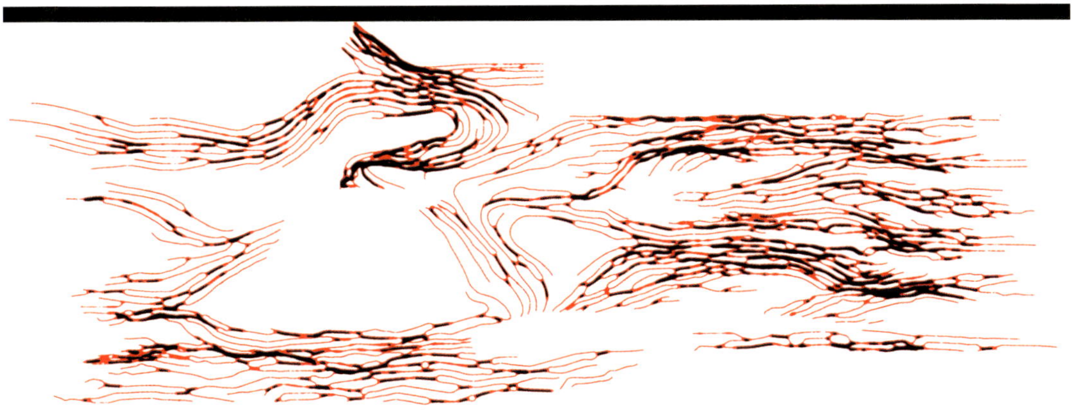

Malibu House, 2011–2013. Structural ceiling pattern.

Emergent order occurs at a larger scale where discernible patterns arise, such as the emergent figure in the Swarm Matter project, where a coherent form emerges from a field of parts. These larger scale patterns include the turbulent flows evident in projects such as NAMOC and the Kazakhstan Symbol or the emergent topology of the Nine Elms Bridge and RMIT Mace.[9] These patterns emerge from feedback that trickles through the entire population of agents and create an expression at the macro-scale.

The generation of intricate form and space from high-population, multi-agent algorithms produces emergent affectual capacities, such as those of the Babiy Yar[10] bronze memorial space or the RMIT Mace, which are inextricably linked to the intensity and resolution of the generative process. These are all qualities and characteristics that emerge from the complex, self-organizing algorithmic process, but which must be teased out through the design intention of the architect.

The behavior of complex systems generates characteristics that reoccur across diverse phenomena in biological, economic, social, and material systems. These characteristics become indicative of complexity. Within this body of work there is an attempt to recognize these characteristics as they emerge through the generative design process and to amplify them. This is not an attempt at imitating the emergent forms and patterns of other systems outside of architecture, but at capturing some qualitatively definable character of emergence. The interest here is not in the purity of this emergent character, but rather in the interaction of these traits with a more diverse set of intentions—an attempt to complicate these characteristics, to strip them of their purity, and enable the projects to take on their own strange specificity.

One strategy for creating this specificity is through the interaction of geometric systems, or substrata (which have bias, tendencies, and behavior), and the complex behavior of algorithms. The intention in drawing out this order from the generative process is to curate a strange, unknown set of qualities. The underlying ordering logics of emergence remain somewhat familiar, or partially recognizable, but emergent character can become something uncanny and strange through its operation within a geometric substrate that is alien to our experience of this familiar order. Unlike biomimicry, this process is not a direct translation of related

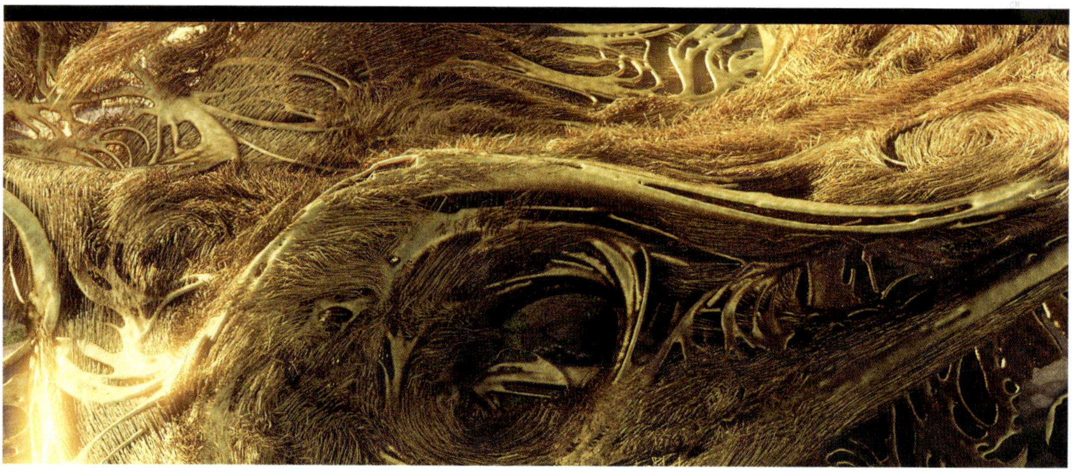

Kazakhstan Symbol, 2013. Detail of the turbulent geometry generated through a volatile behavioral algorithm.

geometric and behavioral logic; instead, it is the interaction of the known logic of emergent systems within a foreign substrate.

Within this body of work there is also a reoccurring set of non-emergent characteristics or tendencies, which are directly imposed without the abstraction of process. These are deliberate architectural decisions that operate through a generative algorithm, but are ontologically independent of emergence. One instance of this is the embedding or synthesizing of parts to create synthetic assemblages, such as the inlaid bodies in the composite projects that compress structure, surface, and ornament into an irreducible whole. Another reoccurring tendency is the creation of spatial ambiguity and frayed topologies, which are typified in the manifold swarm projects, including the NGV Pavilion[11] and the RMIT Mace. These projects are characterized by intricate mass that delaminates, or flakes, into surfaces and unravels at the perimeter of the form, creating a balance between mass and filigree. These architectural strategies operate through an algorithm, but the intention is independent of its process of formation—they are design rather than algorithmic imperatives.

ROCKS AND OTHER DISRUPTIONS

Explicit strategies are used in many of these projects to create a type of monolithic continuum: the building as solid material or as a thick, intricate mass. These are geometries that do not necessarily emerge from the generative process, but are selected to create specific affects. Often these strategies are deployed within this body of work to create mute readings of form, which act as a foil to the highly articulated generative geometry—resisting normative readings of architecture. One such strategy is to import a formal logic from outside of architecture, in order to suppress the normal articulation of the architectural project and disrupt the systemic character of the algorithmic processes. This approach is evident in the adoption of geological forms, such as in the Malibu House and the RMIT Meeting Pavilion, or the hairy geometries of the Kazakhstan Symbol. Similarly, the fibrous assemblages strategy—which is rooted in an understanding of the structure of organic material as heterogeneous assemblages of micro-

Malibu House, 2011–2013. The faceted geological form of the exterior acts as a foil to the intricate ceiling geometry.

fibers—creates a dense, monolithic reading. These strategies are driven as much by aesthetic concerns as by the attempt to delay the onset of known architectural vocabularies.

In many of the projects, such as the Fibrous House,[12] Yeosu Pavilion,[13] and Kazakhstan Symbol, the use of a single material, geometry or color creates a similar monolithic, or unified, characteristic. This does not lead to homogeneity, but rather a field from which differences emerge. It is a conscious formal and aesthetic attempt to move away from the discrete articulation of elements, by emphasizing the role of a single body of geometry that negotiates between different necessities.[14] This strategy is, in part, a response to the emergence of a new construction paradigm of variability—driven by 3D printing and robotic fabrication—that challenges the mass standardization of parts in favor of monolithic and composite construction.[15] The projects with heterogeneous coloration resist discrete articulation by changing color with intensities, rather than indexing tectonic roles or types (such as the tendency of the Yeosu Pavilion to brighten toward the tips of strands).

Generative algorithms play an important role in disrupting normative architectural conventions and tropes. However, it is becoming increasingly evident that, over time, these strategies, regardless of how volatile they are, create their own tropes and traces of indexicality. Expanding on the strategy of *strange feedback*, two strategies have been developed recently in this body of work to disrupt this emerging indexicality through the hybridization of gestural and material behaviors with computational behaviors. *Painterly formation* is a strategy for hybridizing gestural operations and self-organizing behaviors through a feedback that integrates the two into a synthetic process. *Stigmergic robotics* operates at the other end of the spectrum: rather than disrupting the algorithmic behavior with direct intention, it establishes a completely autonomous process based on the feedback of algorithmic and material behaviors.

Through this body of work there is an attempt to create a synthetic and irreducible relationship between various aspects of architecture, such as surface, structure, and ornament. Similarly, the interaction of generative processes and explicit (top-down) approaches is not an attempt to collage the two, but instead to create a synthetic whole that exceeds the properties of either approach. This synthesis is important to the nature of the work; in the painterly

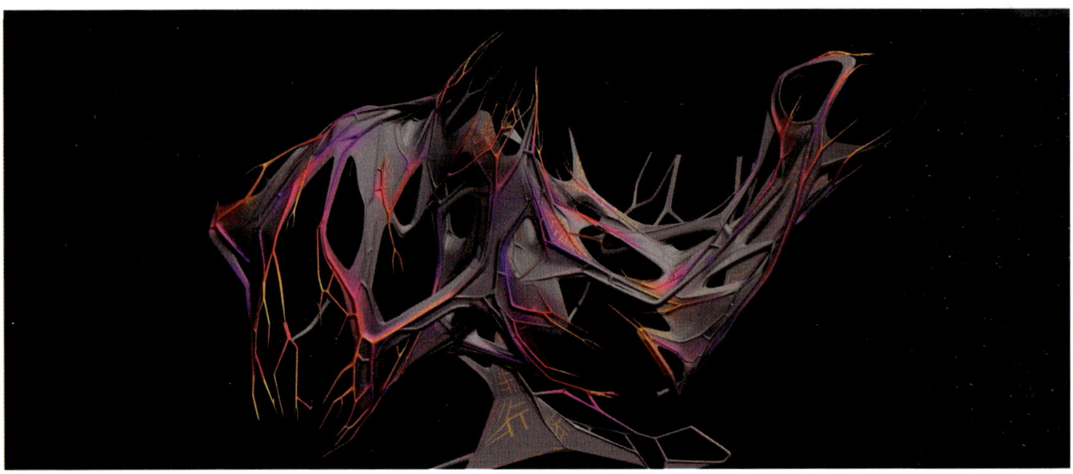

Yeosu Pavilion, 2009. The heterogeneous coloration varies in response to changing geometric intensities.

formation projects, it is only when the object is synthetic and holistic that it acquires strange characteristics and specificity. Otherwise, the reading of the work is reduced to the dueling of known models.

OBJECTS AND THEIR PROCESSUAL CHARACTERISTICS

The design research posited here draws heavily from a processual understanding of form, but without reducing the object to a mere slice through a continuous process of formation. Similarly, the work is concerned with aesthetics, form, objects, and their capacity to affect;[16] however, the concern for objects and their affects is inseparable from process. The outcomes from behavioral processes are not indexical to either the hand of the designer or the operation of the algorithm. Affects, or more precisely the affective capacity of space and form, emerge from the interaction between intention and the emergent behavior of the algorithm. As such, the work is positioned between ontologies of formation and the object.

This ontological difference—between form that is understood in terms of formation, as opposed to object—is articulated by Sanford Kwinter in the article 'Who's Afraid of Formalism',[17] where he states:

Formalism demonstrates first and foremost that form is resonance and expression of embedded forces... The form problem, from the time of pre-Socratics to the late twentieth century, is in fact an almost unbroken concern with the mechanisms of formation, the processes by which discernible patterns come to dissociate themselves from a less finely-ordered field. Form, when seen from this perspective, is ordering action, a logic deployed, while the object is merely the latter's sectional image, a manifest variation on an always somewhat distant theme.

The architectural discourse that has coalesced around *speculative realism* and *object oriented ontology* offers a counterpoint to this processual understanding of the world and the naturalization of architecture. David Ruy warns against the effective dissolution of architecture into ecology: 'Nature is the ultimate milieu, the all-encompassing field of material phenomena. Perhaps architecture's movement from object to field culminates in the vision of the involuted erasure of the architecture/nature divide as a desirable outcome'.[18] In his article, 'Return to

Myriad Wing, 2016. The project was designed through a painterly formation strategy that negotiated between the self-organizational behavior of the algorithm, and the gestural operation of the hand.

(Strange) Objects',[19] Ruy makes a case for object oriented ontology, by critiquing relational approaches where architecture is the product of the field of forces upon it. He describes this as a 'consequence of its context', or an uncontested outcome of its parameters, arguing that attention should be focused on the architectural object rather than that object's relations to a wider socio-political field.

While emerging from a milieu of complex systems and ontologies of becoming, this body of work has developed to privilege the object and its qualities, refusing to defer the value of the object to its process of formation.[20] The specific qualities of the object—those which emerge from, but are not indexical to, its process of formation—render it irreducible to its parts or their relations. Emergence, then, is an important generator of objects that cannot be undermined by their constituent parts and processes. Another approach to this issue is to consider the objecthood of parts regardless of their role in the formation of other objects. John Holland discusses emergence in terms of the interaction of building blocks that generate building blocks at another scale,[21] each of these blocks being objects in their own right, not simply inputs to a relational system. In the Composite Swarm project,[22] the individual agentBodies are not subsumed by the emergent whole of the installation; instead, they lead to the emergence of the whole, while maintaining their individual objecthood and locally specific qualities and characteristics.

It is important to differentiate between a field of relations in the design process and the field of relations occupied by the architectural object. Multi-agent systems are field conditions that do not necessarily respond to a field beyond their own internal relationships. Furthermore, they can be used in the morphogenetic design of an object that is isolated from relationships outside of itself: an object that is evaluated based on its architectural qualities rather than the network of relations from which it emerged.

Within a larger milieu of complex systems and the emergent capacities of self-organization, this body of design research has defined a behavioral approach to algorithmic design. Critical to this research is synthesizing emergence and intention: embedding the architect's intention within the algorithm, and establishing a feedback loop between emergent processes, qualitative judgments and direct architectural decisions. This concern for the role of intention within volatile algorithms has more recently shifted the focus of the research—from a methodological thesis to a concern for the emergence of specific qualities from this process, where the projects and their characteristics are the protagonists of the research. The development of a behavioral methodology has been leveraged to engage emergence with a more diverse set of design intentions that go beyond the systemic in developing a highly specific, possibly esoteric, architecture—an architecture that is inherently tied to its emergent process of formation, but which is defined by its own intricate, complex, and strange characteristics.

1 Intuition is not equivalent to the arbitrary or willful. Rather, intuition refers to a type of complex pattern recognition; it is posited here as a form of encoded knowledge.

2 In reviewing my lecture on the relationship between strangeness and behavioral processes in 2010 (van Schaik 2010), Jan van Schaik drew a parallel to the first performance of Stravinsky's The Rite of Spring when it caused a riot, which van Schaik attributes to the strangeness of the piece: 'Having worked tirelessly to invent chords and tonal relationships that were unfamiliar to the ear, the ruckus was evidence to Stravinsky that he'd achieved the new'.

3 Michael Young describes a related concept of estrangement, which makes no recourse to the new, but instead destabilises the familiar to enable something unfamiliar, or 'other', to arise (Young 2015).

4 Naturalising Architectures exhibited the work of architects including Alisa Andrasek, Marc Fornes, Neri Oxman, and Achim Menges.

5 Steven Johnson argues that systems of interacting parts 'wouldn't truly be considered emergent until those local interactions resulted in some kind of discernible macrobehavior' (Johnson 2001, p. 19.). The issue of what is considered discernible brings subjectivity, or at the very least qualitative evaluation, to the fore.

6 Stephen Wolfram argues that emergence is an unquantifiable phenomenon; the categorization or evaluation of complexity is qualitative and subjective. Wolfram posits four categories of complexity that are qualitative rather than quantitative, arguing that emergence cannot be numerically described. See Stephen Wolfram, *A New Kind of Science* (Champaign, IL: Wolfram Media, 2002), p. 231.

7 Autopoietic is used in this context to describe systems that are self-organizing and regulating without external input.

8 See relevant Project sections and Catalog of Projects.

9 See relevant Project sections and Catalog of Projects.

10 See Babiy Yar Project section.

11 See NGV Pavilion Project section.

12 See Catalog of Projects.

13 See Yeosu Pavilion Project section.

14 The Fibrous Tower is an example of negotiating multiple behaviors within its concrete shell.

15 This is further discussed in the Behavioral Composites section, and is evident in projects such as the NGV Pavilion and Composite Wing.

16 'Affect' is used here in relation to the discourse on the primacy of affects, a description that Jeff Kipnis traces to Peter Eisenman: 'To distinguish post-critical from pre-critical sensibilities and to call attention to the fact that the emotional impact of the work emanates not from the representations of the architecture but from the formal structures themselves, Eisenman termed these new sensations collectively as "affects".' Mark Gage quotes Kipnis in a footnote to his article 'Deus ex Machina: from Semiology to the Elegance of Aesthetics'. Carpo 2015, p. 224.

17 Kwinter 2008, p. 146.

18 Ruy 2012, p. 39.

19 Ruy 2012.

20 This design research doesn't draw on object oriented ontology (OOO), but recognises the relevance of OOO foregrounding the object, rather than rendering it subservient to processes of formation.

21 Holland 1995, pp. 34–37.

22 See Composite Swarm Project section.

STRATEGY

PAINTERLY FORMATION

Painterly Form 1, 2015.

Painterly formation is a strategy that engages painterly operations and self-organizing algorithms in a mutual feedback loop. The interaction of the two creates a hybrid character, combining the complex order of behavioral algorithms with the gestural qualities of painterly operations. The brushing of geometry within digital sculpting software and the reorganization of geometry through multi-agent algorithms interact directly through a mesh substrate. This strategy extends the non-indexical approach of *strange feedback*, which negotiates between top-down surface modeling and bottom-up algorithmic processes.

Strange feedback is a strategy primarily concerned with overcoming the global ignorance of multi-agent algorithms and developing coherent relationships between form and articulation. This formal strategy privileges the control of surface and topology. The shift to digital sculpting techniques and the direct operation of agents on meshes, within painterly formation, redirects the focus from topological to textural descriptions of form. Painterly operations manipulate form without any specific topological control; although non-systemic changes to topology arise through geometric adjacencies during re-meshing processes. Consequently, it is the characteristics of geometry, its poise, directionality, curvature, intricacy, sharpness, and monolithic or fibrous qualities that are the critical criteria in this design strategy.

In creating a hybrid character that is between the painterly and self-organizational, we attempted to escape the indexical characteristics typical of generative processes that rely on a single system. Within painterly formation, the two processes are polymorphic, operating

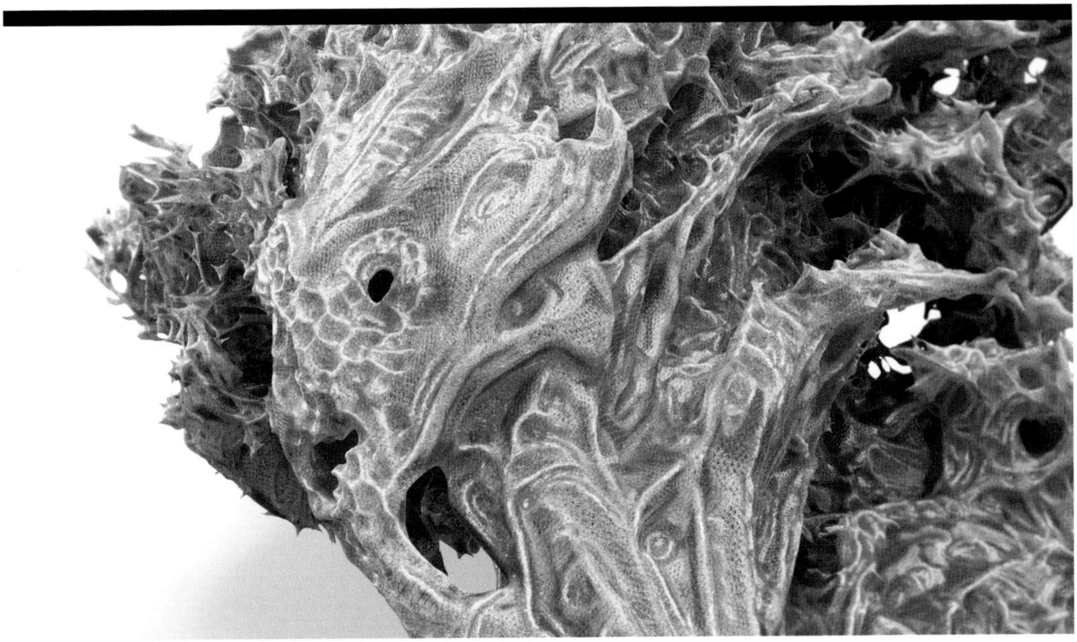

Painterly Form 1, 2015.
Detail.

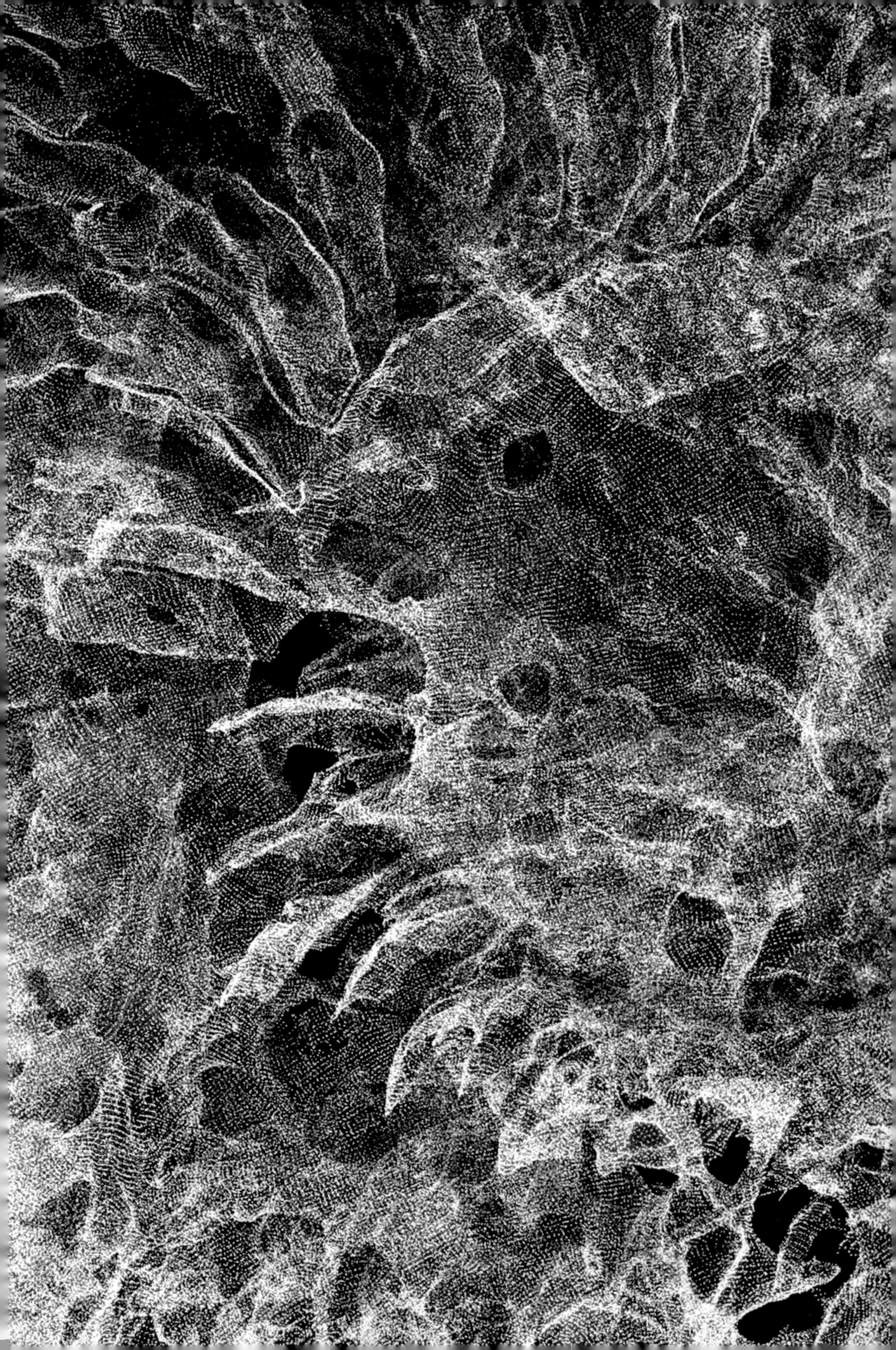

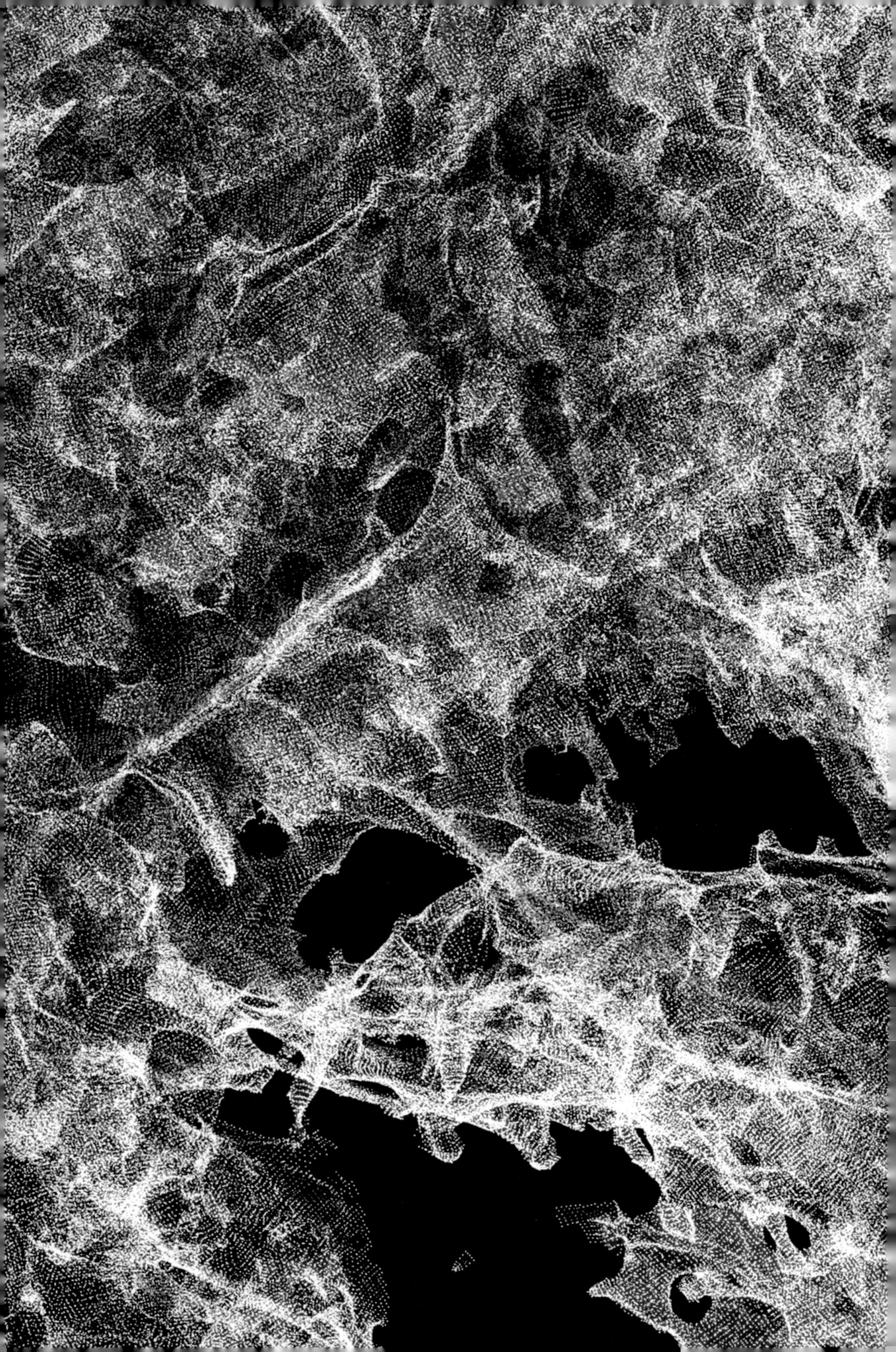

directly and interchangeably on the one mesh. This high-resolution feedback is conceptually similar to the *stigmergic robotics* strategy, which creates a closeness between material and computational behavior through sensor-actuated real-time robotics.[1]

Painterly formation operates directly on the object, both computationally and conceptually. The operations are not deferred, nor do they act as organizational structures to be manipulated later in the design process. Instead, the operations are direct and cumulative. A mesh substrate is encoded with information from both painterly and self-organizational processes. This information creates masks for painterly operations, or triggers procedural geometric operations.

We have designed a series of experimental objects through this approach in an attempt to create an esoteric formal vocabulary. Drawings of these objects were first exhibited at the Technics and Touch exhibition in 2015.[2] *Painterly Form 1* has a discernable silhouette that shifts from clearly articulated lines along the *nose* of the object, to a feathering of the geometry as it becomes more turbulent. The nose of the object is defined by striations that emerge from, and surround, a pocked or dimpled surface. The articulation of the form shifts to a more turbulent, spiky, entangled character as it moves away from the nose. The striations reinforce the directionality of the form, and create a clear correlation between silhouette and articulation. These features exhibit a synthesis of systemic and idiosyncratic qualities, blurring the reading of its process of formation, and positioning it outside of interpretations of either algorithmic or painterly processes.

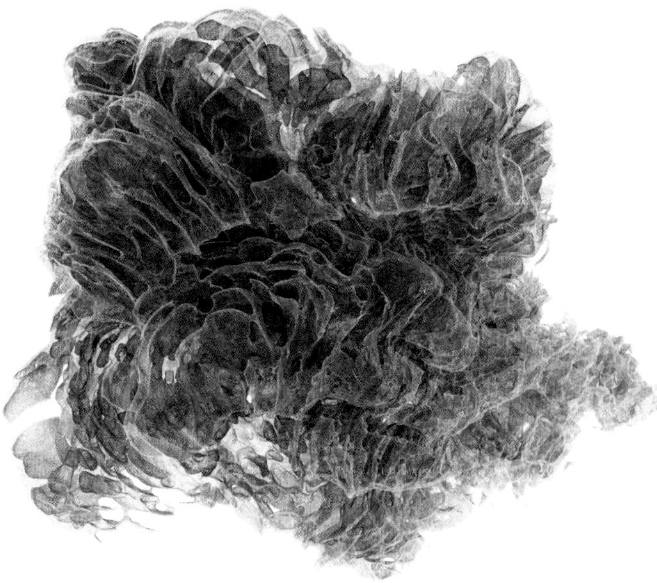

Painterly Form 2, 2015.

Painterly Form 2 is defined less by its silhouette than by the turbulent reading of its flaky topology and highly intricate spatial conditions. These characteristics are generated through algorithmic distribution and painterly manipulation of the form. At a finer grain of articulation, below the scale of surface topology, the object exhibits an embossed rather than a spatial quality. These different formal characteristics are nested at various scales within the object, as opposed to a self-similar or polyscalar approach.

The operations within this painterly formation strategy are layered and cumulative. The non-systemic feedback of the two operations creates formal tendencies within the object, rather than a systemic or indexical consistency. This is an inherently speculative and experimental process. The ambition of this work is to create strange, nuanced, and esoteric formal qualities, arising from a direct concern for the character of the object.

1 This concept is developed further in the Stigmergic Robotics Strategy section.

2 Technics & Touch: *Body-Matter-Machine* exhibition, RMIT Design Hub, 2015-2016, curated by Charles Anderson, Fleur Watson and Kate Rhodes.

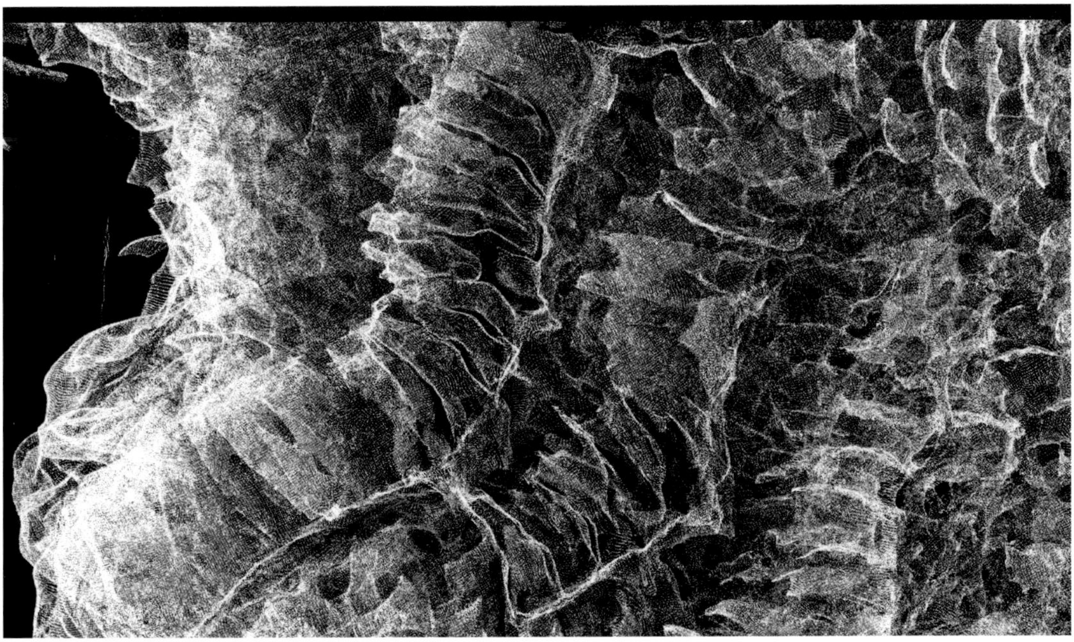

Painterly Form 2, 2015. Detail.

STRATEGY

STIGMERGIC ROBOTICS

Stigmergic Accretions, 2016.
Form study.

The generative potential of volatile physical materials can be leveraged in behavioral processes of formation through an autonomous approach to robotics. *Stigmergic robotics* is a strategy for designing through the interaction of algorithmic and material behavior, where robotics and vision systems are the mechanism of feedback between the two. This strategy exceeds the use of robotics to fabricate algorithmically designed forms, and engages the behavior of material as an active participant in the generative process. Similarly to the *painterly formation* strategy, this stigmergic approach[1] disrupts the purity of algorithmic design strategies, and infuses the work with another set of behaviors capable of generating strange qualities and characteristics.

Robotic fabrication processes in architecture typically operate through a linear relationship, moving from the predetermined digital model to robotic fabrication procedures.[2] An alternative approach is posited here, based on a real-time feedback loop in which there is no predetermined digital model. Instead, agent behaviors are programmed directly to the robot, which operates autonomously – the robot as agent. A simple example of this feedback is the robotic deposition of material, which is subsequently scanned, enabling computational agents to respond to the deposited material and guide the motion and deposition of further material by the robot. This process establishes a conceptual framework for a behavioral or stigmergic approach to robotic fabrication, where the robot/agent affects its environment and the environment affects the behavior of the robot/agent.

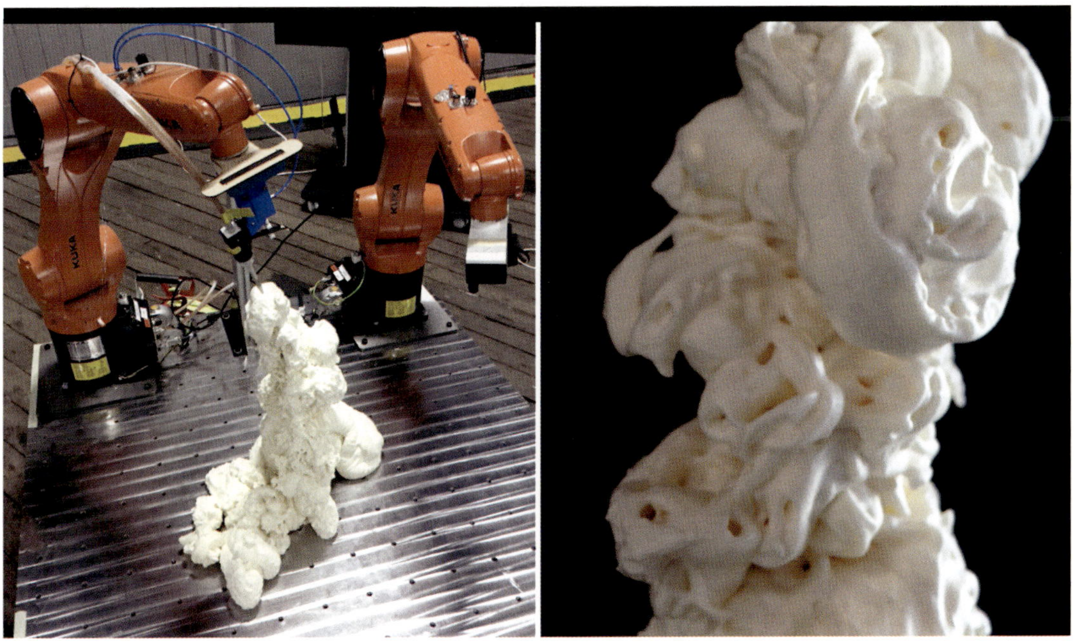

Stigmergic Accretions, 2016.
This real-time robotic cell enables constant scanning while depositing material.

The real-time feedback of sensor and robot enables a closeness[3] of interaction between the behavior of algorithmic agents and physical material that offers a radically different approach to engaging material behavior within computational design. Through the simultaneous interaction of the behaviors of the agent and material, a hybrid of the two behaviors emerges. This strategy is posited as an alternative to the contemporary practice of encoding empirically recorded material behavior as the primary driver of computational design models.[4] This practice risks not only limiting the space of design possibility[5] and the complexity of material behavior that can be engaged with, but it also risks creating a caricature of material by virtue of the limited capacity to simulate its behavior. In opposition, an anti-simulation approach is posited, in which the robot/agent doesn't 'know' the material, it does not attempt to simulate what the material might do, but instead it reacts to the material's actual behavior in real-time. In doing so, highly volatile materials and algorithms can be used without either simulating or conditioning the other's behavior. This approach enables the full richness and volatility of material to actively participate within the behavioral process of formation.

A primary interest in developing this approach is to explore the hybrid characteristics that emerge through the interaction of material and algorithmic behavior. The intention is to generate form that is not indexical to the algorithmic or to the material processes. Through this feedback process, material influences the behavior of the agent, while the motion of the robot/agent conditions the behavior of the material. This mutual interaction infuses the rich

Real-time material deposition.

messiness of material behavior within the emergent order of multi-agent algorithms, thus creating a new set of strange, expressive characteristics.

A highly volatile material, expanding polyurethane foam, was selected to explore this behavioral approach to robotics. Through a series of generative form studies, an industrial robotic arm extruded foam in response to real-time agent behaviors.[6] Strange characteristics were created at two scales, that of local articulation and of the larger emergent form. The local articulation is determined by the interaction of the path and speed of the robot/agent's motion (relative to the speed and continuity of the material extrusion) and the expansion of the foam created by the chemical reaction of its two parts. These relatively simple parameters lead to a wide array of characteristics or expressions that can variously be described as drizzled, whipped, puffed or looped. The generation of larger-scale form is an emergent outcome of the stigmergic system of interaction between the agent behavior and the material deposition.

Creating a feedback loop between computational and material behavior implies the compression of design and fabrication into a single autonomous process. This has the potential to bring into question the linear relationship of architectural design and construction and recast material's subservient relationship to designed form – notwithstanding the many practical complexities that arise from constructing a building as it is designed. However, there is another approach to the integration of material and algorithmic behavior that should be considered: that of engaging material for its capacity as a formal generator at a scale independent of ma-

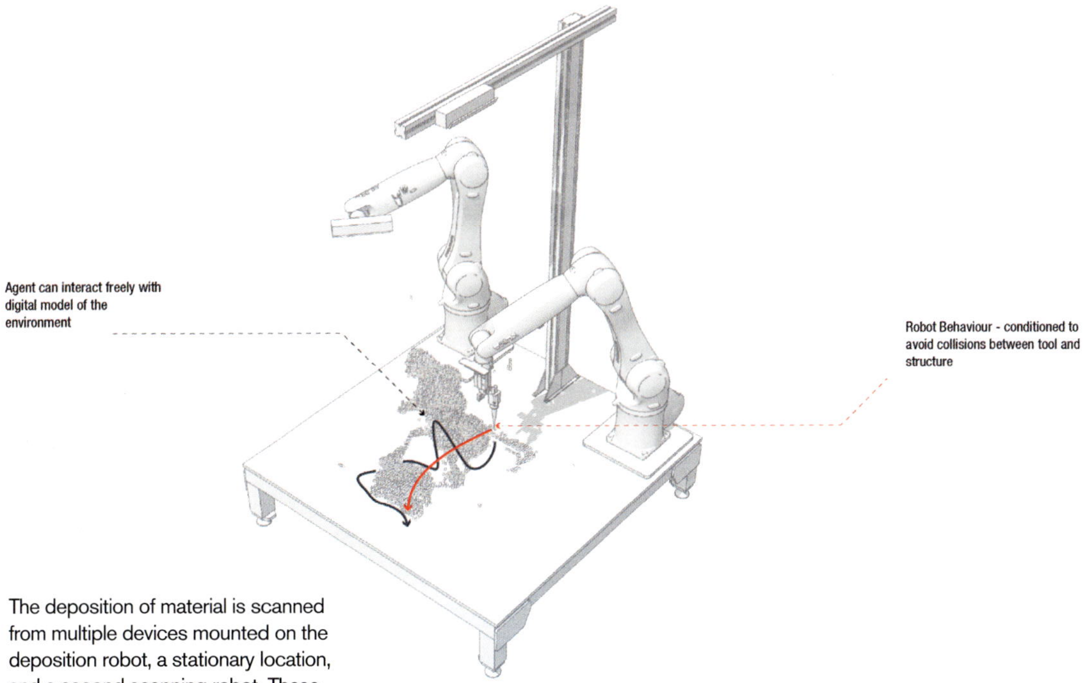

The deposition of material is scanned from multiple devices mounted on the deposition robot, a stationary location, and a second scanning robot. These multiple scans avoid issues of occlusion while scanning complex forms.

terial construction. This approach liberates the generative capacity of material behavior from construction.[7] Material can instead be mined for its abstract capacity to generate form and organizational patterns – an approach similar to the adoption of algorithmic processes in design.

This stigmergic process is the most autonomous of the generative strategies posited within this research. However, the process doesn't operate outside of design intention. The process has the capacity to engage with the full richness and un-knowable behavior of material in generating characteristics that exceed the agent's capacity to perceive them, the generation of which is a primary catalyst for creating this process. The agent is oblivious to texture, flow, gesture, and other emergent characteristics that exceed the agent's simple model of its world, which is described as a scanned point cloud of position and color. The intention encoded within the agent is unable to act on these subtle or subjectively described characteristics. Instead, they need to be iteratively teased out of this autonomous process, through the development of an intuition regarding the relationship of algorithmic design and material behaviors.

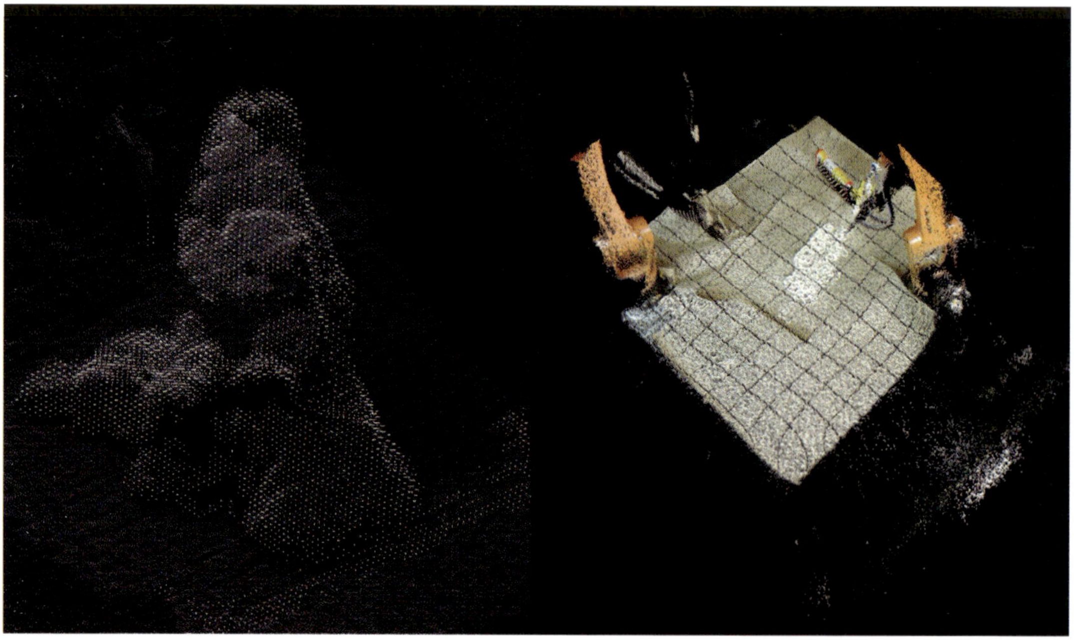

The robot's computational environment is described through a voxel space, which accumulates information from multiple real-time scans.

1 This stigmergic robotics approach was first posited in 2012 (Snooks, 2012a), and described in greater detail in the essay 'Behavioral Composites and Robotic Fabrication' (Snooks, 2013b). These concepts were further developed with Gwyllim Jahn through the papers 'Closeness' (Snooks, 2016a) and 'Stigmergic Accretions' (Snooks, 2016b).

2 There are important exceptions to this, notably the generative application of robotics in the work of Francois Roche and the adaptive approaches developed by Gramazio Kohler.

3 This argument about the closeness of material and algorithmic behavior was developed in an essay written with Gwyllim Jahn (Snooks, 2016a).

4 This practice of encoding empirically recorded material behavior is notable in the work of Achim Menges (Institute of Computational Design and Construction, Stuttgart) such as the ICD/ITKE Research Pavilion 2010.

5 The inherent stability and design limitation of design that is driven by material behavior is discussed in greater detail in the Volatility section.

6 This series of experiments was undertaken as part of the Stigmergic Accretions workshop that I taught at the RobArch2016 conference with Gwyllim Jahn and Cam Newnham (Sydney, 2016).

7 The behavior of material has long been adopted in the modeling process to imbue form with its specific behavior and bias. A notable example is Frank Gehry's use of paper in the design process, which is then built at a larger scale in considerably different materials. The difference that is proposed here is that, rather than the top-down manipulation of material, the material interacts with generative algorithmic behaviors within the design process.

CATALOG OF PROJECTS

NINE ELMS: RETROACTIVE FORM STUDY | 2017–2018
Strategies: agentBodies, manifold swarms, strange feedback.
Design Director: Roland Snooks.
Project Team: Isabelle Jooste, Charlie Boman.

FOLD PAVILION | 2017
Strategies: strange feedback.
Design Director: Roland Snooks.
Project Team: Sean Guy, Marc Gibson, Braden Scott.

MONASH BOULDERING WALL | 2016
Strategies: n/a.
Design Director: Roland Snooks.
Project Team: Marc Gibson, Andres Rivera, Braden Scott.

FLOE | 2017–2018
Strategies: agentBodies.
Design Director: Roland Snooks.
Project Team: Charlie Boman, Sean Guy, Austynn MacHado, Venkatesh Natarajan, Gabriele Mirra.

SENSILAB STUDIO | 2017
Strategies: polyscalar tectonics.
Design Director: Roland Snooks.
Project Team: Sean Guy, Austynn MacHado.

MYRIAD WING | 2016
Strategies: painterly formation.
Design Director: Roland Snooks.
Project Team: Marc Gibson, Braden Scott, Bec DiNapoli.
A collaboration between Studio Roland Snooks and Elenberg Fraser.

SOUTHLAWN | 2018
Strategies: n/a
Design Directors: Roland Snooks, Laura Harper, Mark Jacques.
Project Team: Isabelle Jooste, Max Wight.
A collaboration between Studio Roland Snooks, Laura Harper and Openwork.

MADA/SENSILAB | 2016–2017
Strategies: n/a.
Design Director: Roland Snooks.
Project Team: Mel Iraheta, Sean Guy, Andres Rivera, Marc Gibson, Braden Scott.
A collaboration between Studio Roland Snooks and NMBW Architecture Studio.

SACRIFICIAL SKINS (HAWTHORN) | 2016
Strategies: agentBodies, manifold swarms.
Design Director: Roland Snooks.
Project Team: Marc Gibson, Matt Kohman.

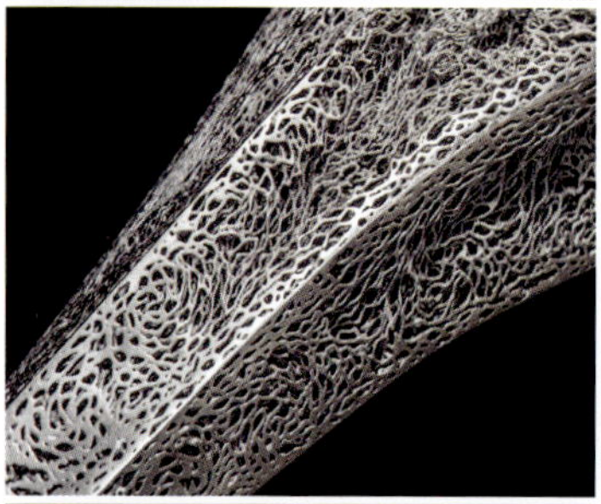

NGV PAVILION | 2015–2016
Strategies: agentBodies, manifold swarms.
Design Director: Roland Snooks.
Project Team: Marc Gibson, Matt Kohman, Susanna Brolhani, Venkatesh Natarajan.

RMIT MEETING PAVILION | 2015
Strategies: agentBodies, behavioral composites.
Design Director: Roland Snooks.
Project Team: Marc Gibson, Ashan Perera, Andres Rivera, Ben Verzijl, Bec DiNapoli.

NINE ELMS BRIDGE | 2015
Strategies: agentBodies, manifold swarms, agency of structure.
Design Director: Roland Snooks.
Project Team: Cam Newnham, Marc Gibson, Drew Busmire, Ben Verzijl.

RMIT MACE | 2015–2016
Strategies: agentBodies, manifold swarms.
Design Directors: Roland Snooks, Scott Mayson.
Project Team: Cam Newnham, Alexander Walzer, Andres Rivera.

PAINTERLY FORMS 1 AND 2 | 2015
Strategies: painterly formation.
Design Director: Roland Snooks.
Project Team: Marc Gibson.

BRASS SWARM | 2015
Strategies: agentBodies, manifold swarms.
Design Director: Roland Snooks.
Project Team: Cam Newnham, Ben Verzijl.

COMPOSITE SKELETON | 2015
Strategies: agentBodies, behavioral composites.
Design Director: Roland Snooks.
Project Team: Cam Newnham, Yian Chen, James Hall, Zhao Fei, Shibo Du, Sebastian Nicht, Wentao Guo, Han Chen, Andre Cheung, Ziyu Meng, Elisa Perez Mosos, Bowen Nie, Jack Bakker.

BLURRED BODIES | 2015
Strategies: agentBodies, manifold swarms.
Design Director: Roland Snooks.
Project Team: Matt Kohman.

FULL BLOWN | 2014
Strategies: agentBodies.
Design Director: Roland Snooks.
Project Team: Drew Busmire, Cam Newnham, Ashan Perera, Andres Rivera, Ben Verzijl, Pei She Lee.

DADA PAVILION | 2015
Strategies: agentBodies.
Design Director: Roland Snooks.
Project Team: Cam Newnham, Hyde Meng.

LAMINAR BODIES | 2015
Strategies: agentBodies, manifold swarms.
Design Director: Roland Snooks.
Project Team: Ashan Perera, Ben Verzijl, Andres Rivera.

COMPOSITE WING | 2014
Strategies: agentBodies, behavioral composites.
Design Director: Roland Snooks.
Project Team: Cam Newnham, Drew Busmire, Amaury Thomas, Pei She Lee.

NGV SLF INSTALLATION | 2013
Strategies: n/a.
Design Director: Roland Snooks.
Project Team: Amaury Thomas, Julien Ybert.

FIBROUS CONCRETE | 2013
Strategies: n/a.
Design Director: Roland Snooks.
Project Team: Amaury Thomas, Jas Johnson, Brad Martin.

SL FOUNDATION | 2013
Strategies: strange feedback.
Design Director: Roland Snooks.
Project Team: James Pazzi, Armin Senoner, Marc Gibson.

ASTANA 2017 EXPO | 2013
Strategies: strange feedback, fibrous assemblages.
Design Directors: Roland Snooks. Robert Stuart-Smith.
Project Team: Zak Kljakovic, Michael Ferreyra, Armin Senoner, Marc Gibson, James Pazzi, Gonzalo Valiente.
A collaboration between Studio Roland Snooks and Robert Stuart-Smith Design.

KAZAKHSTAN SYMBOL | 2013
Strategies: strange feedback, fibrous assemblages.
Design Director: Roland Snooks.
Project Team: Michael Ferreyra, Armin Senoner, Marc Gibson, James Pazzi.

MALIBU HOUSE | 2011–2013
Strategies: strange feedback, fibrous assemblages, polyscalar tectonics.
Design Director: Roland Snooks.
Project Team: Casey Rehm, Armin Senoner, Tommaso Casucci, Marc Gibson.

COMPOSITE SWARM | 2013
Strategies: agentBodies, manifold swarms, behavioral composites.
Design Director: Roland Snooks.
Project Team: James Pazzi, Marc Gibson.

FIBROUS HOUSE | 2012
Strategies: fibrous assemblages, polyscalar tectonics, behavioral composites.
Design Director: Roland Snooks
Project Team: Ryan Wilson, Drew Busmire, Jacob Patapoff, Emily Knapp, Hong Bea Yang, Jose Padilla, Nick Gutierrez, Ashley Ricketson.
Fabrication Team: Jorge Cruz, Adrian Martinez, Cody May.
A collaboration between Kokkugia and Mitchell Lab (Texas A&M).

CLIFF HOUSE | 2012
Strategies: strange feedback, fibrous assemblages, polyscalar tectonics, behavioral composites.
Design Director: Roland Snooks.
Project Team: Adrian Cortez, Zach Hoffman, Stephen Renard, Rafael Vazquez, Andrew Horne, Tyler Nagai, Lyly Huyen, Jorge Cruz, Adrian Martinez, Cody May.
A collaboration between Kokkugia and Mitchell Lab (Texas A&M).

FLINDERS STREET STATION | 2012
Strategies: agentBodies, manifold swarms.
Design Director: Roland Snooks.
Project Team: Adrian Cortez, Farzin Lotfi-Jam, Fleet Hower.
A collaboration between Kokkugia and MvS Architects.

AALTO UNIVERSITY | 2012
Strategies: agentBodies, manifold swarms.
Design Director: Roland Snooks.
Project Team: Adrian Cortez, Michael Ferreyra, Michael Murdock.

NEW TAIPEI MUSEUM | 2011
Strategies: agentBodies, manifold swarms.
Design Director: Roland Snooks.
Project Team: Fleet Hower, Kaicong Wu.

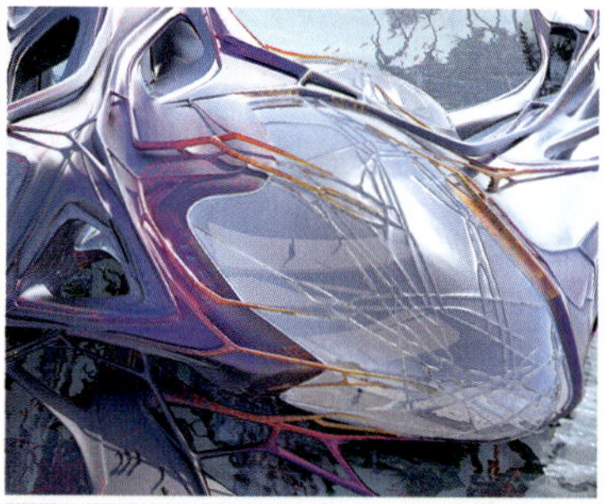

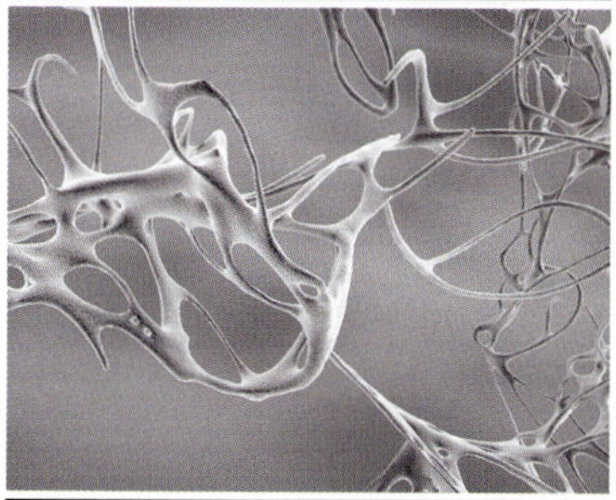
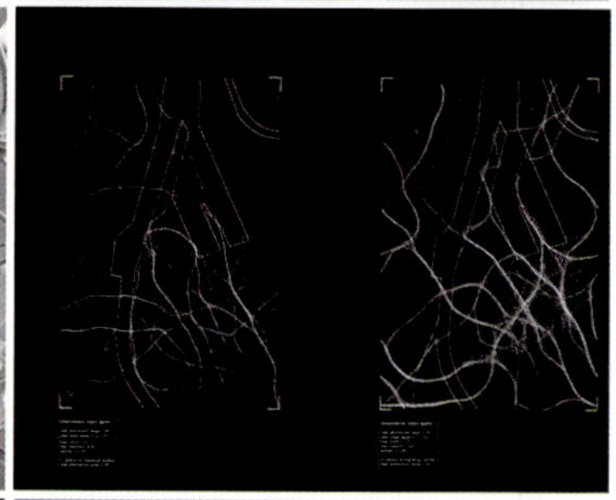

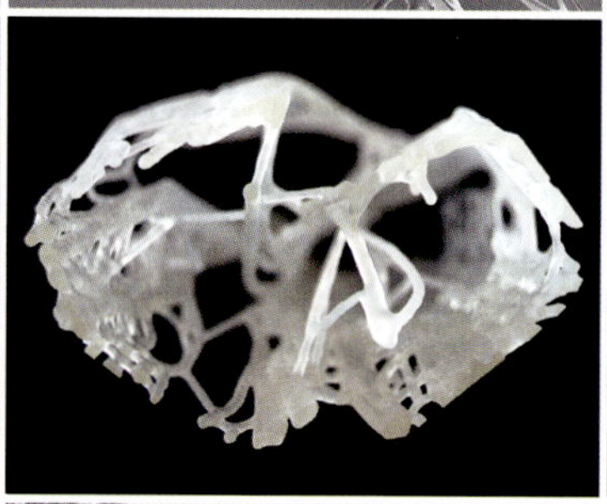

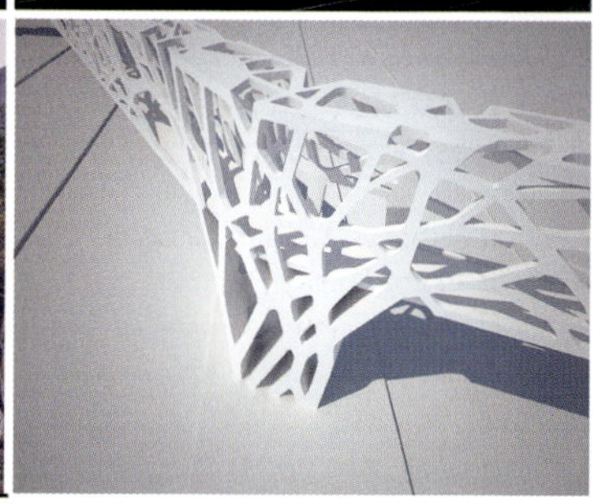

NATIONAL ART MUSEUM OF CHINA (NAMOC) | 2010
Strategies: strange feedback.
Design Directors: Roland Snooks, Robert Stuart-Smith.
Project Team: Nicholette Chan, J Fleet Hower, Xiaotian Huang, Dane Zeiler, Leonid Krykhtin, Edwin Liu, Josef Musil, Ekaterina Obedkova, Casey Rehm, Gilles Retsin, Sophia Tang.
A collaboration between Kokkugia and Studio Pei Zhu.

YEOSU PAVILION | 2009
Strategies: strange feedback, polyscalar tectonics.
Design Directors: Roland Snooks, Tom Wiscombe.
Project Team: Pablo Kohan, Fleet Hower, Ricardo Sosa.
A collaboration between Kokkugia and Tom Wiscombe Architecture.

FIBROUS TOWER | 2008
Strategies: fibrous assemblages, polyscalar tectonics.
Design Directors: Roland Snooks, Robert Stuart-Smith.
Project Team: Juan de Marco.

RIGA AIRPORT | 2010
Strategies: fibrous assemblages, agency of structure.
Design Directors: Roland Snooks, Robert Stuart-Smith.
Project Team: Casey Rehm, Matt Choot, Edwin Liu.

SWARM MATTER | 2009
Strategies: agentBodies.
Design Director: Roland Snooks.
Project Team: Pablo Kohan.

SWARM URBANISM | MELBOURNE DOCKLANDS | 2008
Strategies: swarm urbanism.
Design Directors: Roland Snooks, Robert Stuart-Smith.

LIVERPOOL DEPARTMENT STORE FACADE | 2010-2012
Strategies: n/a.
Design Directors: Roland Snooks, Robert Stuart-Smith.
Project Team: Casey Rehm.
Kokkugia consulting to Rojkind Arquitectos.

FIBROUS TOWER 2 | 2009
Strategies: fibrous assemblages, polyscalar tectonics.
Design Director: Roland Snooks.

TAIPEI PERFORMING ARTS CENTRE | 2008
Strategies: n/a.
Design Directors: Roland Snooks, Robert Stuart-Smith.
Project Team: Brad Rothenberg, Elliot White, Matt Howard.

BABIY YAR MEMORIAL | 2010
Strategies: agentBodies, polyscalar tectonics.
Design Director: Roland Snooks.
Project Team: Casey Rehm, Fleet Hower, Bryant Netter.

TORI TORI RESTAURANT FACADE | 2009–2011
Strategies: n/a.
Design Directors: Roland Snooks, Robert Stuart-Smith.
Kokkugia consulting to Rojkind Arquitectos.

IRAPUATO BRIDGE | 2008
Strategies: n/a.
Design Directors: Roland Snooks, Robert Stuart-Smith.
Project Team: Timo Carl.
A collaboration between Kokkugia and Rojkind Arquitectos.

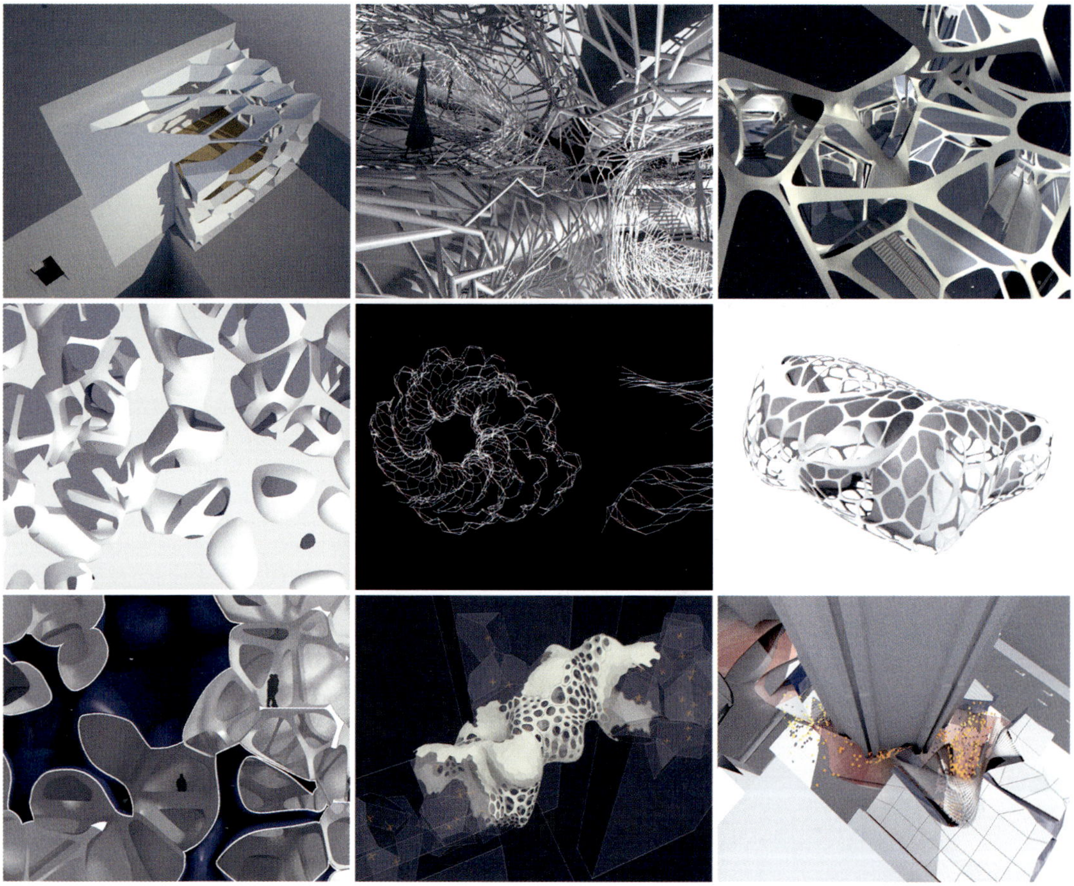

KAY APARTMENT | 2008
Strategies: n/a.
Design Director: Roland Snooks.

FTZ ATHENS | 2006
Strategies: fibrous assemblages.
Design Director: Roland Snooks.
Undertaken as an MArch2 student at Columbia GSAPP.

PARACHUTE PAVILION | 2005
Strategies: n/a.
Design Directors: Jonathan Podborsek, Roland Snooks, Robert Stuart-Smith.

WET FOAM | 2007
Strategies: n/a.
Design Director: Roland Snooks.

RECURSIVE NETWORKS | 2005
Strategies: n/a.
Design Director: Roland Snooks.
Undertaken as an MArch2 student at Columbia GSAPP.

MARS | 2003–2004
Strategies: n/a.
Design Directors: Jonathan Podborsek, Roland Snooks, Robert Stuart-Smith.

iSAW | 2007
Strategies: n/a.
Design Directors: Jonathan Podborsek, Roland Snooks.

URBAN AGENCY | 2005
Strategies: n/a.
Design Director: Roland Snooks.
Undertaken as an MArch2 student at Columbia GSAPP.

EMERGENT FIELD (+ PRE-MAJOR) | 2002–2003
Strategies: fibrous assemblages.
Design Director: Roland Snooks.
Undertaken as a BArch Thesis

GLOSSARY OF TERMS

Some terms in this glossary refer to complex mathematical or computational concepts. Rather than provide a precise technical description, this glossary attempts to describe how the term is used in the context of architectural design.

affect, affectual, affective: refers to the emotional effect of architectural space on the subject. This particular architectural etymology is traced by Jeff Kipnis to Peter Eisenman. (See Strange Specificity section.)

agency of structure: a design strategy developed through this body of work that establishes a feedback between macro-scale structural evaluation and micro-scale, agent-based, heuristic structural behaviors. (See Agency of Structure Strategy section.)

agentBodies: a design strategy developed through this body of work that encodes agent behaviors within the topological structure of a component or body. (See AgentBodies Strategy section.)

algorithm: a set of instructions that coordinates a sequence of procedures or operations. An algorithm is a procedural logic that doesn't necessarily relate to digital computing. However, computers are highly efficient tools for executing algorithms.

behavioral composites: a design strategy developed through this body of work that explores the relationship between behavioral processes of formation and fibre composite materials. (See Behavioral Composites Strategy section.)

Cartesian space/coordinates: a system of defining geometry in space using x, y and z coordinates. René Descartes developed Cartesian coordinates in the seventeenth century.

cellular automata rule 110: a one-dimensional cellular automation that operates on the edge of chaos. Cellular automata is a grid of cells, each with a state (such as black or white). These states change iteratively in response to the adjacent cells.

complex system: a system in which the whole is greater than the sum of its parts. Complex systems operate through the interaction of lower level parts that self-organize in creating higher levels of order.

computation: involves calculation or information processing. It is generally used to refer to digital computation and the use of computers for executing algorithms.

ETFE: a polymer (ethylene tetrafluoroethylene). ETFE foil is used for transparent skins in building construction. It is typically inflated to create the necessary structural rigidity.

emergence: used in this context to describe something discernible arising from the behavior of a system. Complex systems and self-organizing processes can generate emergent patterns, forms, and organisations.

explicit modeling: used in this context to describe the modeling of geometry through direct, causal, linear operations. (Also sometimes referred to as direct modeling.) It is opposed to generative modeling, which involves an abstraction between the inputs and the geometry.

fibrous assemblages: a design strategy developed through this body of work, operating through the self-organization of agent-based strands. (See Fibrous Assemblages Strategy section.)

global: often used in this context to describe the macro-level of a system.

global ignorance: describes the inability of an agent to understand the system of which it is a part. Multi-agent systems are designed to interact locally in order to generate a complex system. (See Volatility section.)

heuristics: a rule of thumb or intuitive guess. Heuristics are used as a shortcut, based on experience, to solve a problem.

indexical: the relationship between an object and its process of formation. In this context, it is generally used to describe a discernible, linear relationship between formation and the characteristics of the object.

isosurfacing: a surface description of a threshold of equal value within a field. It is typically used in computational architecture to extract a surface from a field of values or to wrap lower level geometry, such as points or lines, to create a mesh surface.

l-systems: or Lindenmayer systems, are substitution algorithms that recursively replace, or write a symbol to replace, the symbols of the current iteration. L-systems were originally developed by Astrid Lindenmayer to model the branching growth of plants.

kinematics: describes the motion of geometry. In this context, it specifically describes the motion of geometry with jointed parts, such as a skeleton or robot arm. Inverse kinematics describes this motion relative to an unrestrained point of the jointed system; for example, the motion of an arm can be controlled through inverse kinematics by moving the hand. Inverse kinematics is a common strategy employed in animation software.

manifold surface: requires a complex mathematical description, but it is used in this context to describe orientable, two-dimensional manifold topology. These can be described as surfaces with two discrete sides, or a surface in which the surface normals aren't locally inverted.

manifold swarms: a design strategy developed through this body of work in which a swarm of agents self-organize to create coherent manifold surfaces.

monocoque: a structural system that operates primarily through surface. Eggs and composite fibre airplane fuselages are examples of monocoque structures.

morphology: the study of form or shape. In biology, it refers to the structure and form of organisms.

morphodynamic, morphogenetic: morphodynamic refers to processes of formation that are dictated by influences exterior to the system, while a morphogenetic process generates form through the system's own internal logic.

non-linear: the output of a non-linear system is not proportional to its input. Non-linear is also used to describe the mutual interaction of a system's parts—without hierarchy.

parametric (design, modeling, software, etc.): parametric (or associative) modeling is used in this context to describe a linear relationship between a parameter and geometric manipulation. This logic forms the basis of some contemporary modeling software.

parametricism: a term coined by Patrik Schumacher to describe what he considers to be the next major style after the International Style.

poché: originally a French architectural term that describes the indication of solid elements such as walls and columns that are cut by the drawing plane within architectural drawings, such as plans and sections.

polyscalar tectonics: a design strategy developed through this body of work that produces a self-similar effect where the same generative procedure is repeated at various scales. (See Polyscalar Tectonics Strategy section.)

processual: relates to process, or the study of processes.

reaction diffusion: an algorithmic process that distributes concentrations of substances in space through the interaction of processes of chemical reaction and distribution, often over a surface. This algorithm can be seen in biology, and it possibly plays a central role in morphogenesis. It is argued that this algorithm is responsible for the patterns of animal skins such as those of zebras and tigers.

spline: a mathematical description of a curve that is generally smooth and continuous. The term is adopted from the thin timber or metal strips used for drafting curves. Computational spline geometry is incorporated in many contemporary 3D modeling software packages used in architecture.

stigmergy: a process of indirect communication between agents in a system of swarm intelligence. Stigmergy creates a feedback loop where the agent affects its environment and the environment affects the agent. (See Multi-Agent Algorithms section.)

stochastic: describes a random state of a system. Stochastic systems use probabilistic approaches to problem solving.

strange feedback: a design strategy developed through this body of work that negotiates between explicit modeling operations and generative procedures in a feedback loop. (See Strange Feedback Strategy section.)

swarm intelligence: the local interaction of distributed autonomous agents from which collective behavior emerges.

swarm urbanism: a design strategy developed through this body of work that applies the self-organizing logic of multi-agent systems to urban design. (See Multi-Agent Algorithms section.)

topology: the mathematical study of space and its deformation, with regard to continuity or connectivity. In this context, it is used to describe networks of connection and surfaces that are sometimes described as rubber sheet geometry–as a topological surface can change shape without changing its topology. This understanding had significant influence on architectural form-making during architecture's digital turn of the 1990s.

voronoi: an algorithm for dividing space through the relationship of points. A voronoi is based on lines or surfaces that are equidistant and perpendicular to the two closest points.

voxel: a three-dimensional pixel.

BIBLIOGRAPHY

Abruzzo, E., Ellingsen, E. & Solomon, J., 2007. *Models, 306090 Books, Vol. 11* [Paperback], New York: 306090 Inc.

Alexander, C. et al., 1977. *A Pattern Language: Towns, Buildings, Construction*, New York: Oxford University Press.

Ball, P., 2009. *Flow: Nature's Patterns: A Tapestry in Three Parts*, New York: Oxford University Press.

Bates, D. & Davidson, P., 1997. *Architecture after Geometry: Architectural Design Profile 127*, London: Academy Editions.

Batty, M., 2007. *Cities and Complexity: Understanding Cities with Cellular Automata, Agent-Based Models, and Fractals*, London: The MIT Press.

Batty, M., 2009. A Digital Breeder for Designing Cities. *Architectural Design*, 79(4), pp.46–49.

Brayer, M. & Migayrou, F. eds., 2013. *Naturalizing Architecture – Naturaliser L'Architecture.* ArchiLab 2013, HYX.

Burry, M., 1999. Paramorph: Anti-Accident Methodologies. *Architectural Design: Hypersurface Architecture II*, September, pp.78–83.

Camazine, S. et al., 2003. *Self-Organization in Biological Systems*, Princeton: Princeton University Press.

Carpo, M., ed., 2015. *The Digital Turn in Architecture 1992–2012:* AD Reader [Paperback], West Sussex: Wiley.

Carranza, P. & Coates, P., 2000. Swarm Modelling. *Proceedings of the 3rd Generative Art Conference*, Milan: Generative Design Lab Milan Polytechnic University.

Chu, K., 2006. Metaphysics of Genetic Architecture and Computation. *Architectural Design*, *76(4)*, pp.38–45.

Colletti, M., ed., 2010. *Exuberance: New Virtuosity in Contemporary Architecture*, London: Wiley.

Crutchfield, J. P., 1994. The Calculi of Emergence: Computation, Dynamics, and Induction. *Physica D 75* (1994), pp.11–54. Santa Fe Institute Working Paper 94-03-016.

DeLanda, M., 1995. Uniformity and Variability: An Essay in the Philosophy of Matter, presented at Doors of Perception 3, On Matter conference, Netherlands Design Institute. Available at: http://www.t0.or.at/delanda/matterdl.htm [accessed March 10, 2014].

DeLanda, M., 1998. Meshworks, Hierarchies and Interfaces. In J. Beckman, ed., *The Virtual Dimension: Architecture, Representation, and Crash Culture*, New York: Princeton Architectural Press.

DeLanda, M., 1999. Deleuze, Diagrams, and the Open-ended Becoming of the World. In E. Grosz, ed., *Becomings: Explorations in Time, Memory, and Futures*, Ithaca: Cornell University Press.

DeLanda, M., 2011. *Philosophy and Simulation: The Emergence of Synthetic Reason* [Hardcover], London: Continuum Publishing Corporation.

Deleuze, G., 1993. *The Fold: Leibniz and the Baroque*, Minneapolis: University of Minnesota Press.

Deleuze, G. & Guattari, F., 1987. *A Thousand Plateaus: Capitalism and Schizophrenia*, Minneapolis: University of Minnesota Press.

Ednie-Brown, P., 2007. *The Aesthetics of Emergence*, Melbourne: RMIT University.

Frazer, J., 1995. *An Evolutionary Architecture*, London: Architectural Association.

Hensel, M., 2013. *Performance-oriented Architecture: Rethinking Architectural Design and the Built Environment*, West Sussex: Wiley.

Holland, J.H., 1995. *Hidden Order: How Adaptation Builds Complexity*, New York: Perseus Books.

Holland, J.H, 1999. *Emergence: From Chaos to Order*, New York: Basic Books.

Johnson, S., 2002. *Emergence: The Connected Lives of Ants, Brains, Cities, and Software*, New York: Scribner.

Kilian, A. & Ochsendorf, J., 2005. Particle-spring Systems for Structural Form Finding. *Journal for the International Association for Shell and Spatial Structures, (47)*, pp.77–84.

Kwinter, S., 2008. *Far from Equilibrium: Essays on Technology and Design Culture*, New York: Actar.

Kwinter, S., 2011. The Computational Fallacy. In A. Menges, S. Ahlquist ed., *Computation Design Thinking*, AD Reader, Wiley, pp.211–215.

Leach, N. & Snooks, R., eds., 2017. *Swarm Intelligence: Architectures of Multi-Agent Systems*, Shanghai: Tongji University Press.

Lorenzo-Eiroa, P. & Sprecher, A., eds, 2013. *Architecture in Formation*, Oxford: Routledge.

Lynn, G., 1993. *Folding in Architecture*, London: Wiley-Academy Press, Revised Edition.

Lynn, G., 1998. *Folds, Bodies & Blobs: Collected Essays*, Brussels: La Lettre Voleé.

Lynn, G., 1999. *Animate Form*, New York: Princeton Architectural Press.

Massumi, B., 1995. Interface and Active Space: Human-Machine Design, *Proceedings of the Sixth International Symposium on Electronic Art (155)*, Montreal.

Massumi, B., 1998. Sensing the Virtual, Building the Insensible. In S. Perrella, ed. *Architectural Design: Hypersurface Architecture 68(133)*, pp.16–24.

Mitchell, M., 2009. *Complexity: A Guided Tour*, New York: Oxford University Press.

Otto, F. & Rasch, B., 1996. *Finding Form: Towards an Architecture of the Minimal*, Fellbach, Germany: Edition Axel Menges.

Oxman, R. & Oxman, R, eds., 2010. *The New Structuralism: Design, Engineering and Architectural Technologies*, Wiley.

Rajchman, J., 1998. *Constructions*, Cambridge, Mass: MIT Press.

Reynolds, C., 1987. Flocks, Herds, and Schools: A Distributed Behavioral Model. *Computer Graphics 21(4)*, SIGGRAPH '87 Conference Proceedings, pp.25–34.

Ruy, D., 2012. Returning to (Strange) Objects. *Tarp: Not Nature*, Spring, pp.38–42. Available at: http://issuu.com/tarp/docs/notnature_finaldraft_041012.

Schumacher, P., 2012. *The Autopoiesis of Architecture, Volume II: A New Agenda for Architecture*, London: Wiley.

Silver, M. ed., 2006. *Programming Cultures: Architecture, Art and Science in the Age of Software Development*, London: Wiley-Academy.

Silver, M., 2011. Many From One. *Log* (23), pp.30–33.

Snooks, R., 2012a.Volatile Formation. *Log 25*, New York: Anyone Corporation, pp.55–62.

Snooks, R., 2012b. Roland Snooks / Disguincio&Co. *City Vision*, issue 7 autumn/winter, p.48.

Snooks, R., 2013b. Behavioral Composites and Robotic Fabrication. *In Designing / Education: Proceedings of the 7th International Conference of the Association of Architecture Schools of Australasia*, Diego Ramirez-Lovering, Jacqui Alexander, Alison Fairley (ed.), AASA, Australia, pp.44–61

Snooks, R 2014, *Behavioral Formation: Multi-Agent Algorithmic Design Strategies*, Doctor of Philosophy (PhD), Architecture and Design, RMIT University.

Snooks, R. & Jahn, G., 2016. Closeness: On the Relationship of Multi-Agent Algorithms and Robotic Fabrication. In D. Reinhardt, R Saunders, J. Burry, eds,

Robotic Fabrication in Architecture, Art and Design 2016. Springer, pp.219–229.

Snooks, R. & Jahn, G., 2016. Stigmergic Accretion. In D. Reinhardt, R Saunders, J. Burry eds, *Robotic Fabrication in Architecture, Art and Design 2016*. Springer, pp.399–409.

Turing, A., 1952. The Chemical Basis of Morphogenesis. *Philosophical Transactions of the Royal Society of London, Series B, Biological Sciences, 237(641)*, pp.37–72. Available at: http://www.dna.caltech.edu/courses/cs191/paperscs191/turing.pdf [Accessed March 5, 2014].

Van Berkel, B. & Bos, C. eds., 1998. *ANY 23: Diagram Work: Data Mechanics for a Topological Age*, New York: ANYCorp.

Van Schaik, J., 2010. Kokkugia. *Artichoke (31)*, pp.117–120.

Waldrop, M.M., 1993. *Complexity: The Emerging Science at the Edge of Order and Chaos*, New York: Simon and Schuster.

Weaver, W., 1948. Science and Complexity, *American Scientist*, pp.1–11.

Wolfram, S., 2002. *A New Kind of Science*, Champaign, IL: Wolfram Media.

Young, M., 2015. *The Estranged Object*. Graham Foundation.

Roland Snooks directs the architectural practice Studio Roland Snooks and is an Associate Professor at RMIT University. Snooks' design research explores behavioral processes of formation that draw from the logic of swarm intelligence and the operation of multi-agent algorithms.

Snooks has taught widely in the United States including at Columbia University, University of Pennsylvania, SCI-Arc, and the Pratt Institute. He received a PhD from RMIT and a Master in Advanced Architectural Design from Columbia University, where he studied on a Fulbright scholarship.

In 2004 Snooks co-founded the experimental architectural practice Kokkugia, with the intention of exploring the limits of algorithmic formation and its architectural potential. He directs the RMIT Architecture | Tectonic Formation Lab, which develops computational design processes and robotic fabrication techniques through the design of experimental tectonics.

Snooks' work has been published and exhibited widely and acquired for the permanent collections of institutions including the FRAC and Centre Pompidou.

BEHAVIORAL FORMATION
Volatile Design Processes & the Emergence of a Strange Specificity

by Roland Snooks

Published by
Actar Publishers, New York, Barcelona
www.actar.com

Edited by
Roland Snooks

Graphic Design
Actar Publishers

Copy editing and proofs:
Loma Snooks; Christina Houen

Photographic credits:
All photographs by Studio Roland Snooks and RMIT University except:
Peter Bennetts; pages 154-155, 220.
Paul Rivera; page 226.
Hutchison & Savchenko; pages 29, 31-33, 220.
National Gallery of Victoria (NGV); pages 157, 220.
Eugene Hyland (courtesy of the NGV); page 161.
RMIT University; pages 8, 94-95, 98-100, 107, 214-216.

Printing and binding
Arlequin

Distribution
Actar D, Inc. New York, Barcelona.

New York
440 Park Avenue South, 17th Floor
New York, NY 10016, USA
T +1 2129662207
salesnewyork@actar-d.com

Barcelona
Roca i Batlle 2-4
08023 Barcelona, Spain
T +34 933 282 183
eurosales@actar-d.com

Indexing
ISBN: 978-1-940291-92-5
PCN: Library of Congress Control Number: 2020952317

Printed in Europe

Publication date: 2021